RTÉ Sunday Miscellany

RTÉ Sunday Miscellany

a selection from 2008 – 2011

edited by CLÍODHNA NÍ ANLUAIN

SUNDAY MISCELLANY
First published 2011
by New Island
2 Brookside
Dundrum Road
Dublin 14

www.newisland.ie

ISBN 978-1-84840-086-3

The quotations from the poetry of Patrick Kavanagh are reprinted from
Collected Poems, edited by Antoinette Quinn (Allen Lane, 2004) by kind permission
of the Estate of the late Katherine B. Kavanagh, through the Jonathan Williams
Literary Agency.

The publishers have made every effort to contact copyright owners. If any have
been inadvertently overlooked, the publishers will be pleased to rectify any
errors or omissions at the earliest opportunity.

British Library Cataloguing Data. A CIP catalogue record for this book is
available from the British Library.

Printed in the UK by CPI Mackays, Chatham ME5 8TD

New Island received financial assistance from

The Arts Council (An Comhairle Ealaíon), Dublin, Ireland

10 9 8 7 6 5 4 3 2 1

CONTENTS

March

April

May

JUNE

JULY

August

September

October

NOVEMBER

DECEMBER

INTRODUCTION

Sunday Miscellany is one of Irish radio's longest-running programmes. Its increased audiences in recent times ensure its content is enjoyed by thousands more people than ever before. This anthology is a celebration of that content, heard on the radio and talked about at the breakfast table, in bed, in the car; heard online across the world, or as a podcast wherever we want!

The programme continues to honour the essence of its first broadcast when it went out on air on RTÉ Radio in 1968 and was promoted in the *RTÉ Guide* as part of a brand-new strand of programming designed to have 'greater listener involvement' and 'appeal to listeners of all ages'. Its uncluttered structure – consisting of a weekly choice of brand-new essays and an occasional poem read on air by their authors, interspersed with musical interludes – continues today to lend itself perfectly to all sorts of possibility of content within a now long-proven winning formula, caught between the inimitable brassy sound of Samuel Schiedt's 'Galliard Battaglia', the programme's signature tune.

The period between 2008 and 2011 has been an especially rich one for *Sunday Miscellany*, with such a variety of commissioned contributions and open submissions sent in for consideration, from which I made my selection for the radio programme and, subsequently, this anthology. I intend its content to illustrate how *Sunday Miscellany* captures the national mood and focus: what is distracting, fascinating and captivating at any given time, as well as acknowledging our more personal circumstances and selves expressed through the majesty of trees, the meaning of snow or that place we call home.

My selection here is encouraged by the reactions of listeners to pieces such as those inspired by the election of Barack Obama; the Haiti earthquake; the national salt shortage; the demise of the Irish sugar-beet industry; the diminishment of our banks and of our familiar lifestyles; the emergence of ghost estates; the fiftieth anniversary of the first Irish UN Peace Mission to the Congo and of the Amateur Drama Festival; the first annual National Commemoration Day of the Irish Famine; the bicentenary of the birth of Darwin and the hundred and fiftieth anniversary of the publication of *The Origin of Species*; the seventy-fifth anniversary of The Irish Folklore Commission; the thirtieth anniversary of the first production of *Translations* by Brian Friel; Seamus Heaney's seventieth birthday; ten years of RTÉ lyric fm; the twentieth anniversary of the fall of the Berlin Wall; the retirement of veteran broadcaster Micheál Ó Muircheartaigh; John Henry Newman's beatification; and moving contributions relating to the deaths of such unique and varied figures as Keith Floyd, Alex Higgins and Mick Lally.

As *Sunday Miscellany* runs throughout the year, the anthology is structured in a similar way. The seasons move naturally through its content like the perennials of Valentine's Day in February and *Seachtain na Gaeilge* in March; Easter contributions are followed by contributions about holidays and summer jobs; September is a reminder of how ingrained GAA All-Ireland championships past and present are in the collective imagination; autumn has contributions about Hallowe'en; winter evokes poignant remembrances and abounds with Christmas rituals, seasonality and year's ending.

I would like to acknowledge my indebtedness and thanks to Lorelei Harris (Arts, Features and Drama Editor, RTÉ Radio 1), Ana Leddy (former Head of RTÉ Radio 1), Jim Jennings (current Head of RTÉ Radio 1) and Clare Duignan (Managing Director of RTÉ Radio). Their support and encouragement has made all the difference to this book and to the innovations the programme has introduced in recent years, most particularly bringing *Sunday Miscellany* out of the studio and into the country, which has resulted in some very special live events and, according to our listeners, an edgy and exhilarating radio experience. This is the first *Sunday Miscellany* anthology to cover the period it has hosted programmes across the four provinces of Ireland, and the variety of content here intends to reflect this development. This book includes contributions written especially for *Sunday Miscellany Live* at Listowel Writers' Week; Cúirt International Festival of Literature in Galway; the Mountains to

Sea dlr Book Festival in Dún Laoghaire; the Benedict Kiely Annual Literary Weekend in Omagh; and the Donegal Bay and Bluestacks Festival in Ballyshannon. The contributions from these events in this collection include those by John Banville, Joseph O'Neill, Hedy Gibbons Lynott, Alex Miller, Mary Morrissy, Kevin McAleer and Kevin Barry.

I would like to thank Máire Logue, Maureen Kennelly, Tim Carey, Bert Wright, Bernie Kirrane, Jean Brennan, Traolach Ó Fionnáin and Denise Blake of these festivals, as well as Dún Laoghaire Rathdown County Council, the Peace 111 programme and Omagh District Council, and Donegal County Arts Office. They have contributed to the ongoing success of *Sunday Miscellany*'s quiet nudges towards enhancing tangible links between the programme and the public by including *Sunday Miscellany Live* events in the official programmes of each of these festivals, and making them something not to be missed.

Thanks to Isabell Smyth, Head of Communications, and Michael Starrett, Chief Executive of The Heritage Council; memorable collaborative *Sunday Miscellany Live* events were recorded in Kilkenny City and in Dún Laoghaire and broadcast in 2008. Contributions written for these events by Kerry Hardie, Jason Oakley and Michael Coady, and included here, illustrate the rich diversity of our heritage.

A particularly moving *Sunday Miscellany* project, represented in this anthology in contributions by Brian Crowley and Elaine Sisson, was the recording made by the programme and attended by the public in the Pearse Museum, St Enda's in Rathfarnham, Dublin. In association with The Office of Public Works and Irish Academic Press, *Sunday Miscellany* dedicated a programme to the life and times of Patrick Pearse, recorded on 23 April 2009 – the anniversary of the eve of the day he left St Enda's and headed into Dublin to the Rising. This edition of *Sunday Miscellany*, subsequently short-listed for a PPI National Radio Award, had a particular poignancy when broadcast on the anniversary of the execution of this controversial figure in Ireland's history.

Thanks to Head of Local Arts at The Arts Council, Monica Corcoran, Lucinda Russell, Chairperson of the Association of Local Authority Arts Offices and Sheila Deegan, Limerick City Council Arts Officer, *Sunday Miscellany*'s first collaboration with The Arts Council occurred in 2010. The event was enjoyed by the public and delegates attending '25:25 Arts and Culture in Local Development', a conference in the newly opened World Academy of Dance and Music in the University of Limerick. Celebratory new essays capturing the arts in our daily lives – and written for this *Sunday Miscellany Live* – by Thomas McCarthy, Amanda Coogan and Mary Coll are included in this anthology.

The programme's collaborative events with the RTÉ Concert Orchestra have delivered some wonderful combinations of music and writing to audiences in Studio One in the RTÉ Radio Centre in Donnybrook, and in the National Concert Hall. Gina Moxley's and Brendan Graham's contributions in this collection are representative of these memorable *Sunday Miscellany* broadcasts in 2009 and 2011. While not quite included in this anthology, the many wonderful musicians and singers who contribute to *Sunday Miscellany*, and have become such a rich aspect of the programme, deserve their own particular applause; a particular thanks to conductor Gearóid Grant, Anthony Long, Heather McDougall, Angela Rohan and Michelle McCarthy.

Neither a radio programme such as *Sunday Miscellany*, nor an anthology such as this, could be made without the support of colleagues. I would like to thank Fionnuala Hayes for her invaluable assistance in producing the programme; the RTÉ sound engineers and outside broadcasting crews; Joseph Hoban, Communications Manager, RTÉ Radio; Sarah Martin and Sheena Madden; Malachy Moran of RTÉ Audio Services and Archives, as well as the staff of the RTÉ Library and Sound Archive.

My sincere thanks go especially to Deirdre O'Neill, who so tirelessly and patiently steered me through editing this anthology. I would like to equally thank Aisling Glynn, Inka Hagen, Conor Graham and Edwin Higel of New Island, who all have been so supportive of this and recent *Sunday Miscellany* publications, and who take every care in producing such handsome books. Many thanks to Gráinne Killeen, who worked on the publicity for the book; to Damien Flood for the gorgeous painting for the cover and to Jerome Ó Drisceoil of Green On Red Gallery who made this happen. Finally, I want to thank Brian Fay and our children Nóra and Eoghan for so generously allowing me the time to deliver this latest edition to you, the reader, and my parents Bernie and Eoghan Ó hAnluain who introduced me to *Sunday Miscellany* in the first place.

As a brand-new *Sunday Miscellany* anthology appears and a new period of producing and broadcasting the programme begins, I hope this book is a fine reminder of the wondrous and unique programme that is *Sunday Miscellany*, and that it is read and reread with the equal pleasure that is mine in bringing it to you.

Clíodhna Ni Anluain
Producer
Sunday Miscellany
RTÉ Radio 1
2011

www.rte/radio1/sundaymiscellany

JANUARY

THE MEANING OF SNOW

Liam Aungier

'Isn't there some meaning?'
'Look out there … It's snowing. What's the meaning of that?'
– Chekhov, Three Sisters

Snow is a white rose
Shedding its million petals
On the naked earth.

Open your mouth
And it will settle on your tongue
Like a sacrament.

It loves places we
Disregard, it rests on roofs,
On walls, in gutters.

Rain drips and splashes
In its loud downpour, but snow
Falls without a sound.

It is a memory
Of half-forgotten mornings
Of my boyhood.

Through the hours of night
Even when no one watches
Still it falls and falls.

It makes the earth new,
Cold and white and alien.
The moon is its sister.

It too is mortal.
The evening news has promised
Rain before dawn. So

Come out with me now:
We might discover bird-tracks
Written on the snow.

SALT AND HISTORY

Colbert Kearney

An interesting consequence of the recent cold snap was the sudden reval-
uation of salt when supply fell short of demand and the despised condi-
ment was briefly restored to the paramount position it had occupied for
most of human history. So totally has electrical refrigeration replaced it,
we have to remind ourselves that without salt the human race might not
have survived long enough to invent refrigeration.

Salt was the bedrock of civilisation, as essential to previous centuries
as oil was to the twentieth. A million wars were fought to secure it. No
army could function without an adequate supply of it. A major cause of
the French Revolution was a crippling tax on it that was more than the
poor could bear.

Before humans discovered the preservative powers of salt, meat and
fish could only be consumed fresh, which meant that any interruption of
supply was a shortage that might become a famine. With salting, however,
surplus meat and fish could be stored until required, or transported and
traded wherever there was a profitable demand.

Evidence of the importance of salt survives in the words we still use.
Jesus told his followers they were 'the salt of the earth', meaning that
their virtue could preserve the human race from its inherent tendency to
moral decay. A portion of a Roman soldier's wages was designated his
'salt-money' or what we'd call his 'salary' — at least those Roman soldiers
who were 'worth their salt'. Via Salaria, one of the great Roman roads,
began as a trail down to the salt marshes of the Tiber estuary, and the
growth of Rome, like that of many other great cities, was facilitated by
its access to salt. Liverpool, for example, was developed as a port from

which to export salt from the nearby Cheshire mines. The very names of Salzburg and Salinas tell how these settlements began.

There are two sources of salt. Rock salt is mined in a process so dangerous that being sent to the salt mines was once the severest form of hard labour. Sea salt is produced in coastal factories called salt pans where seawater is heated until the water evaporates and a saline material remains.

Few salt pans have survived in northern Europe, mainly because the need for fuel made it an expensive process. Those in warmer climates could depend on the sun to effect evaporation and some of these are still in operation around the Mediterranean.

In our recent distress we turned to Spain for the salt we needed and first off the mark were shippers in Cork and Limerick. This may have had something to do with the trading traditions of those cities. Limerick was famous for its ham, the preservation and transport of which demanded a secure and plentiful supply of salt. Cork was the butter capital of the British Empire and even more dependent on salt, almost all of which was imported, some of it as the return cargo of ships that carried Cork's salted butter throughout the world.

Because it was required for food rather than icy roads, the imported salt was refined by burning in kilns and this offered those in the lime business an opportunity to expand and diversify; contemporary advertisements and directories record the emergence of a new entrepreneur calling himself a 'manufacturer and chapman of salt and lime', a chapman being a merchant.

One such was James Augustine Joyce of Cork who was born in 1827 and inherited a flourishing salt and lime business from his father.

The Joyces were masons and brick-makers who had come south from Connemara in search of prosperity and had succeeded in acquiring a measure of wealth, property and prestige; but with wealth came the means to indulge what a descendant would term 'an extravagant licentious disposition'. Mid-nineteenth century James Augustine preferred the high life to the drudgery of salt and lime, with the result that he went bankrupt twice, squandering his own and his wife's money and losing the family business in the process.

His only son John continued along his father's primrose path, sporting and playing and drinking as if there was no tomorrow, first as a young buck in Cork, then as an improvident husband and father in Dublin, mortgaging his inheritance to finance his expensive lifestyle. But by 1894 the game was up and he was obliged to return to Cork to dispose of the remaining properties. For company he took his eldest son, another James Augustine, who would recall and immortalise the trip to Cork when he came to write his autobiographical novel, *A Portrait of the Artist as a Young Man*.

Who knows how different cultural history would be had the Cork Joyces resisted their extravagant, licentious disposition? Had John Joyce knuckled down and restored the family fortune, instilling in his eldest son a reverence for office hours and fiscal prudence? Perhaps a Jack or Jim Joyce would have made our television news recently, explaining the logistics of the salt trade in a South Mall accent. In which case we'd never have followed Leopold Bloom on his voyage around Dublin on a fine summer's day in 1904, or have watched with Gabriel Conroy the most famous snowfall in Irish fiction, when 'snow was general all over Ireland'.

THE OLD-AGE PENSION

Pádraig McGinn

I went to the county library in Clones recently to look up the census returns for my grandfather and his family for the years 1901 and 1911. They lived in the townland of Cabragh, near Lough Egish, in County Monaghan, on a small farm. Now Joyce's *Irish Names of Places* translates Cabragh as 'bad, rough, unprofitable land' and, as there were six sons and three daughters in the family, things were undoubtedly difficult. The 1901 census returns indicated that my grandfather was aged forty-two. Ten years later, the 1911 census said he was aged sixty-seven. How, I wondered, had he aged twenty-five years in the ten years between the two censuses? Further research taught me that he was not the only Irish person to have aged greatly at that time; in fact it was quite common and the reason was the 1908 Old-Age Pensions Act.

The British Liberal government, with Lloyd George as Chancellor of the Exchequer, brought in an Act to give a pension of five shillings a week to people of both sexes over seventy whose yearly income did not exceed £21. Lloyd George intended that married couples living together would get only three shillings and nine pence each, that's seven shillings and sixpence in total, but the Conservative F. E. (Galloper) Smith pointed out that a man would get more for living with another man's wife than if he lived with his own, so Lloyd George decided he had to give five shillings to every eligible person.

The passing of the Act led to great rejoicing all over the United Kingdom and especially in Ireland, where the ingenuity of the Irish peasant in hoodwinking the pension officers became the stuff of legends. Percy French and others used the theme in plays, sketches and stories.

The percentage of the population in Ireland who applied for the old-age pension was twice as high as in the rest of the United Kingdom.

One had to prove that one was seventy or more to be eligible for the pension. As the Civil Registration of Births only began in 1864, official proof was often difficult to establish and pension officers resorted to questioning old people as to what they remembered. 'Do you remember the night of the Big Wind?' was a standard question. The Big Wind occurred on the night of 6 January 1839 so if one remembered it, one was over seventy.

Ten shillings a week was a generous allowance for an old couple in 1909 when the average labourer earned ten shillings a week, if he had a job, and nothing at all if he was unemployed. Lloyd George said the pension would 'lift the shadow of the workhouse from the homes of the poor'. The Act was greeted with rapture all over the country and it certainly saved many an old person from the workhouse. Bonfires blazed, bands played and streets were decorated with bunting and flags. Lloyd George was toasted in porter and poteen and a man drove an ass and cart through the street of Ballybay shouting that Lloyd George was the greatest Irishman ever.

No wonder then that my grandfather and many others advanced their ages when the 1911 census was taken. I don't know whether the trick worked for him or whether he managed to deceive the pension officer; he was dead before I was born. But I did hear of one Leitrim lady, a Mary Earley, who got the pension when she was still only sixty-nine. However the pension officer discovered that she was not quite seventy yet and her pension was withdrawn. As she walked home from Drumshanbo Fair one day with her namesake, another Mary Earley who had the pension, the latter affected to be very sympathetic towards her, listing out all one could buy with five shillings and shedding crocodile tears for her neighbour's loss. The younger Mary saw through the false sympathy and, when she could put up with it no longer, exclaimed, 'Ah, what's five shillings anyhow? Isn't it far better to have your youth?'

The Act came into force on 1 January 1909, which was on a Friday. And ever since that day, one hundred years ago, the pension is always paid on a Friday.

ON KEEPING A DIARY

Dympna Murray Fennell

I have a confession to make. About this time every year, I give up on keeping my diary. Whether I have an elegant gilt-edged volume, moleskin-bound, or a cheap bargain-basement version, it's difficult to work up enthusiasm over the minutiae of January life, the flagging New Year's resolutions, the long wait for green shoots; so the diary becomes just a calendar of appointments, a jotter for reminders, a space for doodling.

This year I feel especially guilty, when I think of the great diarist who started his recording 350 years ago, in 1660, and persevered with it for nine years in the middle of plague and fire and an uncertain regime. Young Samuel Pepys faithfully penned his journal almost every night with the light of smoking tallow candles, and would probably have continued longer were it not for his failing eyesight. At a time when a foolish word could have left one in prison, or worse, Sam wrote honestly of his private life and the London of the day, in his own shorthand style, using a kind of French code to detail his many 'dalliances'. He loved the good life, entertaining the 'quality' and especially those who could be useful to him socially, and career-wise. In January 1660 he gave a dinner party, only seven courses, but 'mighty merry I was, and made them all, and they were mightily pleased'. Afterwards there was card-playing, singing and talking, and then 'ale and apples'. No wonder he admitted the next day, that he had such a habit of 'lying long abed'.

He records a great variety of entertainments from attending public executions (though he complained about not getting a good view at the beheading of an old republican). Later he saw his first cock-fight, and then came home to 'an extraordinarily good dinner'.

After the dour days of Cromwell, the theatres re-opened, and Sam went regularly, both to the traditional drama and the roistering new Restoration comedy; he noted with approval the first appearance of a woman actor. There was still a slight 'whiff of sulphur' about theatre-going, and in a New Year's resolution in 1661 he took an oath to abstain from 'wine and the theatre' with the added advantage that he would 'save enough and get rich'. He worried about his finances, and chided his young wife Elizabeth over the household accounts; she retorted by accusing him of 'gadding abroad to look after beauties'.

He had a good position as secretary to the navy, though he admitted he knew little about ships; there was a bit of trouble when some of his enemies accused him of embezzling funds; he was brought before a tribunal, but his attending at court paid off – the king intervened on his behalf, and all was well. Considering he was one of those who cheered at the execution of the king's father, he was lucky to have tacked around when he saw the way the wind was blowing, and was on board when Charles II was brought back from exile. He wore his new velvet coat to the coronation, and was so impressed by the 'show of silver and gold that we were not able to look at it'; there was much partying afterwards! Later when he saw the king in a 'plain common riding-coat and cap, he seemed a very ordinary man'. The king's mistresses were assessed very candidly, and his behaviour to his queen deplored. Sam admired the virtuous Queen Catherine, and sympathised with her lonely position – she is one of the few characters in his chronicle who escapes criticism – but he was not impressed by the new beverage which she introduced to court: tea. The coffee-house was more to his liking; there he enjoyed the political and social gossip of this exciting new world.

This busy life was interrupted slightly by the outbreak of plague in 1665. Sam took precautions by chewing tobacco and being careful about his wig supplier, in case the hair used had come from a corpse. He sent Elizabeth out of the city for safety, and at the end of the year he conceded, 'I have never lived so merrily as I have this plague year, because I never got so much.'

Life was more upset the following year by the Great Fire, and Sam was delegated to tell the king. Charles passed on the responsibility to the Lord Mayor, and Sam went home to save his wine and Parmesan cheese by burying them in the garden; later he consoled himself by 'having an extraordinarily good dinner'.

Three hundred and fifty years later, Samuel Pepys', picture of his life and times makes fascinating reading, and could be an incentive to those of us who abandon the diary-keeping at the first hint of boredom; who knows but that today's mundane and ordinary record might be a gold-mine for the social historian of tomorrow.

DRIVEN TO DISTRACTION

Clodagh O'Donoghue

Every year for the last ten years, I have made the same New Year's resolutions.

I used to write them down. I would make my list, confident that, as the year went on, I would be able to tick each item off as I accomplished it. Then it began to emerge that one resolution remained unticked at the end of every year, and had to be put at the top of the new New Year's list. Eventually, I stopped writing it down and merely made a mental note which, in recent times, has become more of a desperate plea – please let this year be the year I learn to drive.

The problem is I'm no good at doing things that I'm no good at. It's a character flaw, I know, but if something does not come easily to me, I am liable to throw in the towel sooner rather than later.

Now, this did not present too much of a problem when I failed to learn to juggle, as I had never really intended running away to join the circus. Nor was it too much of a drawback when I proved not to be a natural swimmer, as an ability to swim is not strictly necessary for getting from A to B. Driving, however, is a different matter. You can extol the virtues of walking as much as you like – talk about how it keeps you trim, and clears the head, and gets the endorphins flowing, but when you are trying to get two children back and forth the mile and a half to school in the pouring rain, these protestations sound a trifle hollow.

It's not that I haven't put in the effort to master driving. I have severely tried my husband's patience as we have made endless trips to a wide variety of industrial estates where, with me at the wheel, we have crawled around, alongside lots of other L-plate drivers, who have doubtless gone on to become proficient motorists with full licences whereas I, tragically, have not.

I have also, I am embarrassed to say, taken more than fifty lessons with professional driving instructors. Yes, that is fifty. My first batch of lessons was with an instructor whom we will call 'Billy' – not his real name – who was a rather stylish young man in his early twenties with girlfriend troubles. Our Saturday morning lessons would go something like this:

Hi, Billy, how are you today?

Not so good. Check your mirrors. First gear.

Oh dear, I'm sorry to hear that.

Yeah, she's not talking to me again. Signal and moving off.

Is she not, Billy?

No, not since last Thursday. Second gear. Take the next left.

What's it about this time?

Oh, the usual. Me working too much. Third gear. Evenings. Weekends. Squeeze the brake. And stop at the lights.

Now, instead of spending my lesson feeling bad that I was keeping Billy away from his girlfriend and trying to make helpful suggestions about buying his girlfriend flowers and cooking her a romantic dinner, I should have pointed out that I was paying him a substantial fee to teach me to drive and, after twenty-one lessons, I still hadn't a clue. And that, in fact, I should be charging him for listening to his problems and providing guidance. Shortly afterwards, Billy and I parted company. As, possibly, did he and his girlfriend.

And, as another January dawned, I signed up with another driving school and another instructor. This one took a little longer to start telling me his life story but, by about lesson 12, I had heard about a chequered past, some unsavoury friends, at least two estranged relationships, and his hopes and aspirations for the future.

It is nice to discover that I am clearly a good listener, but my sympathetic ear has proved something of an expensive and time-consuming liability.

I have had nine lessons with my current instructor, whom we will call Paul – because that is his real name – and I am thrilled to say I know nothing about his personal circumstances, his marital situation, or his living arrangements. In fact, I know nothing about him at all. Refreshingly, our sole topic of conversation is driving and the imminent test.

Obviously, I know that my failure to master driving is not the fault of my previous driving instructors, and that my own lack of tenacity, determination and self-belief are to blame. But it is coming up to ten years now that I have been taking lessons, which is a nice round number. And I am about to take my third test, which could prove third time lucky. I am full of hope. Wish me well.

AN UNEXPECTED GIFT

Barbara Scully

The recent snowfall, which caused such travel chaos, also brought with it some unexpected and beautiful gifts.

The uncommon arrival of such deep snow inserted a large comma into the normally manic days preceding Christmas. The kids' school was closed, I wouldn't drive and so life took on a whole new way of being. Lighting an afternoon fire and making bedtime hot-water bottles became essential and were reminders of a previous, simpler way of life. As Christmas neared, I made two shopping excursions facilitated by my husband and his jeep. Knowing I wouldn't be venturing forth again forced me to focus on essentials as opposed to striving to create festive perfection. It was my most relaxed Christmas week ever. Trudging through snow to Mass on Christmas Eve was an added magical bonus of the Arctic weather.

But more than all that, I just loved the special quiet that a thick blanket of snow brings. That uniquely snowy hush as the earth is wrapped up in frozen whiteness. I was tucking my children into bed one night when my youngest said, 'Mom, listen. What's that sound?'

I stopped and listened. As I whispered 'that's the foghorn on the end of Dún Laoghaire pier', I was whisked back over forty years to my own childhood bedroom in Blackrock, about a mile from the sea.

How many nights did I lie in my bed listening to that very same, regular sound as it floated out over Dublin Bay? If I listened very closely, way off in the distance, the Dún Laoghaire foghorn was answered by the one on Howth Head. I used to wonder about what ships might be in the bay, hearing the low drone of the foghorns. Who were on these ships?

Where were they going? Were they safe? Was the sound of the foghorn reassuring to them or did it sound an ominous warning?

I used to imagine a young deckhand, a boy perhaps a little older than me, on board one of these ghost ships of my imagination. Was he wishing he could be home, tucked up safely in his bed as I was?

Back then I was in national school in Monkstown where I was very lucky to have a wonderful teacher, Mrs McGloughlin, who was steeped in local history and folklore. She often told us the stories of eighteenth-century shipwrecks that occurred just off the coast of Dún Laoghaire and Dalkey. Her stories were vivid and totally captivated my childish imagination. She told us that many of the victims of these tragedies were buried in the old graveyard on Carrickbrennan Road. So, as I lay there on those winter nights, my mind also wandered to their ancient headstones and I wondered if these lost souls could hear the mournful tune of the foghorn. Perhaps if they had been able to hear a foghorn, back on the night their ships sank, their lives could have been saved. According to my teacher, many of them perished because in the foggy confusion they did not realise just how close to the shore they were.

'What are you thinking, Mom?' brings me back to my daughter's bedroom. 'I'm thinking about how much I love the sound of the foghorn and how we have never heard it before in this house.'

What a wonderful gift the snow delivered – a last chance to fall asleep to the comforting, regular, heartbeat of the foghorn on Dún Laoghaire pier.

On Tuesday, 11 January, Ireland's foghorns, having outlived their usefulness, will be switched off for good. I doubt I will be alone in missing their lonely yet comforting call on winter nights.

BURIED

Joe Kearney

Maps and buried treasure: the stuff of boyhood dreams.

I still recall, with a clarity that surprises me, the day our neighbour, Catherine, propped her bicycle against the front windowsill, released the spring from her carrier and brought a small parcel into our kitchen. How was I to know that the contents of that parcel would change me forever and would fuel an obsession governing the rest of my life? I don't know why she did it. Catherine never repeated the gesture but, looking back, I'm glad she did. She offered me three tattered, hardback books. I'll never forget them. They were *What Katy Did*, *Treasure Island* and Gibbon's *Rise and Fall of the Roman Empire*.

Here I was, an only child in 1950s Ireland, living in a house on a by-road, off a byroad, our nearest neighbour a good half-mile distant; no TV, no Nintendo Wii, no Gameboy, just the Bush radio up there on the shelf and the *Dandy* posted to me from an aunt in England each week.

Ours was not a literary house. As far as I can recall the only books we possessed were my grandmother's pension book (and that was tucked away in a biscuit tin beneath her bed) and a couple of prayer books stuffed with novenas and memory cards. It didn't take me long to work out the order in which I'd tackle these new possessions. The Gibbon's looked daunting, the *Katy* book a bit too girlie...but *Treasure Island*? Oh! *Treasure Island*: that was the real find, the repository of pure, literary gold.

I sailed into a world of pirates, buried treasure and maps. I entered the world of Jim Hawkins, Billy Bones, Squire Trelawney and Long John Silver. My daytime musings and my night-time dreams filled up with Captain Flint's pieces of eight and the creaking timbers of the good ship *Hispaniola*.

At the kitchen table, I drew my own maps, substituted local townlands for the topography of *Treasure Island*; imagining Caribbean waters washing over the inland shores of Ballinashig, Modeshill and Attattinoe. When I climbed into the upper reaches of the big chestnut tree, the swaying branches became my crow's-nest. Below my eyrie, the wind tossed the meadowed fields until they resembled an angry sea. It rippled the grasses into a green tide; the distant tractor became a Spanish galleon stuffed to the gunwales with jewels and plate.

It was a slow read, my first novel. But long before the *Hispaniola* sailed back to England, laden with Flint's doubloons, long before they rescued Ben Gunn and reformed the mutinous Long John, I was hooked, not just on this manuscript but on the entire world of books. However, this newfound obsession would not go unnoticed. It carried a domestic price:

'That child will ruin his eyes from all that reading.'

'Would you for God's sake put down that book and go out in the fresh air to play.'

'I can get no good of him, at all. He has his head shoved in a book night, noon and morning.'

I was nine when I finished *The Rise and Fall of the Roman Empire* and still remember it as a dull read compared with Stevenson's *Treasure Island*, but nonetheless it was a book. It was a place of the imagination, a place I could enter whenever I liked. If I dug between its pages I would unearth treasure, sooner or later.

That initial, imaginary voyage on the *Hispaniola* happened over fifty years ago; it was the first embrace in my lifelong love affair, my first literary kiss!

Squire Trelawney's ship was named after a real place. There is an island called Hispaniola. In the early seventeenth century, this island became a regular stopping point for Caribbean pirates. It is believed that much pirate treasure is hidden beneath its volcanic soil. All you need is a map with a skull and crossbones, and dig at the spot marked with the red 'X'.

In 1665, under the reign of King Louis XIV, the French colonised Hispaniola. It was given the name Saint-Domingue but that would later change. Nicknamed the 'Pearl of the Antilles' it became the richest and most prosperous colony in the West Indies and one of the wealthiest in the world.

And now, Hispaniola is back again in the news; it has returned to haunt the world – the stuff of nightmare instead of the inspiration of boyhood dreams. This time around, digging is also involved. But there are no maps to point the way; the digging is desperate. The excavation is for bodies and not pieces of eight. The treasure being sought is that most precious, and most fragile of all: human life.

The Island of Hispaniola is divided in two: the Dominican Republic to the south and, in the north, a country called Haiti.

FACEBOOK FAME

Sue Norton

If I can believe my Facebook page, I am more popular than I realised. It seems that every time I log on, someone else I once knew is looking to 'friend' me. Usually the invitation for Facebook-friendship comes from a former classmate. Curiously, though, I am certain I wasn't this sought after back in high school or college. In university during the mid-1980s, I was a girl with friends, sure, but hardly a girl at the centre of things. Yet people I barely knew back then are seeking to connect with me now.

I have a feeling this pursuit of me has more to do with the desire for popularity of my former acquaintances than with any long overdue popularity of mine.

But I am keeping an open mind.

It's just that every time I see the thumbnail photos of friends on my Facebook wall or on someone else's, I am reminded of the taxidermied lion heads that adorn the trophy walls of victorious hunters: the more you have up there, the more accomplished you seem. It's the thrill of the kill, I guess.

My niece, who is 20 years old, has 365 friends on her Facebook wall. One for every day of the year, I suppose. She is Facebook-fabulous. Her father, my brother, has four Facebook friends. And one of them is her.

But I predict that he, too, will soon be vanquishing more friends. It's just a matter of time before a low headcount on your Facebook wall makes you feel self-conscious.

Maybe that's why Facebook has become so popular. It's competitive. It now has 200 million members. And if you are one of them, you know that many of these users are middle-aged or older. Yesterday I was joking with a friend – over coffee, by the way, not on Facebook – that the site has become so prevalent that if I were to wake up one morning and discover that my own father had sent me a friend request, I'd barely be surprised. And my father has been dead for eight years.

But oh how I would love to see him post status updates on his heavenly wall: 'heard the distant trumpets of angels before dawn this morning'; or, 'mulled around the Pearly Gates this afternoon meeting interesting newcomers.'

Because this is the other curious thing people do on Facebook: they don't just get in touch with their old high-school sweethearts, they broadcast their latest musings and reflections to everyone who's interested. And quite remarkably, many of us are. There are over 400,000 users of Facebook living in Ireland. If you aren't one of them, you know someone who is. And if you were to visit the pages of your friends and relatives, you might find yourself scratching your head at the sheer frivolity of their preoccupations. Ordinarily busy people, your own closest associates are pausing throughout the day to let their Facebook fanclub know when they've had a nasty brush with a taxi-driver or been driven to despair by the complexities of their child's algebra homework.

It seems we middle-agers are quite the attention seekers. We go about our low-profile lives commuting to work, shopping for groceries, attending PTA meetings, walking the dog, and then the glow of the PC monitor catches our eye and – bam! – we're divesting ourselves of our frustrations and jubilations to any of our acquaintances with a passing interest.

Perhaps this impulse is not all that different from the simple wish to share a few pleasantries with the postman or to gossip with the school traffic warden. It's swift and gratifying. But, on the other hand, when I chat with my acquaintances or friends in person, I feel I'm actually *giving* them something. I'm giving them attention. But when I post my musings on my Facebook wall, I have a funny feeling I'm *looking* for attention.

So really it's not the same thing at all.

I'm bracing myself for the day my pre-teen son asks me if he can join Facebook. Social networking sites can be such a Gargantuan waste of time. No doubt I will worry that his homework will suffer, that his outdoor activities will vanish, and so on. Very likely, he will ask to join MySpace or Bebo, because they draw a younger crowd. And as I prepare for this eventual conversation, I find myself really hoping he will ask to join Bebo just so I can look at him contemplatively and say, 'Ah, Declan, to Be-bo or not to Be-bo, that is the question…' I just want to see him roll his eyes and turn away, before he breaks a smile.

I can't do *that* on Facebook, now can I?

THE FRAUNHOFER LINES

Mark Joyce

In 2001 a group of Irish artists worked with the famous American artist James Turrell in the National Sculpture Factory in Cork. We had volunteered to help him with a new piece of work in the Sculpture Factory on Albert Road. The piece in question was a complicated machine, 'The Ganzfeld Sphere', which the audience would climb inside one at a time. Turrell had brought specialist technicians with him, so we simply scraped and sanded walls and floors in readiness for the exhibition.

James Turrell was born in 1943 in Los Angeles, and is best known since the 1960s for working with artificial light, but he knows a great deal about any kind of light.

He regularly flies gliders in the high desert air of the south western United States, and indeed his conversation that day glided over the scientific, art historical and literary aspects of light, air and the gaseous atmosphere that envelops the earth. He knows a lot about these things, and we listened.

He had a copy of the French aviator and author Antoine de Saint-Exupéry's book *Wind, Sand and Stars*, written after an air crash in the Sahara. De Saint-Exupéry survived only to dissappear finally over the Mediterranean Sea at night in 1944. Turrell was interested in the descriptions of the relative brightness of the starlight in the desert and at sea.

Stars, he explained, appear as a milky white point of light; they twinkle because of refraction in our atmosphere, and they are 'white' because of the hydrogen gas in their make-up. The younger and fiercely hot stars have a bluer colour like the hottest gas flame.

Turrell felt, and we all agreed with his laconic West Coast view, that we Earthlings were lucky to live on a planet at just the right distance from a mellow yellow middle-aged sun. Someone asked him just how did he know what the stars are made of, being so far away.

'It's the Fraunhofer lines,' he explained.

The Fraunhofer lines: now where had I heard that before? It was the mid 1970s, and a friend of mine had a father who was a scientist. We went to his laboratory on a quiet weekend; it was full of the bulky technology of that era. My friend's father showed a group of us 9-year-olds some cool stuff, deep freezing everyday objects in liquid nitrogen, cupping mirror-like pools of mercury in the palm of his hand. He showed us powerful laser beams and magnets with immense hidden forces, and finally a spectrometer.

As we looked into the lens of the spectrometer we saw a series of colours, with dark threads in between. 'Those are the Fraunhofer lines,' he explained. 'They are the missing bits of the visible spectrum.' Their darkness was the absorbative deep darkness of outer space.

He told us the extraordinary story of Josef von Fraunhofer, the 13-year-old Bavarian orphan who had been pulled from the rubble of a factory collapsed in Straubing in 1801 by the Prince Elector Maximilian of Bavaria. The prince somehow noticed the boy's genius and sent him to the monks of Benediktbeuern Monastery to study optical glass manufacture. Fraunhofer became the greatest scientific glass maker of the age and, using his own lenses he studied the visible spectrum. He found 574 dark threads or lines, gaps in the visible spectra which had been absorbed by particular gases on light's journey from the sun to earth. By analysing any star with Fraunhofer's spectroscope, scientists could now identify what materials were present even at such impossible distances.

'What are the stars?' asked everyone from Aristotle to Joxer Daly.

Josef von Fraunhofer answered this ancient question. With modern spectroscopy, the 540 Fraunhofer lines have grown to over 10,000. Fraunhofer died aged just thirty-nine from the cumulative exposure to the toxic ingredients of optical glass manufacture. But he left a legacy in the metaphorical power of the most fundamental contrast of the sunlight and all the colours visible to the human eye with those dark Fraunhofer lines, the darkest dark, the total absence of colour.

He also gives his name to the Fraunhofer Gesellschaft, the German-based global scientific research organisation which pools and reseeds research with the profits gained from its members' patented discoveries.

A PLACE IN THE BRONX

Iggy McGovern

To come into real estate in these recessionary times may be a mixed blessing. I was recently offered possession of New York property that has been in the family for almost ninety years. Granted, it is small – bijoux, I think, would be an estate agent's description – but isn't everything in that crowded city? There's lots of green space which is well looked after and it's very quiet, hardly a living soul to be seen, although it does come with some pretty interesting neighbours; notably the Irish-American mobster Vincent 'Mad Dog' Coll and 'Lady', the jazz legend Billie Holiday.

By now, you will have guessed that this property is located in a grave-yard, Mad Dog having departed this life in the early 1930s, helped on his way by former associates, and Lady in sadly reduced circumstances fifty years ago this year. It is indeed a grave, or at least a share of a grave, and it's in The Bronx. St Raymond's Cemetery lies at the intersection of the north–south Hutchinson River Parkway with the east–west Cross Bronx Expressway. In spite of that, it is a surprisingly peaceful spot, as if the nearby traffic intentionally slows down as a mark of respect; I should say spots, for there are actually two cemeteries, the old and the new.

The grave is occupied by my paternal aunt, Helen McGovern, and her brother Thomas, natives of the parish of Glangevlin in County Cavan; a parish where there are so many McGoverns that the triple nam-ing system is employed to this day. They are 'Thomas-Oineys', after their father Thomas and his father Eoin, the latter a survivor of the Famine. Helen and Thomas Thomas-Oiney were part of the steady stream of emigration just prior to the establishment of the Free State.

The grave is a three-berth and I have been given the job of filling the empty space, at least figuratively. Senior members of the family argue that a grave is too valuable to lie empty, and since none of the family now lives anywhere close to St Raymond's it should be passed on to someone else. This is not an easy task and I have not yet succeeded, indeed I have barely started; an initial transatlantic telephone approach to the cemetery authorities was less than helpful. 'Have ya got the deed? Ya gotta have the deed.' No, I had to confess, I had not got the deed, nor did I have dates of burial. I rang off feeling like a grave-robber.

I still have not got the deed, although I have some ideas as to where it might be. For now I have to be content with a site inspection. A business trip to the States affords a long weekend lie-over in New York. Monday morning I take the Pelham Bay local to East 177th Street, transferring to the Q44 bus to alight at Lafayette Avenue, and begin the long headstone-lined walk to the cemetery office. There the telephone voice is embodied as an elderly woman who, if she suspects that I am the other half of that fitful conversation, decides not to acknowledge it. I still don't have proper dates, but as the computer says there are five Helen McGoverns and only two Thomases, and one of those is from the nineteenth century, we agree that the other must be our man. But of course, he's not here in the new cemetery and so begins the much longer trek to the old.

By the time I get there, I'm running against the clock and the departure of flight EI108 back to Dublin, so there's no possibility of stopping by the graves of Mad Dog or Lady, nor those of the welterweight champion boxer Benny 'Kid' Paret, or of the infamous Mary Mallon, better known as 'Typhoid Mary'. Instead, I go straight to section 12, range 8 and grave 117 where I read 'Thomas McGovern, March 10, 1921' and Helen McGovern a lifetime later in 1984. And I am moved to small tears for what the headstone cannot tell: the shadow on the Thomas-Oineys. That Thomas never made it to the Bronx alive, catching scarlet fever on the boat, dying in isolation on Ellis Island, barely as old as the century. And that his sister, just three years his elder, had the unenviable task of claiming the body for burial.

And I am, there and then, decided that only someone who has weathered an equal amount of pain and loss deserves to share this place in The Bronx.

SATURDAY NIGHT HAMBURGER

Mary Rose Callaghan

A steamy Saturday night, and we drove into town for a hamburger. Four women were in the air-conditioned car. My American cousin, Lillian, myself, and two other Red Cross volunteers: Alice, who was a black, and Pam, who was a white Mississippian. It was August 1969 and Hurricane Camille had left a trail of destruction along the Gulf Coast, the worst until Katrina. The American Red Cross had set up a refugee camp in an army base near Hattiesburg, a town north of New Orleans, and Lillian, who worked for the Red Cross, was in charge of recreation. She was a tiny thirty-something, who had gone to UCD in the 1950s. After a hard week, she was hungry and wanted to relax. We tried one seedy drive-in after another with no luck. Looking back on it, we seemed to be repeatedly ignored. But perhaps they were just busy; it was a Saturday night after all.

'Maybe we should go back home,' Alice said. Like all the volunteers, she was in her early twenties. We were staying together, sleeping in bunks, eating army food, but having nightly guitar sessions and singing songs of liberation: Bob Dylan and Joan Baez.

As we failed to get service, Alice was getting more and more nervous. 'Why don't y'all make popcorn?'

'But I want a hamburger!' Lillian insisted.

I had wanted to visit America all my life, and that summer I had a student visa. It had been a bizarre trip. I had taken a bus from New York to Las Vegas and had been in LA on the night of Sharon Tate's murder. I was now travelling cross-country to Florida, where my mother had grown up. I had broken the journey to volunteer. It was relief to get out of the car.

I don't remember any adult refugees, although there must have been many. All week I played with the children, telling them Irish stories and braiding their hair, supervised by armed, white National Guards, who kept asking if I liked that 'kinda work'. I said I did. I was planning to be a teacher and, although shocked by their poverty, I enjoyed the children's quirky humour.

All summer I had survived on pancakes and maple syrup, so had put on a stone. That night I was looking forward to a hamburger too, with maybe a milkshake and some fries, as the Red Cross was paying: a thank-you for all our help. If only we could be served. Finally we pulled into Joe's Place, a rural truck-stop café at the side of Route 59.

Conversation stopped as we entered and found a table in the all-white café. Men in overalls whispered to their wives. A middle-aged waiter wiped our Formica-topped table and gave us menus and glasses of iced water – all except Alice.

Lillian asked for another menu.

'We don't serve nigger folk, Ma'am,' the waiter said. His skin was pitted with acne and he had ugly teeth – unusual for an American. Of all the waiters who have ever served me, I was to remember his face.

Alice began to tremble, and stood up.

Lillian put a restraining hand on her arm. 'But you're breaking the law!' she said to the man.

He looked back with hatred. Without saying a word, we all got up and trooped out into the sweltering heat. 'God bless you and your company,' the whole café chanted.

Martin Luther King had been dead for over a year, and two Civil Rights Bills had been passed. That summer an American had landed on the moon. 'How many roads must a man walk down, before they call him a man?'

As we stood outside, inhaling gas fumes mingled with smells of hamburger, the cops screeched up. A big fat sheriff got out of the car, fondling his gun.

Lillian ran over. 'I want to report that café for breaking the law. They wouldn't—'

'Lady, that's your problem.'

'But the law?' she said.

He pulled down his Stetson and waved his gun. 'Move on, Ma'am!'

Although from Florida, Lillian had never experienced segregation like this, and kept assuring me that it wasn't America. We drove back to the camp in shock. The law meant nothing. Pam apologised to Alice. 'That café just made a liar outta me.'

I haven't thought of the incident for forty years. But when Barack Obama was sure of being elected at about three o'clock on the morning of last November 5th, I remembered that night.

ELECTION NIGHT IN HARLEM

Colin Murphy

'House of Justice' said the banner sign above the window. And under it, in smaller letters: 'No justice, no peace'. A big woman in a black suit stood at the door. 'We're having a watch night,' she said. 'Come on in.'

Earlier that day, I'd spent a spare hour in the ballroom of an old hotel on the Bowery, downtown. There was a desk for registration, and a small group being trained, and then, along every wall and scattered on the floor, there were people talking on mobile phones and scrawling notes on sheets of paper. The bar was unmanned and empty, and the chandeliers unnoticed.

At the help desk, a young woman approached the twinkle-eyed official. 'I keep getting French speakers,' she said. Behind her, a man was pacing the room, talking earnest French into his phone.

'Yeah, that's a French-Canadian retirement community in Florida,' said the official. 'We've got a bunch of numbers for them.'

'They'd all vote for Obama if they could,' said the young woman.

The room hummed with good intentions, with newfound camaraderie, with sexual energy. The people in charge hadn't met before they'd started volunteering for the Obama campaign – just days earlier, in most cases. This was one of Manhattan's five 'phone banks', tasked with getting the vote out, using volunteers and their phone credit. It was like a cross between a call centre and a rave, with people getting high on volunteerism, and beaming at each other.

As it happened, there wasn't a black person in that ballroom that afternoon. And there wasn't a white person in the House of Justice that evening.

This was a beacon of a different volunteerism: a more old-fashioned, hard-won community spirit that combined political and civic activism with the gospel – both the religious and musical varieties. Chicken wings and rice were being served by a prickly old lady at one end of the room; two oversize televisions were broadcasting the latest state-by-state results at the other. A man took to the microphone. 'Barack Obama: 150; John McCain: 95', he said, giving the latest total in the electoral college vote. They cheered.

'It certainly looks like there's gonna be a new day in the United States of America,' he said.

I wandered outside and fell into conversation with an elderly gentleman. He introduced himself as 'Jenkins Washington, born in the clayhills o' Georgia', and talked of growing up in the south in the 1940s. 'We didn't have nothing. In the house where I grew up, you could just lay in at night and see the stars,' he said.

'They used to hang black people back where I was,' he said.

'This is a wonderful time for America, 'cause the change is coming,' he said.

He spoke of sitting around the family hearth at night in Georgia, singing, and I asked him what they sang. He laughed to himself, and the laugh became a low growl. He started to sing, an old Negro spiritual: 'There's a bright side somewhere, oh Lord. Don't you start until you find it,' he sang, slowly and reverently, standing outside the House of Justice on 145th Street.

From inside, there was a tremor. Jenkins Washington was still talking; whatever momentous change might be happening on the television was just a moment's backdrop to a rich life story; he didn't want it to interrupt his telling of that story. But I forced a break in our conversation when the door opened and someone said, 'He did it.'

I pushed my way back in, against a stream of people rushing out. It was suddenly bedlam. A woman cried. A young woman ran around the room, seizing people, laughing. Young men ran outside shouting, 'Obama'. A woman took the microphone on the small stage; bent almost double, she wept biblically. 'Lord, we know we're not perfect, but thank you, Lord,' she cried. The man who had earlier addressed the room took the mike again. He shouted: 'I am!' 'I am!' they chorused. He shouted: 'A history maker!' 'A history maker!' they replied.

There was respectful quiet for John McCain's concession speech, and then a DJ played James Brown's 'I'm Black and I'm Proud'. 'We did it, black people,' he shouted.

And then it was Barack Obama's moment. When he thanked his wife, Michelle, the women around me cried. His speech was echoed in this small room with murmurs of 'thank you, Jesus' and whoops and cheers. A woman sang in a low falsetto, simply 'well'.

I found Jenkins Washington outside again later, as his family aimed for home. 'I'm thinking of putting my gospel group back together,' he said. And then his daughter and wife bundled him into the car, and they left, and I caught a cab downtown. On the street, people were standing out, drinking, talking, cheering, dancing. On the radio in the cab, someone was telling the disc jockey that this was the end.

UPDIKE AND THE KING OF POP

Bert Wright

When John Updike died of cancer at seventy-six, it felt more than usually shocking, almost like a death in the family. Several people I spoke to felt the same way. When you've lived with a writer most of your adult life, the voice, the style, their ideas on art and the world become part of your mental furniture. Somehow the idea that all this should come to an abrupt end seemed like an offence against nature. Mid-seventies is no longer old and Updike still looked good, a faded-to-grey version of the immensely colourful writer who had once blown us away with his racy blend of intellectual fireworks, lush prose, and lubricious musings. Here surely was a forever-young oldster who would stay the course and still be producing great work into his dotage. Disease, however, is no respecter of rank or reputation and Updike was fated to miss out on the dotage.

Still, I have the books and some good memories of meeting Updike on a beautiful summer's day in 1997. Behind me in my office there is a photograph of Updike and I taken in the projection room of the old Brattle Theatre in Harvard Square where Updike was about to give a rare reading. I was directing the Harvard Square Book Festival at the time. Updike was to be in town to receive an award and so, in spite of his fabled aversion to public appearances, I decided to chance my arm and wrote to ask if he might consider giving a reading. He responded quickly and kindly, expressing particular curiosity about venues.

I suspect it was the choice of the Brattle that clinched it because for Harvard students of a certain vintage, the Brattle was where, of a Saturday evening, undergrads in blue jeans and button-down Oxfords would squire their dates to the latest European art-house movies. Back came his response – if it was the Brattle he'd be pleased to do it and would I please collect him from Harvard at 3.00 p.m.

Like a freshman on a first date, I arrived an hour early. The speeches were over and Updike was patiently fielding softball questions from the assembled students. He looked ill at ease, anxious to be gone, and so when he was done I introduced myself and together we escaped into the dappling sunlight of Harvard Yard. Trouble was, he had cut his engagement a little short and we were way too early for the Brattle gig. How to kill an hour with your favourite author? Some dilemma! Perhaps he'd fancy a beer? Nah, too bold. A spot of lunch, then? Doubtful, he'd just pulled an apple from his pocket and was carelessly munching away like Tom Sawyer on his way to meet Huck Finn.

On we strolled, with Updike invoking the ghosts of old student hangouts long since laid to rest in the name of progress. His manner was easy and affable, but I suddenly dreaded running out of conversation. Dare I ask him the sort of questions fans love to ask, about Rabbit or Bech or how he found the time to write so many darned words? Risky, I thought, but then, lightbulb moment, I remembered that, like me, Updike was a keen golfer. So amid the leafy environs of Harvard, we discussed the great Scottish golf courses we'd played and the hour was soon put to the sword.

Up in the Brattle projection room Updike, a long-time film buff, let his eye linger lovingly on the round metal reel-cans, checking the titles on the faded labels. He read brilliantly that day – poems, short stories and other bits and pieces – engaging the home-town audience with his usual grace and diffidence. He was enjoying himself and there was I grinning like a lunatic in the wings. Afterwards we shook hands and he thanked me. I ventured some dumb golf line about keeping the head down and off he went, descending with a wave into the bowels of the Charles Hotel car park. Of course, I never saw him again but, once upon a time, Updike and I hung out and that's one for the grandchildren.

Just before Christmas I was boarding a flight back from London. As I was stowing my bag in the overheads a young fella lumbered up the aisle looking slightly the worse for wear. He stopped within feet of me and bellowed for the entire plane to hear, 'Hey, you're Michael Jackson's mate; seen ya on the telly?' He might just as well have shouted 'this guy just groped my wife' because every head turned in my direction. As I slunk into my seat, I was, for once, grateful to Ryanair for the sardine-packed conditions and the refuge they afforded me. But yes, I had met Michael Jackson in 2006, when his handlers booked a private shopping expedition in the bookstore I was managing in Dún Laoghaire. Had Michael become my 'mate'? Not exactly; we exchanged about six words and one exceedingly limp handshake. His kids were pretty cute, I remember – boisterous but polite and much more normal than their names might suggest. My overriding impression, however, was one of pity; pity for a guy who could only take his kids out under cover of darkness, pity for the sad, sable-clad little waif who had once looked so young and vital in his Motown heyday.

Updike and The King of Pop – two all-American heroes so different they might have been from different planets. One chose the cool sequestered vale of the literary life, the other the roar of the madding crowd. Meeting the former meant so much more to me but my kids, as you might suppose, disagree.

THE OLD FOLKS

John F. Deane

How strange the power of the imagination. How is it, when we are young, we cannot see that a day will come where we will be old, and tired, and unable to move at the pace we would like to move. Now I am seen by my children and by a younger generation, as one of 'the old folks', a grandfather, a man who moves slowly and finds it not too easy to climb over a gate or clamber down a cliff to the sea's edge. Yet, in my time, how I loved to climb and clamber, higher always, and higher. As if there were no end to the world. As if there were no such thing as growing old. I sat, often, high and hidden among the top branches of a pine tree, swaying with the winds that came glorying in off the Atlantic. I sat and dreamed, and did not know I was young, for such a word did not impinge on me. What I was aware of, even then, was the sense of irreparable loss that was beginning to grow within me as I tried to come to terms with the death of my own grandfather, one of the old folks whom I loved and had lost.

Even today, such is the strength of the imagination, I can become that child again, and even younger, and can climb the steep stairs in the old grey house, not as adults climb, but on the outside of the banisters, clinging on, rising along my own Matterhorn, and I can hide (though half a century ago) in the brush-and-broom cupboard while they call my name. From the top of the stairs I can see the landing window, and follow the long view over field and furze and scutch-land to the pier; I can touch on the window-ledge the dried-out lacecaps of pink hydrangea, as they gather talcum powder of dust and the husks of flies. Gathered for their delight by those who were the old folks around me then. Nor have I need to kneel and pray for souls in Purgatory as I still watch the old man crumbling plug tobacco in his cardboard hands, still hear the woman's voice as she sings 'the violets are scenting the woods, Nora', as both grandfather and grandmother together beckon me to the front door, to marvel how the fuchsia blooms, those *deora Dé*, are the Christ's blood and how the sun has laid a silver pathway out over the sea.

As I sat in the crow's-nest of the pine tree after the sad day of my grandfather's death, I watched grandmother come out into the yard and stand, silent and heavy in herself, and I saw her respond to the angelus bell that came ringing from the monastery half a mile away. I saw her genuflect, And the Word became flesh, then bless herself again and move slowly back into the house. It was her loneliness, I know, and her efforts to come to terms with that loneliness, that stirred some sense of real compassion into my young bones. At Mass I would like to kneel beside her. She plumped her missal with little missives to the dead, their photos in black and white, all smiles, all beautiful, while she whispered prayers and harvested indulgences; I loved the small-growth-rustling of her rosaries, beads clicking softly against the polished wood of the pew.

Now she lies in sunshine, under peony and lavender; she it was who had taught me how to pray, to think about Jesus, that child who was to grow up, too, who made me think about putting the self-rending God back together again: all the king's horses, all the king's men… The day the cortège passed along our road I saw how every house drew curtains down against the passing; she taught me, by abandoning me in death, how obdurate are the dead, taking with them so much of our dependent lives as we constantly remember them. About her grave, mother-of-pearl dragonflies are shivering in sunlight.

The old folks. How their passing has emptied a once loud and bustling townland of life and movement, leaving the world to browsing cattle, to rushes and hedgerows, to silence. After the old man's death, grandmother, reaching back in her age to the nineteenth century, as he had done, took charge of the mysteries, the joyful, sorrowful, and the glorious; she had retired into blacks and greys, for out of darkness, she would say, we come, and into darkness we must go. Each night we knelt, the rules of recitation fixed; after the last 'glory' and 'amen', the silences; elbows hard against the hard seat of the chair, knees sore against the flagged floor, we floated into our privacies. I watched her face, the old flesh, talced and spotted, closed eyes lifted as if she would see beyond the darkness of our fall, to a bright redemptive country where those she had borne and loved walked again, unhurt, the Christ walking, too, and I saw tears ease themselves onto her cheeks till her whispering was the whole structure of the mysteries, the words and the Word, flesh distilled to grief and love, and all this gravity a straining towards the invisible.

Now that I have become a grandfather myself and have reached the top of a different kind of tree than those I climbed as a child, it is something of enormous wonder to me to hold in my arms my first grandchild, Emily Maria, to see how her tiny fingers wrap themselves around my large thumb, and I find myself quieted utterly, the mysteries hanging about me having become almost tangible, the long and powerful thread leading down through the generations something like the golden chain on an old rosary, handled, loved, and scarcely understood.

TROUBLE BREWING

Fiona Price

In common with most Irish families growing up in the 1970s, the drug of choice in our house was always 'the cup of tea'. It was the first response to any minor calamity and an integral part of every celebration. In fact, each significant milestone reached in the day – from arriving home with the shopping, to finishing the ironing – was another reason for someone to suggest, 'Stick on the kettle there, we'll have a nice cup of tea.'

Like the rest of the nation, we happily drank gallons upon gallons of tea, dutifully collected our Minstrels, and emptied our used tea leaves through a strainer into the sink.

Then, all of a sudden, everything changed. Tea bags appeared in ads on the telly and arrived in bulk on the supermarket shelves. We shunned them at first, of course – in loyal support of Mum, who had instantly deemed them to be 'another one of those new-fangled gimmicks' and 'an awful waste of good money'. However, in common with the rest of the country's households, we eventually gave in and then enthusiastically joined 'the tea-bag generation'.

In the years that followed, it became second nature to 'use'. We used square-shaped bags with extra perforations, round bags with the chimpanzee seal of approval, one-cup bags with clever drawstrings, and we even had a brief dalliance with pyramid shapes. Whatever method was in vogue, we continued to inject ourselves with our daily dose.

When I finally moved away from home and on to college, my first investment in the flat in Rathmines was naturally – 'a kettle', turning student digs instantly into a home away from home. My addiction carried me safely through the exam-cramming sessions, the late-night parties, and early-morning hangovers of student life, and then on to the first steps of the career ladder.

Before long, the Celtic Tiger began to miaow and I started to notice her cubs on the street, stealthily padding by with plastic bottles full of water. Why? I wondered. Could they really be *so* thirsty that they can't wait until they get home to make a cup of tea?

Despite these obsessive water-guzzlers on one side and the health-conscious, probiotic fans, delicately sipping thimbles of milk on the other side – I stuck religiously to my tea-drinking habit throughout the 1990s. Even a four-year stint in the States failed to tempt me to embrace the 'cup a cawfee'. On the contrary, while away, my fix of choice began to take on even greater powers of comfort. The regular parcel of 500 tea bags, sent from Ireland, became a care-package that, for me, blended family concern with warm, nostalgic thoughts of home.

I sometimes wonder just how large a part these tea gifts played in enticing me back to live here once again. But what a different world I returned to. 'Professional' tea-drinkers had taken to the street en-masse, bearing cardboard cups of the steaming brew on their way to the office.

In the home too, the average Irish kitchen cupboard had taken on the Celtic Tiger's stripes, piled high as it was with packets of orange and cinnamon infusion; lemon and ginger; peach and passion fruit. Not to mention the various blends of green tea, Moroccan mint tea, dandelion detox, slimming Pu-erh and calming chámomile.

Now, as I watch late-night clubbing giving way to the Sunday tea dance, breakfast rolls and three-euro muffins are making way for packed lunches in tinfoil, with a slice of mum's tea brack for afters. Even the nation's economists have stopped studying the *FT* and have taken to reading their tea leaves instead; while our TV chefs cheerfully remind us all just how easy it is to turn out a batch of fairy tea cakes for less than the price of your bus fare to the charity shop. I can't help feeling a strange sense of déjà vu. Perhaps I'll make that bus journey and invest in a couple of three-tiered cake-plates and a rose-festooned set of Gran's best china cups and saucers. With invitations to sophisticated dinner parties now about as likely to arrive in the post as a hefty dividend cheque, I fancy it's time – once again – for some 'afternoon tea'. Anyone else for a hot drop?

FEBRUARY

BUDDY HOLLY: MY FIRST ROCK HERO

John Boland

Like Don McLean, I can't remember if I cried when I read about his widowed bride, but I do recall that my sister was inconsolable when news of Buddy Holly's death came through on the wireless in the kitchen of our Kenilworth Park house.

That was only to be expected, as Buddy Holly was my sister's first hero. Being younger and belonging to a sterner sex, I was somewhat less desolated at the thought of the air crash which killed Holly, Richie Valens and the Big Bopper on 3 February 1959. I wasn't yet old enough to comprehend what such a death, indeed any death, meant, and I obviously didn't share my sister's adolescent yearnings for this bespectacled, brown-eyed, handsome man.

Yet the sense of loss was considerable for me also because, if Holly wasn't an object of longing for me he was certainly my first rock hero. I had never really cared for Presley or Fats Domino, but when I heard 'That'll Be the Day' by the Crickets, I was hooked on this new music.

Our father, a devotee of Nelson Eddy and Jeanette MacDonald and a man who scorned the new-fangled sound, was bemused by the musical tastes of my sister and myself, though he indulged us in a roundabout kind of way. We had to be in bed by mid-evening, but on Sunday nights at 11 o'clock he would tune in to Radio Luxembourg and put the volume at a high enough level to be heard by us from the upstairs landing, to which we crept from our beds, listening in rapture to our heroes. He never mentioned this selfless act of his to us, nor we to him, but I still feel an immediate if somewhat uncharacteristic rush of fondness towards him whenever I recall it.

It would be easy now to let a beguiling nostalgia cloud my judgement of what I heard then, but I think I can maintain a sufficient distance to assert that Buddy Holly remains for me among the greatest and most influential of rock stars.

Presley came before him, of course, and has to be given pride of place for historical and sociological reasons – he created the climate in which it was possible for others to discover and nurture their talents. But I think that Holly's influence – as a songwriter, vocalist and guitar player – has proved to be more pervasive and lasting. Certainly the music that followed on from him would have been subtly different if he hadn't existed.

The influence lies, of course, partly in the songs he wrote, mostly in conjunction with manager-producer Norman Petty, and a listing of those of them that immediately became rock staples and have remained so makes for an astonishing achievement, considering Holly was only twenty-three when he died: 'That'll Be the Day', 'Peggy Sue', 'Every Day', 'Oh Boy', 'Maybe Baby', 'Listen to Me', 'It Doesn't Matter Any More', 'Well All Right', 'Rave On', 'Raining in My Heart', 'True Love Ways', 'Peggy Sue Got Married', 'It's So Easy'. And bear in mind that few people in rock were writing their own songs at that time.

But the influence is not just to do with the songs themselves, and his importance in another area was summed up by Mick Jagger, who said: 'Buddy Holly, as far as I'm concerned, was the only original white rock and roller. All the rest borrowed from the blacks, even Presley.' And if you listen to Presley and Holly that becomes very clear. Presley was essentially putting a white man's gloss on black music, but Holly created a white person's rock music, less sexually aggressive than Presley, more playful, full of sophomoric yearnings that Presley's style never encompassed.

Then there's the voice. That's more playful, too, lighter, more jaunty – though given depth by the drawling style that stretches and bends the vowels and also by that characteristic hiccup. It's a vocal style that has been much imitated, from the Beatles onwards.

Beyond that, there's the guitar style, played very fast on a downstroke and placed very close to the microphone, so that the sound of the plectrum is picked up. Indeed, there's a real awareness of the importance of the studio and what could be achieved there. That, too, has influenced a whole generation of musicians.

For all these reasons, Buddy Holly remains for me one of the most important and enduring figures in pop music, and I think my sister and myself got an inkling of his lasting greatness as we listened to him by stealth on that upstairs landing in Harold's Cross.

A JOYCE SONG

John S. Doyle

The city of Zurich in Switzerland has recently been voted the best place in the world to live. There are many reasons why this should be so; apart from the money the city has other forms of wealth. It has two rivers and a lake, hills to the back and mountains in the distance. It is a small and handsome city, and the centre is easily managed, on foot or bicycle, by tram, bus, boat, train, even funicular. On warm evenings there are people swimming in the lake, cycling and strolling along the shore to meet friends, play music, eat grilled sausages and drink beer. The city is well used.

The writer James Joyce might well have agreed with those who voted for Zurich; it was there he spent the years of the First World War. Later, while living in Paris, he frequently returned to Zurich, to visit friends and to attend a doctor for his troublesome eyes. And it was thanks to Swiss friends that Joyce was able to get out of France during the Second World War and return to live in Zurich. He died there less than a month after arriving, in 1941.

There are many traces of Joyce still visible in Zurich. Down near the lake, at Bellevue, is the Café Odeon, where he used to drink. Around the corner is a restaurant he patronised, the Kronenhalle, still owned by the family that helped Joyce get the necessary permits to travel to Switzerland at the end of 1940.

The Joyces moved around a lot. The Zurich James Joyce Foundation's website gives details of twelve addresses for the writer in the city, including the hospital where he died – the Roten Kreuz – and the cemetery at Fluntern, further up the hill, where he is buried.

Unlike many cemeteries, Fluntern is a beautiful place, given over to mature trees and bushes, the grass verges well kept by gardeners. It is a surprise to come upon the statue of Joyce at his grave, a figure sitting quietly in the shade. Made by the American Milton Hebald, the sculpture is a piece of great charm, in an angular pose which fits the gaiety and elegance of descriptions of the writer.

Fritz Senn, the eminent scholar who set up the Zurich James Joyce Foundation, was present in 1966 when the statue was put in place, and told me he met Giorgio Joyce, the son, on that occasion.

I had called on Fritz Senn at the foundation to deliver a piece of sheet music connected with Joyce. The music was for the song 'Invisibility', whose refrain figures in the early pages of *Ulysses*.

For a long time not much was known about the song except that, as it says in the book, Stephen Dedalus remembered that his mother heard old Royce sing it in the pantomime of *Turko the Terrible* and laughed with others when he sang:

> I am the boy
> That can enjoy
> Invisibility.

Some years ago, in a junk market at Cumberland Street in Dublin, just off Parnell Street, I came across the song, in a suitcase full of old sheet music. The six pages gave the verses and melody, and the ornate cover revealed that the song had been 'sung with great success by Mr E.W. Royce in the popular pantomime *King Turco the Terrible*, at the Gaiety Theatre, Dublin'. The song tells of the advantages of being invisible: 'to consult an attorney and disappear when he speaks of fees', and 'to travel by rail in the limited mail and vanish at "tickets please" '.

'Invisibility' duly found its way into print again, in an essay by a Harvard professor which showed how the words of the song throw light upon certain aspects of *Ulysses*. And the song was recorded in time for the big exhibition at the National Library celebrating the centenary of the day on which the book is set, 16 June 1904, Bloomsday.

But the fragile pages of the old sheet music needed to be preserved. Zurich, James Joyce's resting place, and the place where he wrote much of *Ulysses*, seemed a good home for the song, and when I sent Fritz Senn an email suggesting this, he said the Joyce Foundation would be glad to have it. So one morning last year my wife and I presented ourselves at the old town house in the Augustinergasse, and handed over the music, not before singing him a verse and chorus.

HOSPITAL BEDS

Anne Sharpe

At times we are all drawn to a kind of mental stocktaking. Lost in minutes of passing reflection we stand back briefly to find our bearings between and around whatever life swirls towards us. At that considering juncture old sayings may spring to mind, the summarised wisdom of ages that has stood the test of time. Or, better still, some telling image or anecdote can poignantly or humorously ease out and slip through the layers of memory to hit home with fresh impact.

Years ago when I was attending a French course for adults, the teacher introduced us to the nineteenth-century French poet Baudelaire in her own humorous way. She began with a little philosophical aside, an anecdote which at the same time she was just as quick to belittle. Yet you couldn't help seeing how seriously she took it all as well. I remember how offhand and casual she was, this elderly French nun moulded and shaped by her love of a literature she had long made her own. And her tone was so respectful, her phrasing so measured, even if she did reassure us at the end of the story that, of course, life wasn't really like that, shrugging it all off in that elegant way of hers.

Did she think that we wouldn't be able to take it, that we'd flinch and recoil before setting off home, perturbed? Certainly, she went through the routine of taking the harm out of things, while this is my own elaboration of her remembered words.

Baudelaire, she claimed, described life as a series of hospital beds, one great long row after row of them, extending as far as the eye can see. Every human being in the world is confined: the same fate for each, whether old or young, rich or poor. For one way or another, every single one of us lies in our own particular hospital bed, wrapped passive under blankets, still and waiting. By now a focused stillness had taken over the room, perhaps each one of us ready and eager for more. You could have heard a pin drop while the teacher continued steadily.

For each person has a separate disease of his or her own, something so unique to herself that its very difference seals her apart from her neighbour. Now one person's bed happens to lie beside the radiator up close and comfortably warm. In that position he or she is directly facing the occupant of the bed under the window. Suddenly stabbed by resentment, he or she wonders what is wrong with that person over there, what could she have to bother her with her bed just under the window? Meanwhile at that very moment the second man or woman is gazing enviously back at the radiator man. It's well for him, didn't he fall on his feet, the lucky man, it must be wonderful to have a bed beside the radiator.

And there the teacher left us hanging, silently amused I think, as she gauged the response, letting the images hold. Then she gave that dismissive shrug of hers again, as if what she had just shared with us meant nothing; nothing of account or relevance; nothing to bring away or ponder over – until, with the uncertainty within the room, she broke out into a smile and the beginning of rueful laughter brought the group together and the episode to a close.

THE IRISH APE:
DARWIN'S MISSING LINK

Joe Kearney

There's no row like an old row.

When Charles Darwin published his book *On the Origin of Species*, it is unlikely that he realised he was about to ignite one of the greatest international scientific debates of all time. His book arrived amongst the inquiring minds of Victorian society and was sold out in the space of one day. He summoned forth an image of man's origins that shredded any notion of the Garden of Eden. His theories regarding natural selection and the struggle for life were read at a time when the map of the world was turning 'pink' due to the expansion of the British Empire. The idea of 'survival of the fittest' was a notion mirroring a nation that itself was aggressive, competitive and challenging.

Contrary to popular belief, Darwin was careful to avoid the question of human evolution. In fact, the word evolution never occurs, but interestingly the last word in his book is 'evolve' and that single word becomes as potent as the final 'yes' of Joyce's *Ulysses*. Darwin writes of the changing progression of plants, insects and animals, but any suggestion that apes and man have a common ancestry was left for others to voice. What Darwin, in fact, produced was an argument that other scientists could use in the ensuing row.

The debate might have intrigued the public at large, but it divided the scientific community. Naturalists and theologians became engaged in heated exchanges over the evolutionary relationship between man and ape. What was needed was strong evidence of the so-called 'missing link' and – hey presto – in walks the Irishman.

Within the pages of popular British newspapers 'The Irishman' morphed into the 'Simianised Celt', a person depicted as some form of giant ape. The Irish were, after all, Britain's first colonial subjects and for centuries its most troublesome.

Within the Victorian mindset it was easy, therefore, to characterise our nation as being largely composed of people who were uncivilised, violent, ignorant and drunk. In 1862, *Punch* magazine argued that the missing link was not to be found in Africa but, instead, resided closer to home amongst the lower districts of London and Liverpool. The magazine informed its readers that adventurous explorers need venture no further than Britain's slums if they wished to find evolution's 'missing link'. *Punch* solved the origin of the species with the following quote, 'It comes from Ireland, whence it contrived to migrate; it belongs in fact to a tribe of Irish savages; the lowest species of the Irish Yahoo.'

Around this period, a gentleman called John Tenniel, who was the original illustrator of Lewis Carol's *Alice in Wonderland*, became the chief cartoonist for *Punch* magazine. He specialised in depicting Irishmen, and particularly Irishmen representing the Fenian movement, as bloodthirsty ape-monsters who threaten a matronly, buxom cartoon of Britannia. But apart from the Irish, Darwin himself also came in for vilification in the pages of *Punch*. The scientist's hirsute appearance leant itself to his frequent depiction as some form of ape-like monkey-man.

A mere decade prior to the publication of Darwin's book, the appropriately named missionary Thomas Savage was credited as the first European to set eyes on a gorilla. Here was a beast similar to humans in size, appearance and social behaviour which would challenge the Victorians' notion of themselves.

In the thinking of the time, this ape represented man's darker, wilder and more primitive self. And under the circumstances, it was easy enough to make the evolutionary leap from the gorilla to the Irishman.

This year we have the rare pleasure of a double celebration: Charles Darwin was born on 12 February 1809, and in May we celebrate the 150th anniversary of the publication of his book *On the Origin of Species*. His last years were spent at home in Downe, Kent. Here he was at his happiest, growing peas and beans. His last published work is entitled *The Formation of Vegetable Mould Through the Action of Worms*. The book deals with the relationship of earthworms to soil fertility. And to me, this seems a highly appropriate subject for the man who opened a can of worms that has led to the longest-running debate in the history of human mankind.

THE AMERICAN COUSIN

Bernard Farrell

When I was young, my father loved to tell us stories about how our lives would change as soon as we won the Sweep – which, in the 1950s, was like winning today's Lotto. 'We'll all be living like Maharajas then,' he would say, despite the fact, as my mother used to remind him, that he never bought a Sweepstake ticket in his life. She, on the other hand, would tell us different kinds of stories – romantic, heartwarming tales about her family and how they had overcome adversity to find eventual happiness. Her favourite one – and one that my father used to doubt ever happened – was about her granduncle, Michael-John.

The story always began the same way – Michael-John, a young farmer in County Kilkenny, walking down the boreen, gently herding a prize cow to the market in Castlecomer, watched by his mother who called after him to be home in time for dinner. She remembered him calling back that he'd be home in plenty of time – and that was the last she ever saw of him.

Many years later she discovered that, with the money from the sale of the cow and some savings, he had travelled on to Cork where he boarded a ship to New York with the sole intention of following the girl he loved. She and her entire family had left three months previously without giving any address and just a tender declaration that she loved him and hoped that someday, somehow, they would marry.

It took him ten months of working, searching and questioning other Irish emigrants in the confusion of nineteenth-century New York before he eventually traced the family and got her address. But when he went to the house, he heard that, four months earlier, the family had left for the West Coast to seek a better life in Denver, Colorado.

At this point, my mother would digress into descriptions of death-defying adventures as Michael-John crossed America, through the corn-fields and the prairies and beyond the Rockies, to Denver, where his search began all over again.

This time, in a smaller population, his discovery was quicker but it came with even greater heartbreak. For when, at last, he stood face-to-face with the love of his life, it was to hear her tell him that six months previously, having abandoned all hope of ever seeing him again, she had married, settled down, and was now expecting to begin her own family.

How Michael-John showed, or hid, his devastation we can only de-duce from the fact that he chose to live on in Denver, where he married an American girl, raised his family, lived, worked and died. My mother would then conclude the story with the romantic detail that his house in Denver was within sight of where his lost love lived and, although he often saw her, he never spoke with her again.

My father's reaction to this story was always the same; it was, he said, 'a bit too far-fetched to be true.' But all that changed one morning when, out of the blue, a letter arrived at our house, postmarked 'Denver, Col-orado', from a descendant of the mysterious Michael-John, telling us that he was coming to Ireland in the summer to trace his roots and would love to meet my mother and her family.

My mother was delighted at the prospect of meeting an American re-lation, while my father immediately abandoned all stories about the Sweepstake and instead switched to tales about the Californian gold rush and how many Irish settlers had headed out West and how some of them didn't reach California, but staked their claims in gold-rich towns like Denver, Colorado where, we were left to assume, they all lived like Maharajas!

So when our American visitor eventually arrived – a tall man with per-fect teeth and a wide smile – he was greeted with open arms. And we lis-tened as he and my mother discussed Michael-John and we heard her story confirmed in every detail. And after dinner, my mother played the piano for him and my father played the violin and my sisters sang and I recited a few poems and he smiled and applauded and raised his glass in numer-ous toasts. And when he was leaving, he was still smiling, thanking us for our hospitality and saying he would return to see us again, very soon.

He never did. Just as, a century earlier, his ancestor, Michael-John, had disappeared down a boreen, promising to be back for dinner, so our American relation disappeared into the night, never to be seen again.

If my mother was disappointed, she never showed it but, thereafter, we heard less of her romantic stories and none of Michael-John. My father dismissed it all as a great experience and reverted to his stories about winning the Sweep. But they never forgot the American. And even in later years, when they were both more concerned with age and its aches and its pains, I remember how my father could still make my mother laugh heartily by just suddenly and innocently asking: 'And no word, I suppose, from Colorado?'

WHEN ROMANCE IS IN THE AIR

Catherine Foley

The two of them came in at 9 o'clock once a week to the bar where I worked. Their whispered imprecations and concerned entreaties at the door always created a certain awed expectancy within. Heads turned to view their progress as they pushed through that heavy squeaking door.

They were big people who moved slowly, cumbersomely even. Their bodies seemed to sway elegantly from side to side as they came down along the narrow bar, step by careful step. They seemed to mimic the great milking beasts of the farm where they spent their lives. Arriving at the counter, they would stand and wait for me to serve them. There was a definite aura of glee about the pair of them. Although well into their middle years, they were newly wed.

Her face would light up at the sight of me and she'd bend her head slightly to one side and smile with pleasure when I went to take their order. He would stand slightly behind her in the darkened passageway. He'd come close if she looked to him to furnish an answer. Even I, in my blinkered state of youthful indifference, could see he was a handsome man with a fine mouth, smiling eyes and a manly bearing. He always wore a suit and a dark trilby with a short trim. They looked well together.

Her voice, deep and velvet-like, would caress me like a cat. 'Hello, Catherine. How are you?' I remember her warmth and her friendliness. And it was clear she had taken pains to dress up for the occasion – with a dab of rouge reddening her cheeks and a garish line of lipstick along her mouth. Usually she sported a military-style suit and sometimes she wore a hat, its netting pulled forward jauntily over her forehead. A paste brooch often decorated her lapel.

But with all the wisdom of my nineteen years, I used to view this woman and her soft-spoken husband in a slightly pitying way. I thought her innocent and simple, although I kept these preconceptions to myself. But when she put her handbag on the counter, her eyes twinkling at me, full of the fun and excitement of being out together for a drink, I didn't fully appreciate how happy she was in her newly married bliss or how beautiful and lovely she was.

She'd give me their order then, 'A pint of Guinness and a vodka and slimline tonic,' and she'd chat to me while I prepared the drinks.

She leaned in close one night to tell me about their romance. I don't think I believed her. Secretly I dismissed her story, thinking she was away with the fairies. But she told me how they'd lived on neighbouring farms until she wrote him a letter one day suggesting he call up to the house so they could talk about getting married. She asked a mutual neighbour to deliver the letter. That's how she proposed to the shy farmer, and he accepted.

'I asked him to marry me,' she said, watching my reaction. 'I did,' she said, seeing my disbelief, her great rheumy eyes reflecting the light that bounced off all the bottles ranged along the shelves.

Recently I revisited the pub where I had worked that summer long ago. It was dark and cold outside. Ice covered the roads and the sky was heavy with snow. Very few were out that night.

There were just three men drinking at the counter inside: all bachelors having a quiet drink in the dead of winter. I ordered our drinks and we got talking to them. One of them sketched us a story of unrequited love! It was his own story but he brushed it off lightly, as if broken hearts are meant to be lived with and endured. Romance trembled in the air, and the press of solitude was dispelled. I looked at this big, lonely man and I recalled the couple I used to serve in the pub.

Did they remember them? I asked. The other men nodded. They did know them, and remember them. They are both gone now, they said.

'Do you know that she proposed to him?' one of them asked me. 'Oh, she wrote to him,' the man at the counter continued. 'She gave the letter to a neighbour who lived between the two of them. She wrote, asking him to call down to her so that they could discuss marriage.' We all savoured the wonder of it then.

'And do you know,' said the man at the counter, 'the neighbour who delivered the letter was a bachelor too and he couldn't understand why she hadn't asked him.'

We all laughed at that and sipped our drinks. Love was in the air that night when I recalled the couple who used to put on their finery to come to the pub for a drink, where they would twinkle in the gloaming, exuding happiness.

BANK CRISES

Jackie Nugent

I think Shane O'Reilly was the first boy I ever loved. I didn't realise it at the time, but looking back from the perspective of years later the signs were all there. I loved the way he looked; the floppy black hair that was always getting in his eyes. I loved the way he spoke; his father was a bank manager and they had moved from County Down to live above the bank in our town, so Shane spoke with a clipped Northern accent that was far superior to our bogger accents – I didn't even know I had a bogger accent until Shane let me know. I loved that he told me things he didn't tell anyone else. Like when the IRA held up the bank and got away with loads of money. He told me that the men hit Mr Davis – who worked behind the counter – and made his nose bleed. Of course Shane was in school, like me, when the raid happened and it was all over by the time we got out at dinner time, but he heard his mum and dad (Shane called his mammy and daddy 'mum' and 'dad') talking about it and then he told me everything on the way back to school. But most of all I loved that he was the boldest boy I had ever met. I didn't always approve of his boldness, like when Miss Griffin had her back to the class and was writing on the board and he would drop his pen on the floor so that when he stooped down to pick it up he could look up her skirt – I didn't like that – and I told him I didn't like it. Then he would say he was sorry, and it gave me a funny warm feeling in my stomach.

I knew Miss Griffin didn't like Shane the day she told us all to draw a picture of Jesus's triumphant entry into Jerusalem on Palm Sunday. None of the rest of us could draw to save our lives, but Shane was an artist – a real artist. He could draw things and people just like they looked in real life – not like the pictures the rest of us made. Miss Griffin went mad when she saw Shane's picture and started shouting at him that his picture was sacrilegious (I never forgot that word) – and all because Shane had put lots of Draculas and Frankensteins (Shane loved to draw Draculas and Frankensteins) in the crowd that was watching Jesus riding along on his donkey. But the thing is, the donkey looked like a real donkey; the Jesus looked like a real Jesus and the Frankensteins and the Draculas all looked like real Frankensteins and real Draculas – and I couldn't understand how Miss Griffin couldn't see that. I knew then she didn't like the picture because she didn't like Shane for looking up her skirt when her back was turned.

It was on Jennifer McInerney's tenth birthday that my admiration for Shane reached new heights. The McInerney's were the richest people in our town and Jennifer always had great parties – there were loads of drinks and sandwiches and biscuits and cream buns laid out when we all arrived. Everyone knew you were supposed to eat the sandwiches first and the buns and biscuits afterwards at a birthday party – well everyone except Shane. While the rest of us dutifully reached for the sandwiches, he grabbed a handful of cream buns and started stuffing them in his mouth before anyone knew what was happening. He started to laugh – nearly choking himself – when he saw the looks on the faces around him. Ham sandwiches, with bites missing, remained suspended in mid-air as the rest of the partygoers looked at him in stunned horror. Mrs McInerney started hitting him with a tea cloth – this only made him laugh and choke even more – then Jennifer McInerney burst into tears. I just looked at him thinking he was the most amazing person I had ever met in my life.

That summer of Jennifer McInerney's birthday party was the last summer the O'Reillys lived in our town. Mr O'Reilly got a new job in a big bank in Dublin and the whole family moved up there. At first Shane said he wasn't going to live in Dublin but he went in the end. When he was gone it was like someone had switched the light off in my life. I couldn't bring myself to walk past the bank for ages after that. If I was sent up the town for a message I'd cross the street before I came to the bank and wouldn't cross back again until I had passed Brennan's chemist and then I'd do the same thing – but in reverse – on the way home. I hated the bank for a long time back then. Eventually I did recover, but after the trauma of any bank crisis, things are never really the same again.

PASSING THROUGH

Ted Sheehy

It was 8 o'clock. Two girls left the Centra and idled their way up the village. The day was thinning into a cold evening with the falling light. Crows in their thousands took wing from the woods in the demesne as the last of the sun dipped behind the houses.

Rooks and jackdaws called and wheeled about the sky – a myriad of ragged, black things turning between the rooftops and the heavens.

Below them the lights went on outside the chipper. An old tractor sputtered up the hill. The usual Sunday evening stream of red rear lights ran eastwards in steady convoy towards Dublin. Ghostlike behind the car windscreens the dimly lit faces passed on through, countless eyes tracking the car in front.

How many times had I passed that same main road myself? Had I ever caught sight of myself here, on this footpath in some strand of the possible future? Did I ever see myself, from here, the younger man behind the wheel of one of those countless cars?

Overhead, the crows grew silent and broke off their flight. They settled on the ridge tiles of the roofs, and on chimneys. They settled on parapets and aerials. Everywhere on the skyline they settled in twos, each pair a discrete black silhouette.

The two girls idled on up Chapel Street. One made a face and the other laughed. They went on past number 22, paint peeling around the spotted chrome numerals on the door. The day was drawing in, a chill coming to the evening air.

I was headed out the other way, taking the quiet road out from the crossroads. To my left a woman pushed a buggy up the narrow school lane, heading over the rise for home, somewhere this side of the horizon light.

Across the road, in the cul-de-sac, the windows of the empty new houses shimmered with reflected light – pink and purple shot through with the darkness behind the panes. Out front, dispersed amid the rubble, clustered stalks of thistle and dock, nettle and scutch gave some notion of where there should be gardens.

Along the road-side, builders' and auctioneers' posters peel away from backing boards mounted on weathered wooden posts. The faded 'for sale' signs advertise an empty promise from what is already another age: 'four-bed semis with "un-suites".'

That's 'un' suite as in un-inhabited, un-sustainable, un-fathomable; three words that may describe the future of the village itself. Before long it will be bypassed, cut off from its hinterland so that people in faraway places can cut their journey time across the country.

Further out this road I'm on, if I follow it in my mind's eye, I see the empty houses of an earlier generation dotted over every townland, their inhabitants mostly driven out by poverty into the unskilled labour market of post-war Britain. Their crumbling houses with their blind windows and empty hearths testify to the stupidity of the rhetoric of the time. And if we travel further, further out this road into the hinterland, we will pass one of the possible birthplaces of the poet and playwright Oliver Goldsmith.

Goldsmith's 1770 poem, 'The Deserted Village', was written as a re-action to the agrarian changes then sweeping rural England. Those changes marked the hardening division between labour and capital, a process consolidated during the Industrial Revolution and persisting on into the present day.

How can it be possible, I wonder, that a 239-year-old poem should seem so relevant in Ireland today? Can it be that we are mostly ghostlike behind the wheel, blind not just to the past or to the future, but blind to the world we are passing through?

As Oliver Goldsmith in his poem 'The Deserted Village' wrote:

> Ill fares the land, to hast'ning ills a prey,
> Where wealth accumulates, and men decay:

Princes and lords may flourish, or may fade;
A breath can make them, as a breath has made;
But a bold peasantry, their country's pride,
When once destroy'd, can never be supplied.

AUDRE HANNEMAN:
A MOST REMARKABLE WOMAN

Kevin Casey

A most remarkable woman died recently. Her name was Audre Hanneman and, for many years, she lived in Kansas City, Missouri. It is improbable that you will know her name, unless you are interested in the writings of Ernest Hemingway. But if you are and have ever read a critical study of his books, you will have found the name Hanneman sprinkled copiously throughout the footnotes.

In 1967 she published an encyclopaedic book, *Ernest Hemingway: A Comprehensive Bibliography* and then, eight years later, a *Supplement*, almost as large. These two books, with a total of almost 1,000 pages, contain a quite astonishingly meticulous record of Hemingway's publications, from his very first stories in his High School magazine to each and every item that appeared after his death. And not just his writing but the writings of others about him – every review, every news item in newspapers and periodicals, all of the secondary material that makes it possible to study an author's writing and follow the pattern of his professional life.

So if you want to know where a short story first appeared, or what novel first sold well or the dates of publication of translations of these novels into more than fifty languages, you consult Hanneman.

Very good, you might think, but that's what academics are paid to do, that's why archivists and librarians are given the time and conditions to achieve these things. And that's what I thought, having owned the books for many years and consulted them often without really having the curiosity to wonder who Hanneman was. Then I got to know her a little and to discover the remarkable circumstances in which these books were actually produced.

Audre Hanneman was born in Iowa in 1927 but, when quite young, moved with her family to Kansas City. Because of family circumstances she wasn't able to go to university. Instead, while she was still a young woman, living at home, looking after her invalid mother, she embarked on a somewhat earnest task that was very much of its time: she decided to read every title on a list of 100 best novels. About a quarter way through this task she came across Hemingway's *A Farewell to Arms* and a magnificent obsession was born. Not only was her life changed by the force of Hemingway's writing, it was also changed by her determination to track down everything ever written by and about him.

She had no special training for this task: she trained herself. At first she worked in local libraries and local bookshops and in the offices of the *Kansas City Star* where Hemingway had been employed as a cub reporter. Then, using whatever time and money she had to spare, she travelled to other libraries and other possible sources.

Later again, while working in New York city in a number of mind-numbing secretarial posts – for a while, for example, she typed the name and address labels that were gummed onto mail-order magazines – she spread her net more widely and travelled to libraries throughout America that housed special collections.

It is worth remembering that she did this without any encouragement or any financial aid and without any help of any kind. An academic undertaking a similar task would have grants and a team of research assistants. She travelled with nothing but her ever-expanding folders.

It's also worth remembering that all of this work was done long before she had any access to a computer. There were no online databases; nothing could be simply Googled. She had to discover a primary source each time.

Eventually, Carlos Baker, a Princeton professor who was working on the authorised biography of Hemingway, became aware of her work and helped her to shape it. After many vicissitudes, the two volumes were published by Princeton University Press.

Their excellence and authority have never been questioned since then. But recently, although her work is always acknowledged as a source, I couldn't help feeling that she had not been given the attention that she deserved. She returned to Kansas City where she lived, more or less anonymously. She looked a little excluded.

If she had held an academic position she would almost certainly have had more public acknowledgement. So it was particularly good that when the Hemingway Society chose Kansas City for its annual conference two years ago, Audre Hanneman addressed it and was given a long, standing ovation. She was very, very pleased.

Her Hemingway scholarship, achieved with such difficulty and such singular purpose, is certain to survive as long as there is any interest in one of the twentieth century's great writers.

BUYING IRISH

Colbert Kearney

The other day I was taken aback to learn that President Obama's much-heralded plan to restore the American economy had originally contained a stipulation that those benefiting from his capital injection should undertake to 'Buy American'. Novel though this might have seemed to Americans, it rang nostalgic bells for Irish people.

The Irish state was born into protectionism: we were at economic war with a major power and many believed our only hope was that *sinn féin amháin* would buy what *sinn féin amháin* had produced. Back in the 1950s and 1960s vestiges of the patriotic era lingered and some of us remember being sent to the shops having been warned not to come back with anything not made in Ireland. The early 1970s brought the 'Buy Irish' campaign, based on the old-fashioned idea that if we bought goods made in Ireland we'd keep Irish workers in jobs and off the dole queue. In many ways it was the last blast of protectionism, because when we joined the Common Market, currently called the EU, we forfeited the right even to think of discriminating against our European neighbours. As ever we did our best to circumvent the new legislation. The Irish Goods Council believed it was entitled to promote Irish produce as long as it stopped short of demoting non-Irish produce. A decade later their successors hoped that a Guaranteed Irish sticker was a guarantee of quality that the Irish customer would choose even if the product was a few cents more expensive than the imported competition. In the giddy days of the Celtic Tiger such parochialism seemed to have gone out with crossroads dancing and the button boots, but in the wake of the economic tsunami patriotic commentators are again criticising those who are lured across the border by fabulously lower prices, thereby putting Irish retailers at risk.

Talk about economic cycles: almost 300 years ago, when Jonathan Swift arrived back in Dublin to take up his appointment as Dean of St Patrick's Cathedral, English legislation had ensured that Irish corn was more expensive than imported English corn and, as a result, Irish farmers tended to abandon the production of corn and concentrate on breeding sheep for wool. But in order to prevent the Irish woollen industry from threatening its English counterpart, London introduced more legislation to hamper its development, with disastrous results for employment in Ireland, not least among the weavers who operated within the vicinity of St Patrick's Cathedral.

In the immediate aftermath of his installation, the new dean did not seem too concerned about local industry. He had his own grievance to nurse; for though most would have seen his deanship as a promotion, for Swift himself it was a calamitous disappointment. He felt betrayed by the Tory politicians in London in whose cause he had exercised his matchless talents as a satirical spokesman; instead of rewarding him with a bountiful bishopric in England, as he had hoped, they had sent him back to Ireland to die, as he put it himself, like a poisoned rat in a hole. For, though born and educated in Dublin, Swift had been at home in London, the capital of English culture, among the movers and shakers, political and literary. To return to Ireland was to go into exile in a country beset by wars and famines, inefficiency and profiteering. Little and all as Swift thought of the Anglo-Irish who allowed themselves to be bossed by London as if they were, in Swift's words, 'one of their colonies of outcasts in America', he thought even less of those he termed 'the savage old Irish' who had been dispossessed physically and legally by the Anglo-Irish.

Dean Swift was not one to take things lying down. To his own personal resentment was added the savage indignation he experienced when he looked around him. As he wrote, 'Whoever travels this country, and observes the face of nature, or the faces, and habits, and dwellings of the natives, will hardly think himself in a land where either law, religion, or common humanity is professed.' In both cases the major share of blame lay with London where, coincidentally, Swift had perfected the art of political satire.

In 1720 he published his pamphlet, *A Proposal for the Universal Use of Irish Manufacture*. When he got into his stride, few escaped his lash: the English for their superior attitude, the Irish for their ineffectuality and gutlessness, landlords for their profiteering, even Cromwell for his destruction of churches, but its kernel was an appeal for Irish self-reliance to frustrate English exploitation.

Not that Swift assumed the Irish were capable of defending themselves in this way. 'Is there,' he asked, 'virtue enough left in this deluded people to save them from the brink of ruin?' He thought it 'wonderful to observe the bias among our people in favour of things, persons and wares of all kinds that come from England' and so he didn't sound too hopeful when he imagined the Irish parliament enacting a ban on the 'wearing [of] any cloth or stuff in their families, which were not of the growth and manufacture of this kingdom.' In such circumstances he could entertain an even more radical counter-protectionism.

I heard the late Archbishop of Tuam mention a pleasant observation of somebody's; 'that Ireland would never be happy till a law were made for burning everything that came from England, except their people and their coals.'

Though he had taken the legal precaution of placing the suggestion at two removes from himself, the sentiments would come down through the generations as his, establishing him as a champion of the Liberties and a founding father of Irish nationalism.

Towards the end of the pamphlet Swift alludes derisively to a new idea that was doing the rounds in Dublin: the setting up of a Bank of Ireland. Traditionally Swift has been criticised for his short-sightedness in not welcoming such an institution but, were he in touch with Ireland today, he might feel somewhat vindicated. He wrote:

> I cannot forbear saying one word upon a thing they call a bank, which I hear is projecting in this town. I never saw the proposals, nor understood any one particular of their scheme ... I hear only of a monstrous sum already mentioned ...and the jest will be still the better, if it be true, as judicious persons have assured me, that one half of this money will be real, and the other half entirely imaginary.

This would seem uncannily prophetic to President Obama and indeed to the ranks of world leaders faced with the task of clearing up after the recent bubble-burst.

MISSING THE BEET

Margaret Hawkins

I had never seen a sugar beet until I married and moved to Wexford, but from then on the root crop that was once called 'white gold' put its own work rhythm into winter.

It's the sights and sounds that I remember most. The green tractor-pulled harvester speeding up the drills of the back-lane field, belts grasping the beet from the loosened soil, sending leafy tops in a constant stream to the left, while at the same time the beheaded beet dance-trooped their way to the top of the elevator, the first few to fall off making a clunking sound as they hit the bottom of the collecting tank.

There were more revs and clatters as the harvester stopped periodically to tip its tankful into the trailer waiting on the headland. Then it was off to the yard where it was tipped once again, the beige-brown pile on the cement now growing bigger by the hour.

Days later, the beet would again bounce, this time up the elevating chains of the cleaner loader to knock off the excess soil, the tractor and its driver working late into the evening, driving back and forth, forth and back to put up the load for an early start to the beet depot in Wellington-bridge.

For farmers all over Ireland, not just in Wexford, where one quarter of the national crop was grown, the beet dockets arriving in the post in early September signalled the beginning of what was called 'the campaign'.

From October to New Year the tractors and trailers could be seen on the Duncannon Line, convoying their way to the railway station depot, the queue spilling backwards into the village of Wellingtonbridge on wet days, dry days, cold days, crisp days, waiting to have their loads assessed for tare and sugar content.

Later the same beet would jickety-can its way to the factory towns of Thurles or Mallow where the sugar was finally extracted.

The pulling of the beet was the culmination of many months of work. From ploughing the ground in the spring, to spreading the blue-grey limestone that was quarried in Ballyellen and tipped in mini Sugar-Loaf shapes at field gates, to harrowing the ground, to sowing and fertilising.

Early summer meant walking the fields, a prayer escaping to the wind for the right mix of sunshine and showers that year, eyes peeled for wireworm and wireweed, red shank and leatherjacket, chickweed, scutch grass, dead nettle and lamb's quarter that could suffocate plants and profits.

Then there was the tillage farmer's satisfaction of seeing the beet leaves meet in the drills and, as summer ran into autumn, the leaves opening their arms to the sun so that the heat could soak down and sweeten the waiting root to the level of fourteen teaspoons of sugar per beet.

The silence of the winters now makes me want to remember the crop, to mark its absence, even three winters after its passing. I feel the urge to peel back the thick skin of its history, to reveal a milky glimpse of what was once a sweet story of success.

Sugar beet, I know now, wasn't just a twentieth-century crop in Ireland. Although the first factory opened in Carlow in 1926, sugar beet had been grown in Achill and Antrim as far back as the 1840s, and in 1851 the Royal Irish Beet Root Sugar Company had been set up in a move to break the country's dependence on imported cane sugar.

Although that company wasn't successful in the long run, intelligent men on the Irish Industries Commission in the 1880s knew a good crop when they saw it.

'A moist climate with moderate sun is what the beet requires and such is the climate of Ireland,' pronounced one Mr Baruchson.

But sugar beet's European history goes back much further to the time when the Berlin scientist Margraf discovered a technique for extracting sugar from beet in the 1700s.

The Irish later had a hand in the scientific development of the industry as well with Trinity professor John Hewitt Jellett inventing an analysing prism in 1860. This made it possible to determine the sugar content of beet by means of a rotating ray of light.

On the mechanisation front the Irish also later played their part through the development of machinery to sow and harvest the crop – designs that were subsequently sold worldwide.

It's the silence of the winter that still jars. There's sadness at the loss of the crop that once brought pastoral and industrial man together, as the sugar beet industry's chronicler, Michael Foy, once put it.

There's sudden unease too when the eye falls on obsolete machinery in the shed – now mechanical monuments to times past – and my ear still somehow expects to hear the clatter of the cleaner loader in the yard, the tractor and its driver working late into the evening, driving back and forth, forth and back, putting up the load for an early start.

It's then that a sudden sigh escapes to the wind for the crop and the industry that has passed in the night and the work rhythm that has gone out of winter. It's then that I know that I too, am still missing the beet.

EDNA

Monica Henchy

Listening to Edna O'Brien being interviewed by Miriam O'Callaghan recently on RTÉ radio when she mentioned the parties she liked to give brought me back many years ago to when we gave a party for Edna in our house. It happened like this. Kieran Hickey, the well-known film-maker, was making a sponsored film on the National Library, when he spotted Edna, who was researching James Joyce at the time, working at a desk under one of the green lamps in the library. He spoke to my husband, who was the Director, and said, 'Do you think Edna would agree to feature in our film and give her views on the Library? She could add so much to it, both factually and visually.' My husband spoke to her as a fellow Clare person and she replied, 'I'd be only too delighted to participate.' He then spoke to me, saying: 'She's been very generous with her time. Should we take her out to dinner?' I said, why not to dinner in our house and let her meet the Trustees of the Library (among whom I remember Terence de Vere White, F.X. Martin and Mary Lavin as well as Kieran, the instigator). 'But have you forgotten,' my husband, being the more cautious type, said, 'that Terence gave her recent book *Mother Ireland* a slating in *The Irish Times*?' I said, authors are used to such ups and downs, and I don't think Edna is a prima donna.

So I phoned Edna and asked if she would mind if I invited Terence as well. Her reply was, 'I'd be charmed to meet him.'

The long-awaited night came. Edna was first to arrive, delightfully punctual. She swept in on a wave of diaphanous skirts and her striking red hair flowing around her shoulders. Terence was next to ring the bell. I went out, followed by our little dog, Pell Mell, who jumped up on

Terence who immediately lifted him up and put him around his shoulders for comfort as he looked distinctly nervous. 'Is she here yet?' he whispered. 'Yes,' I said with a smile. 'She's waiting inside for you.' I brought him and put him sitting beside her on the couch. They kissed each other affectionately on the cheek as if they had been friends all their lives.

At dinner Terence and Edna had some lively conversation across the table and the other guests were alternatively joining in or listening. Tactfully, nobody mentioned *Mother Ireland*. I only wish we had a hidden tape recorder (I don't think we even had one at the time). If we had I'm sure my children would have used it. To my relief everyone was chatting amicably. I did not get all of the repartee as I was busy serving the meal and giving instructions to my daughters who were acting as waitresses and eavesdropping at the same time, but they assured me afterwards that the conversation was great. It gave me such pleasure that my guests were really getting on well together.

When it came to moving back to the sitting room, where, as a good hostess, I tried to change the seating, Terence asked if he might sit in his original seat on the couch with Edna. In fairness, apart from the odd *tête-à-tête*, they did join in the general conversation, which must have been entertaining as the guests did not start to move until 1 a.m., saying that they had not enjoyed a party so much for a long time.

Two days later I had a charming letter from Edna which I still treasure and an invitation for both of us to her play on at the Abbey. Terence phoned to thank me for being so brave. My husband looked at me quizzically and said, 'Congratulations. You took a big chance. There could have been recriminations once the wine started flowing, but you got away with it.'

MARCH

A LATE INTERIOR

Gerald Dawe

In an old photograph
of my mother and grandmother,
I see the look of my daughter.
Nineteen forty-seven,

the two women smile,
arms delicately linked –
one the same age as the century,
the other turning twenty.

In the darkened window,
in the neatly falling lace curtain,
before sunburst and cloud cover,
whosoever took the photograph

is just about discernible –
my soon-to-be-father father,
in his new postwar life or,
more likely, the man-to-be my uncle –

goofy-toothed, sleeves rolled up,
skinny as a rake, making faces
at this little family before
they all go back in again,

through the dim hallway,
by the monk's bench,
good chairs and grand sideboard
to the light of a painted scene.

THE LAND OF SPICES

Mary Coll

I was exiled on a regular basis from the classroom for talking and quickly discovered that loitering in the corridor was fatal, inevitably leading to a close encounter with the head nun, followed by yet another phone call home.

If you were smart though you could disappear entirely from the radar by slipping under the stage in the Boarders' Hall where sanctuary was guaranteed among the baskets of old props, discarded sets, and very carefully guarded packets of purple Silk Cut. Under the stage was the private domain of the senior boarders, boarders more than most needing a place of refuge, a place to share secrets, a place to keep their well-thumbed copies of *Rich Man Poor Man*, *The Valley of The Dolls* and *Cosmopolitan* – a syllabus which would complete my education far more effectively than the conjugation of Latin verbs. I spent a great deal of time there, and it was many long months before I ran out of racy diversions and terminal boredom drove me to rummaging through the pile of dusty hardbacks abandoned in the back corner. I had never heard mention of Kate O'Brien in a Laurel Hill classroom, but I instantly recognised the infinite possibilities of the forbidden pleasures which *The Land of Spices* might contain and which I, like every pupil of the school, knew had been banned by the Irish censor. *Banned*. A banned book in the hands of a convent schoolgirl was a form of exotica beyond even my wildest imaginings, which after a term of Jacqueline Susann and Irwin Shaw were pretty wild by anyone's standards.

It was a dark red hardback without a dust jacket. I could only guess what the original cover must have looked like and was more than happy to judge it accordingly. For the rest of the week I was consumed by the story of Anna Murphy and Helen Archer, set in my very own school, in the well-waxed corridors I ran through on a daily basis, peopled with a world of nuns and pupils immediately familiar. I had myself ejected from so many classes I'm surprised I wasn't expelled, such was my enthusiasm to reach the end of a story so sordid that it had threatened a nation's moral integrity. Of course at the tender age of sixteen I completely missed the depravity that had so enraged the censors.

The line, 'She saw Etienne and her father in the embrace of love' went right over my adolescent head, so that I reached the end puzzled and perplexed but with a very clear understanding, for the very first time, of what it feels like to have your own place transformed by the imagination of a writer and the alchemy that occurs when the familiar is given a new life through the magic of fiction; how it holds a mirror up for you, making it possible to see everything with such clarity. This shocked me more than any of the athletic goings on in the Hollywood Hills; really good literature is that potent and subversive. It would take many years, many more novels and a great deal more maturity for the full implications of Kate O'Brien's writing to make any sense to me, hindered as it was by her absence from the shelves of the City and County libraries. Lost. Hidden from view. A writer silenced, cut off for decades from her readers, it was a crude, cruel and unnatural punishment.

By the time we returned to Laurel Hill in September all was changed, a new broom in the Reverend Mother's office had swept everywhere clean, the boarders regrouped at the rear of the gardener's tool shed, and I suspect the contraband went into the adjacent ever-glowing brazier, but *The Land of Spices* proved far more enduring, it had taken hold in a place where banning and burning can have no real effect; it formed the kindling of my own imagination, and all down the years I have endeavored to keep it safe.

Church bells beyond the stars heard, the soul's blood,
The land of spices, something understood.

A PLACE TO DREAM

Amanda Coogan

I was out, free of school and home and teenage angst, bursting my way out of Dublin and landing in Limerick in 1989, a fresh-faced eighteen-year-old. Every weekend *Scrap Saturday* on RTÉ Radio 1 told me I was in stab city. It constantly rained in great waves of misty, steel blue, the labyrinth of Georgian grey streets providing a background to my vivid orange pelted flares and brightest pink crêpe top that suddenly I was allowed – no, encouraged – to wear. I was now an art student.

In those days Limerick School of Art and Design was based around the Locke Bar; I mean Georges Quay, The Granary and Bruce House. The painting department in Bruce House was my base. From its front door on Patrick Street you could smell the delicious reek of oil paint and linseed oil and rabbit glue size.

Upstairs on the third-floor studios every day we practised or explored alongside our teachers. We'd drop into the store to buy paint, see Richard Slade applying thick impasto paint to canvases, and we'd ask each other how he could afford to use so much paint. Bob Baker's structuralist red, blue and white grid paintings lay around and we'd endlessly discuss if he used masking tape or could he paint those lines, that straight, by hand. I'd mix colours on my palette looking for a particular blue and walk to the end of the studios to check out the colours Jack Donovan was using on his current painting, and occasionally we'd pop into Charlie Harper's office on the pretence of college business, but really to take a peek at the dancing figurative drawings he was working on. The world of possibilities opened out in front of us: ripe and exciting.

The painters Paddy Graham and Tony O'Malley were our heroes. My pal Michael Canning and I ran across O'Connell Street one day and presented O'Malley with a freshly made canvas we just happened to have with us under our arms. It was an homage. London's Young British Artists and Damien Hirst's sharks in formaldehyde had yet to emerge. We had a 'shark lady' in a ball dress in Dorothy Cross's sculpture. The soft smooth bronze head of the shark, its intimate size, like a finger, stirred something in me I couldn't quite understand but ignited my liquid excitement.

Every Friday morning we ventured outside our normal part of the city, past Cruise's Hotel, its dining room wallpapered with varnished leaves, and up to Pery's Square. Limerick City Gallery of Art: there was our Aladdin's Cave.

Paul O'Reilly, the gallery's then director, was charged with enlightening our teenage minds to the visual arts. His great theme was that of 'active looking' versus 'passive looking'. The back room of the gallery was hung saloon-style, paintings hung up and down the wall seemingly higgledy-piggledy. The bold yellows and greens of William Leech's *Fields by the Sea* hung alongside Camille Souter's sun-bleached canvas, *Washing by the Canal*; the paintings conversing with each other, talking to us.

To look, O'Reilly told us, is to try to see. He guided us to considering visual art beyond the ocular immediate or, as he called it, the literal-visual. Jack Yeats's *Chairoplanes* blew our minds; the flash of movement, of a moment, caught in the canvas. The mess of colour, the stroke of the artist's movement, all read through squinted eyes and heady hearts.

Twenty years later, my pal Michael reminds me that the best way into active looking is, funnily enough, to *listen* to works of visual art. Climbing up the thick wooden stairs of the gallery every week I'd turn left into a spacious, light-filled room to listen. In the big white room only one painting seemed to hang, Paddy Collins' *Rising Swan*. To lie on the floor in front of it for hours was to peer into a treasure trove. My memory of the painting differs shockingly to the images of it I see now twenty years later. It begs the question of who completes a work of art: the artist or the viewer? The literal-visual of it or is it the experiential of that piece of art? The experience of this painting was mother's milk to my formation as an artist.

The beauty of its bluey greyness, the swirl of the paint around the swan: some days it was scraps of grey paint applied with a palette knife, and on other days it was a hazy pulsating womb-like form. A moving, shifting, possibility of meaning – a site to dream. The bold slash of white paint in the middle of the swirl – possibly representing the swan, the Children of Lir, the beauty and myth of the animal – and for me a flag, a wave, a cave.

ANNIVERSARY

Noel Duffy

We walk along the oak-lined paths
your tight-paced step soon leaving Dad and me
behind to the mumble of our casual words.
We find you motionless by the boundary wall.

Twenty-five Novembers have now passed
and still each one you have mourned for her,
your damaged child too soon gone from you,
your daughter of twelve days of infant life.

Mother, I have wished with every breath
to restore her to you, strong and whole.
I who was born from those days of loss,
for the small child lying in the angel's plot.

WINIFRED M. LETTS

Cathleen Brindley

The recent death of the actress Blánaid Irvine reminded me of the many times I had heard her recite the poems of Winifred M. Letts on Ciarán Mac Mathúna's RTÉ radio programme *Mo Cheol Thú*. And the name Winifred Letts in turn called up a further set of memories because, at an early age, I came to know her work, not as a poet as she is usually remembered, but as a writer of children's books. The fact that she wrote for children is never mentioned. I was given two of these books by my grandmother when I was very young and I began to wonder what I would think now of these stories which I had enjoyed so much long ago.

A search through the attic discovered them both – they had not been thrown away and had survived the many moves in my life. These stories about Pomona Thompson – aged about twelve – and her family were originally broadcast on the BBC and, because of their popularity, Winifred Letts was encouraged to bring them out in book form. The first of these books, *Pomona and Co.*, published in 1934, recounts the adventures of Pomona and her brother and sister who lived with their mother and artist father in rural Herdfordshire. Of more interest to Irish children was the next book, *Pomona's Island*, published in 1935. Pomona goes with a friend and the friend's young governess to spend some months on an island on Lough Erne in a house inherited by her friend's father. They lead a magical outdoor life there, learn to row a boat, go hunting and fish in the lake. Pomona even finds an ogham stone in a thicket on an island and is congratulated by a visiting archaeologist. The stories are lively and well told, the children come to life, and Letts' love of the Irish countryside is very apparent and shines through. But to our eyes now, these books, especially the Irish one, are to a certain extent curiosities and period pieces. The Irish book portrays a completely Anglo-Irish society and atmosphere. When Pomona hesitates to accept the invitation that means leaving her family for several months, her governess cheers her up with these words, 'You will still be in Northern Ireland and will be singing the National Anthem and shouting "Up King George".' When I was young and read these books I was too young and ignorant to notice this and I just wished that I could have an island holiday on an Irish lake just like that.

Winifred Mary Letts had a mixed heritage. She was born in England in 1882 near Manchester. Her father Ernest Letts, a rector, was English, but her mother, Isabel Ferrier, was Irish, and, although her early education was in England, the Irish link was maintained by frequent holidays in Knockmaroon House near the Phoenix Park – her mother's old home. After her father's death she and her mother returned to Ireland and lived in Blackrock while Winifred attended Alexandra College. Trained as a masseuse, she worked during World War I as a nurse in army camps in Manchester. She started writing in 1907, mostly stories and dramas, but in 1913 she published her best-known book of poems, *Song of Leinster*. This was followed by other collections of poems, *Hallow-e'en and the Poems of War* in 1916, and *The Spires of Oxford* in 1917. Versatile and prolific, she kept up an almost annual output. In 1926 she married a widower, William Henry Foster Verschoyle of County Kildare, and they lived in Fitzwilliam Square and County Kildare. After his death in 1943 she returned briefly to England, but Ireland drew her back again and she lived in Killiney, County Dublin until moving in the last years of her life to the Tivoli Nursing Home in Dún Laoghaire, where she died in her ninetieth year on 7 June 1972.

I went out recently to Rathcoole, a village on the Dublin–Kildare road, to visit the Church of Ireland graveyard. The graveyard surrounds the small church which dates from 1737 and I confidently expected to find her name within or near her husband's family grave plot. Her husband's name is on the plinth of the imposing pink granite monument that marks the Verschoyle family burial place. But search as I would, her name is not there or on any other gravestone. The church records, however, show that she was buried there, though her grave is unmarked. The day I visited Rathcoole was bright and sunny, and the quiet graveyard was full of snowdrops – just such a day as she described in her poems.

THE ROUND WINDOW

Karl O'Neill

In the early days of the Northern Troubles, my father put a round window in the gable end of our house.

We lived in the centre of Armagh, in Abbey Street, the first house on the lower end of one of the city's seven hills. It was a small street, steeply rising past the Unionist Hall, Methodist Church, Catholic Parochial House, and on the top the Church of Ireland Cathedral, the grounds of which are supposed to contain, as the song has it, 'the ashes of Brian Boru'. A bloody past seeped down through the soil of Armagh over the centuries and the Troubles of my childhood were a mere staging post on the graph of history. Parades, riots and bombs pepper my pre-teen memories.

In the late 1960s and early 1970s, it must have been a good time for glazers. Our windows regularly had to be replaced following explosions. I particularly remember sitting on the carpet in the front room, between two windows, listening to a Cliff Richard single on my sister's mono record-player, when an enormous bang was followed by the two windows smashing either side of me. Jumping up with fear and an odd excitement, my 10-year-old hand opened the front door to find a quivering young British Army squaddie cradling his rifle in the doorway, seemingly hiding from the billowing smoke engulfing the street. A car-bomb had gone off outside the post office, not fifty yards away. Perhaps this squaddie, and the others who began to appear to me in the thinning smoke, had been moving down the street to inspect the suspicious vehicle.

The post office was a regular target. Just as close was the City Hall, a fine building that housed among other things my first library, an orchard of delights. I was in Geography class at my Christian Brothers School when the City Hall was blown up. Glazers were already putting in new windows in our house when I got home that afternoon. The City Hall was destroyed and for over thirty years became a car park.

That front room where I listened to my sister's records was kept almost like a museum, scrupulously tidy, not a room for horse-play. Guests were shown into the front room. Antique furniture, an old grand piano, a library, and a severe-looking portrait of my father dominated the room, with two armchairs, one red and one green, facing each other at either side of the fireplace. It was here my future brother-in-law had to undergo the task of formally requesting from my father my sister's hand in marriage. A labour of love indeed.

It was in the corner of that front room that my father had the round window installed. At about head height, it wasn't a large window, about two feet in diameter. But what made it memorable was the stained-glass centre-piece, a red hand. *Lámh dhearg.*

My father loved history, and was proud to be *an* O'Neill if not *the* O'Neill. My two older brothers had been christened Con and Shane. By rights I ought to have been named Hugh, but my father, whose name was Charles, was going through his German period at the time, and had the bright idea of sneakily calling me after himself, using the German form of his name, Karl, with a K. My mother recorded that the parish priest at my christening was not best pleased.

'You can't call an O'Neill, a great Irish name, after a Hun! You might as well call him Hitler!'

But my father was not for turning and, under protest, the priest baptised me in the name of the Hun. Subsequently my father would introduce me as having been called after Karl Marx. I was never able to figure out which one of the Marx Brothers that was.

The round window, with a protective wire mesh covering the outside, could be seen from a good distance away in the main thoroughfare, English Street. The display of the Red Hand of the O'Neills remained there until well after we had left the North for Dundalk, where I finished my schooling, with deliberate family contrariness, at the only Protestant school in the town.

Of course there is an allegiance to the Red Hand that has a more sinister aspect and I often wonder if my father was somehow playing to both sides of the house, as it were.

Future tenants removed the stained glass, but a round window remains still, plain and transparent, as it should be perhaps – there are enough bloody hands in our history.

AN CAISLEÁN I MIONNLACH

Mairéad Ní Choneannainn

Feiceann muid anois ar fud na tíre seanfhothracha idir chaisleáin agus tithe móra á naththógáil agus á nathchóiriú. A bhuíochas sin don fhuíollach airgid a fhaid is a sheas sé chun fiúntas dar n-oidhreacht agus dar ndúchas. Anseo le hais na Gaillimhe tá sean-chaisleán gur cheart a chaomhnú agus an scéal tubaisteach a chuir deireadh leis tar éis breis is trí chéad bliain a mheabhrú.

Cois Coiribe ar bhruach thoir anall atá an baile tuaithe Mionnlach suite, i bhfoisceacht trí mhíle de chathair na Gaillimhe.

Ba limistéar beag iargúlta é fadó gan mórán de mhaoin an tsaoil ag na tionóntaithe agus iad ar a ndícheall leis an gcíos a íoc leis an tiarna talún, An Blácach, eiseann agus a mhuintir go sámh galánta sa chaisleán ar bhruach na habhann, ag fáiltiú roimh na huaisle chuig cóisir is ceol. Ar bord bád as Gaillimh a thagadh na daoine seo, chun dul i dtír suas staighre cloiche go doras an chaisleáin. Bhíodh sé de nós freisin, ag an mBlácach Lá Bealtaine cuireadh a thabhairt dá chairde eile chuig an áit chun an garraí agus an choill a fheiceáil. De réir sceálta ba mhór an cháill a bhí ar áilleacht na háite. Thaitin le daoine móra i gcónaí dul i gcaidreamh ag tabhairt féile ar son féile, cuairt ar son cuairte. Is minic mar sin a bhíodh na Blácaigh iad féin as baile go minic. Ar thuras dá leithéid a bhíodar i 1910. Bhí an bheirt imithe go Baile Átha Cliath. Sa bhaile sa chaisleán bhí iníon an tí, Miss Eleanor Blake, bean ós cionn an dá scór blian, chomh maith le foireann seirbhíseach mar ba ghnáth, cócaire agus, cailín aimsire.

Thuas ar bharr an tí ar an gcúigiú stór i seomara beag cúl a chodail an bheirt cailín. Beirt dheirfiúracha a bhí iontu. Taréis obair an lae dualgas ar leith a bhí ar an gcailín aimsire, Annie Browne, lampa ola Miss Blake a lasadh gach oíche agus é ag éirí dorcha, agus é a fhágáil isteach ina seomra. É sin déanta ag Annie ar an 26 de mhí Iúl i 1910 chuaigh sí suas ina codladh suas san áiléar, sa seomara beag agus an cócaire Delia Earley sa leaba eile in éineacht léi. I lár na hoíche dhúisigh Annie agus mhothaigh sí balla deataigh. Nuair a d'oscail sí doras an tseomra scanraigh sí leis na lasracha ag luascadh aníos. Ní raibh aon bhealach éalaithe ag an mbeirt chailín, i ngéibhinn, thuas san áiléar ach amach an fhuinneog chun seasamh ar leac taobh amuigh cúig stór ón talamh thíos.

Ansin a bhí siad ag screadaíl gur bhailigh na fir timpeall chun fóirthint orthu. Gan dréimire sách fada ní raibh aon rogha acu ach léim síos, rud a rinne siad nuair a shocraigh na fir carnán féar tirim ar an talamh. Maraíodh Delia ar an bpointe agus leagadh Annie gan bhrí, gan mothú. B'í an mhíorúilt gur mhair sí, gan dochtúir le fáil aici go luath. Ní raibh seans ar bith ag Miss Blake ina seomara thíos mar ba chosúil gurbh é an lampa lasta a bhí aici a chur tús leis an dóiteán.

Is deacair a chreidiúnt anois gur réab an tine gan srian le taobh an uisce, ach ní raibh gléas nó córas ar bith ag na comharsana gur tháinig na saighdiúirí ón mbeairic ón Rinn Mhóir ach bhí sé ró-dhéanach. Bhí an tine imithe thar fóir ar fad le truscáin agus gléasanna tí ag pléascadh thart timpeall.

An lá ina dhiaidh is ar éigin ar éirigh leo corp Eleanor Blake a aimsiú. Is sa reilig ar chnochán ard i ngar do fhallaí an chaisleáin atá sí curtha agus an leac os a cionn le feiceáil fós.

Maidir le Annie Browne, tar éis breoiteacht an-fhada san ospidéal d'fhan sí tamall lena muintir sular thug sí na cosa léi as Gaillimh chun dul go Meiriceá. Ansin, bhain sí saol sárchúramach di féin, áit ar phós sí. Ach ní dhearna sí dearmad ariamh ar dhóiteán an chaisleáin, agus taréis breis is trí scór bliain scríobh sí litir go stairí san Ollscoil i nGaillimh, ag cur síos le cuimhne cinn ar imeachtaí na hoíche úd mí Iúl 1910.

THE SWALLOWS OF CAPISTRANO

Mae Leonard

It is a sweltering Sunday in Los Angeles and my uncle has designated it for the Mission. We're on our way to the San Juan Capistrano Mission. I look longingly at the signpost for Malibu and Laguna Beaches and I sigh. But the Mission is the mission and we drive on between tall date palms with the Pacific glistening away to our right. As bird-shaped signposts perched along the roadside guide us all the way to Capistrano, my father begins to sing 'When the Swallows Come Back to Capistrano' and my uncle hums along with him.

Whatever the other twenty Missions of California have to offer, Capistrano tops them all with the phenomenon of the swallows. On 19 March, the Feast Day of St Joseph, crowds gather at the old Mission of San Juan; tourists, pilgrims, archaeologists and scholars come to walk under the canopy of the restored ancient arches, view the ruins of the old church and listen to the Mission bells. Television cameramen, radio broadcasters, newspaper reporters and magazine writers also come to report the return each year.

The Mission was founded towards the end of the eighteenth century by Spanish Franciscans and, once established, became a place of work and education for the native Indians. Then in 1821 Mexico won her independence from Spain; California's new governor was totally opposed to the Franciscans, and by the end of the nineteenth century all the old missions lay in decay. It was then that Fr John O'Sullivan, an Irish-American priest, came to the Mission of San Juan Capistrano. He was suffering from tuberculosis and had been sent to California to recover. The place so enthralled him that he vowed to restore it and restored his health at the same time. To his absolute delight he discovered that the swallows arrived back to nest in the Mission on 19 March every year – it was his birthday. Thus on that day it became a ritual for his friends and neighbours to rise at dawn and sit with Fr O'Sullivan in front of the mission to await the return of the swallows.

Ornithologists came to study the nesting habits of the swallows sometime before 1915 and reported to the magazine *Overland Monthly* that the birds, in great quantities, built their beehive nests into the crevices of the ruined Mission. It was in 1930 that the story of the Capistrano swallows finally found its way into print. A collection of tales, legends and stories named *Capistrano Nights* written by Fr O'Sullivan was published. One story told of a previous padre becoming angry when a local hotel owner destroyed the swallows' nests because the birds were too noisy for his guests. The good padre somehow managed to get the birds to follow him back to the Mission and they've come there ever since. They migrate every autumn to Goya, Argentina some 24,000 kilometers away, and winter there until 18 February when they begin the return journey that takes thirty days, arriving – like clockwork – on 19 March at the San Juan Mission at Capistrano.

Having read *Capistrano Nights*, the editor of the *Los Angeles Times* announced the return of the swallows in his column each year. Although nobody could be absolutely positive that the birds would show up on time, a radio reporter decided to cover the event live in 1936. His listeners were not disappointed when he announced 'the skies are blackened with swallows' and the Mission bells rang out to welcome them. The announcement of the swallows' return is printed every year, even in the Irish newspapers: a sort of symbol of hope.

It was on 19 March, seventy years ago in 1939, that songwriter Leon René was waiting impatiently for his wife to cook breakfast. 'Honey,' he said, 'the swallows will be back at Capistrano before my breakfast is ready.' And suddenly a melody sprung into his head. 'When the Swallows Come Back to Capistrano' was born and became a huge hit that turned the eyes of the world on the old Mission.

Our long day in Capistrano leaves us quiet with our thoughts on our journey back to Los Angeles, and my father and uncle softly sing as the sizzling sun slips down into the Pacific.

TEA TIME EXPRESS

Sheila Maher

The arrival of a Tea Time Express cake into our house was a big deal. Even though any cake my mother ever made was lighter, fresher and more real-tasting, a 'Tea Time' was a proper treat. It was when there was an extended family gathering that one usually appeared. A thoughtful, more affluent relative would arrive into our house and proudly hand Mum the fancy red box, with the yellow ribbon tied in a bow around it. 'Oh you shouldn't have!' Mum would say, as she placed it squarely on our countertop.

I hovered close to my mother's elbow when it came to cutting the Tea Time. I loved the ceremony of untying the ribbon (to save it for some other use), lifting the lid on the box and catching my first glimpse of the cake. My favourite bit was when Mum removed the cake from the clear plastic wrapper and left this aside. As she cut the cake, I scraped my finger along the inside of the wrapper and scooped up any icing and crumbs that had stuck to it. Some icing yielded a better result than others. The fondant icing was the best, as it clung to the wrapper in large chunks that my greedy fingers would scrape up before Mum had a chance to replace it back on the cake. If there was a big gathering in the sitting room, Mum sliced the cake in its entirety. The slices were carefully placed, slightly overlapping, on a fancy doilied plate.

There was the Strawberry Layer and the more exotic Pineapple Layer – we never got the chocolate one for some unknown reason. But when the Australian Layer arrived, it immediately became my favourite. Mum only ever put one layer in her cakes; four or five layers, interspersed with jam and the sweetest butter-cream, meant a slice of Australian Layer dissolved easily in my mouth. There was even icing on the sides of these cakes, so that every piece was generously endowed. With other cakes no one wanted the heel, the crust, the hard, dry bit at the edge. With the Tea Time, there was a fight for the last piece. It was to here the excess icing had oozed and lodged during the cutting; sometimes there was more icing than cake on the last slice.

When visitors came, Mum prepared her trolley. This was a gold trolley with two shelves that she got as a wedding present. On the top shelf she placed cups and saucers, a milk jug, sugar bowl and a plate of sandwiches; some egg, some ham. On the bottom shelf was a plate of Viscount Biscuits in their inviting green and orange foil wrappers, Cadbury's Chocolate Fingers, some Scottish shortbread and now the plate of Tea Time Express. Mum wheeled this laden trolley into the sitting room, like a cross between a stately pram and a tea lady's trolley. From here she served her guests with a generous supper, washed down with several cups of tea. As children we were told to keep our hands off until guests had eaten their fill. I sat on the arm of a chair and waited patiently. I tried to stay focused on the conversation buzzing around me and answer questions that were asked of me, but my eyes were drawn to the last remaining slice of Tea Time cake, slightly damaged but very inviting, languishing on the smudge-covered doily. I was hoping everyone else had forgotten about it.

During a lull in the conversation, Mum started to tidy up; she placed all the dirty cups and saucers and empty teapot back on her trolley and wheeled it into the kitchen. Disguising my greed as helpfulness, I followed her and offered to wash the dishes so that Mum could return to the sitting room and relax with her guests. Gratefully, she accepted my offer. My siblings were delighted to be relieved of washing-up duty. As soon as the sitting room door shut and I was certain I had the kitchen to myself, I pounced on my haul. I greedily gobbled the heel of the cake, before anyone could interrupt me. Alas, this much coveted slice of cake was not as good as I had anticipated. I sucked the icing from each of my fingertips, to make sure I had not missed the taste in my haste to eat it. The sugar in the wedge of icing was the only flavour I could identify; it overrode any that existed in the sponge and jam. This was a disappointing result for all my patience and deviousness, and in return for that sad slice of cake I had a sink full of dirty dishes to wash.

SHIRTS FOR BOOKS

Peter Sirr

I stop at the corner of Clare Street and stare. Surely? But of course it's not there, the bookshop has vanished, even if there's still a corner of my brain that expects to see the green-painted book barrows under the awning on the street outside as I cross over from Merrion Street. Instead, I find myself looking at expensive shirts: the lilac button cuff, the blue Cadogan, the Cavendish light blue stripe. Greene's is now Henry Jermyn, the London shirtmakers and court tailors. Inside, where the books and post office used to be, you can see the neat shelves of business shirts. I find myself reluctant to accept the visible evidence of the new life of this corner shop. I can still see the bookshop so clearly in my mind's eye that the shirts keep receding to reveal the slightly chaotic downstairs section, with its small selection of new books and a queue in front of the post office window and, in September, queues of harassed parents with their long lists of school books. There are no queues today, no fervent shirt-buyers scanning the shelves.

The death of a second-hand bookshop always hits hard. There are never that many of them to begin with and they are rarely replaced, so that one more opportunity to idle among familiar shelves disappears. Maybe someone has died and their relatives have sold off the library; there might be a clutch of poetry or French novels of the 1930s or a dictionary of agricultural terms or an account of medieval travelogues you have to climb the ladder to pull down. Regular bookshops push their predictable lines of new titles by the currently favoured, but the real joy is the second-hand shop because, dingy and dull though the stock might often be, its true offering is surprise, the random encounter with a book placed there, you imagine, by some serendipitous god exactly so you should find it. These are where the unsought, life-changing books are stored, the books you would never have thought to search out.

Proper bookshops can often seem like retail outlets where the products happen to be books. Or there are antiquarian shops where books are slipped into plastic covers and converted into outlandishly expensive fetish objects. On the other hand, there are civilised refuges of the unexpected, like the half-hidden one at the end of a narrow corridor past a doctor's surgery. The bookshop part takes cash, but if you want to use a card you must take your docket to the record shop man at the other end who appears from his stacks of vinyl to apply the technology.

Now we're getting somewhere: must and old books and half-forgotten music and a complex retail experience. A portal through which you can leave the city and the fixed trajectories of your life. This is something else which the shirts will never replace. Bookshops are mental spaces, they are places for thinking and dreaming; the best of them have an atmosphere that makes them seem like the outward embodiment of the inner life. The physical proportions, the disposition of the shelves and the smell of old books all seem like extensions of the imaginative life; they leave an impression that can be entered and re-entered long after you have left.

They are part of what Susan Sontag calls 'the geography of pleasure', 'like the sexual hunt – another reason for strolling about in the world'. She was writing about Walter Benjamin, who was a devoted collector, whose books were also portals into the rooms – in Berlin, Naples, Danzig, Munich, Moscow – where they had been bought. No one will hold a shirt in his hand and fall into a reverie about the shop it was bought in, or will idle away hours in a department store browsing the socks and trousers. A wardrobe is not a library, no matter how well stocked. Bookshops are like parks or museums, spaces where public and private collide, where the inner and outer worlds become porous – another Benjamin term – and admit each other. And both are hospitable to the solitary wanderer; they are constructed to serve solitude.

At one point in my life I used to fantasise about running a second-hand bookshop, reading books about it, gathering all of the technical information, thinking about stock management and computer systems. All of that was far too real, whereas what I wanted was a kind of private city, or an officially sanctioned privacy. So impractical was the impulse that I'm sure, had anything actually come of it, that my wish would have been granted. It would have been a perfect licence for idle reverie. It is, though, one of the reasons I am jealously attached to the freedom of bookshops and why they are the first port of call in any city I visit. And it's why I am standing outside here now, trying to magick the shirts out of their bubble on Clare Street, and whoosh the books back in.

THE GATE LODGE

Susan Stairs

In the summer of 1987, when our first child was three months old, we rented a quaint redbrick and cut-stone gate lodge, close to Killiney Bay. Having lived in the city centre for a number of years, we looked forward to walks along the beach on fine evenings and weekend trips out to Bray or Blackrock on the Dart.

The gate lodge – hidden from the road by an eight-foot-high wall – sat just inside heavy wooden gates at the top of a tree-lined avenue. At the far end of this avenue stood the big house – a huge Victorian Gothic mansion, complete with a tower from where, we had heard, there was a stunning view of the bay. The occupants of the big house owned a pair of inquisitive Great Danes who roamed freely around the grounds on the lookout for mischief, lolloping excitedly up the avenue to the gates at the mere touch of a hand on the latch.

Returning home with our young son in his buggy, I always approached the gates with a huge sense of trepidation, for although I'd been assured that Great Danes were quite benign and playful, I was nevertheless terrified of this pair of kidney-coloured beasts. Heart thumping, I'd lift the metal latch as silently as I could, opening the gates the tiniest amount. On a good day, I'd be greeted by the sound of their paws on the gravel as they scrambled up the curving avenue on their long legs. If I was quick, I'd close the gate, run to the gate lodge, heave the buggy into the hall and slam the door shut before they arrived. I'd look out the window from my sanctuary to see them sniffing around the front door, tails wagging dejectedly before they'd slink back through the trees looking for something else to satisfy their curiosity.

On a bad day, however, gently opening the gates, I'd be greeted by two wet black snouts feverishly attempting to poke their way through the gap. Petrified, I'd ease the gates closed and stand outside, waiting for the beasts to retreat.

If, after ten minutes or so, I hadn't heard them running back down the avenue, there was nothing for it but to swing the wheels of the buggy around and start walking again. Down Military Road, breathing in the salty air, right onto Seafield Road with the glorious expanse of the bay to the left, onto Killiney Hill Road and on around towards home again. A circular loop of about a mile. Arriving back, I'd slip through the gates and into the house to the sound of those great paws pounding up the avenue.

One day, a year after we'd moved in, the gate lodge was broken into. We returned home to find our front door open and the place ransacked. The items most missed were pieces of my jewellery: the tiny gold cross and chain I'd been given for my First Communion; the engraved silver bangle I'd received on graduating from secondary school; and the one-of-a-kind silver bracelet that had belonged to my auntie Mary.

Another item we missed was a painting. We'd opened a gallery in 1986, exhibiting work by new and well-known Irish artists, and the painting was a damaged one we'd been asked to repair. A large oil, with a two-inch tear down its middle, it depicted a majestic white sailing ship on a choppy, turquoise sea. We hadn't given its owner any deadline for its completion and had mislaid his contact details. We'd simply have to wait for him to get in touch so we could break the news.

As the months passed, the imminent arrival of our second child prompted us to think about moving back to the city and purchasing a home of our own.

After finally obtaining mortgage approval, we put in an offer on a house off South Circular Road; it was accepted, and we were set to move in February 1989.

On the appointed day, we loaded our belongings into the removal van and prepared to say goodbye to the gate lodge. My husband decided to have one last look around before we left and, for some reason, climbed up the mossy, stone steps that led to the flat roof of the coach-house adjoining the gate lodge. And there, to his surprise, under a layer of wet leaves, lay the painting of the white-sailed ship. Why it ended up there, we will never know, but I like to think that maybe the Great Danes had a part in it. Perhaps they chased the burglars up onto the roof, and the painting got left behind in their haste to get away from the beasts.

Incredibly, despite having lain exposed to the elements for nine long months, we were able to fully clean and restore the painting of the white ship on the turquoise sea. When its owner finally got in touch, we were relieved to be able to tell him that yes, his painting was ready for collection. And he was absolutely delighted with the result. I often wonder what he'd say if he knew of the sailing ship's secret sojourn on the coach-house roof at Killiney Bay.

Our baby girl arrived one week after we moved into our new home and she is now almost twenty-one years old. We still live in the city, and I am still afraid of dogs.

BIRDS

Evelyn Conlon

In the same way that not everyone reads a bundle of poems every month, not everyone watches birds. Although, mind you, if the birds all disappeared one morning you'd be surprised at how quickly the radio lines would be jammed. There would be people who would stand to attention, not knowing why they were suddenly inexplicably in mourning; they would stand quietly listening to *something*. But there would be others who would jump to the phone believing that sharing the shock would relieve it. That's bad shock. But there's such a thing as good shock; surprise it might be called, or delight even. And that's what happens when a person sneaks out early in the morning to see an assortment of Australian birds rising for the day. I mention Australia, not because I casually or without reason or thought hop down there, but because I've just been sojourning around the place in pursuit of the lives of girls who went there before our time, but more about that another time.

You see this thing about not being a birdwatcher. And being sure that you're not. Well, many of us are birdwatchers without knowing it. And if not a watcher then certainly a listener. There can be a moment of deliciousness before the alarm goes off, particularly on an Irish spring morning, a moment when we don't know that what has actually woken us is a swallow tweeting – ah, that lovely word before it was stolen, and remember when wireless was what shook out stories of wet and dry batteries and had men listening to football matches at shop windows. Of course it mightn't have been a swallow, it could have been a thrush; you don't have to know the name of a bird for it to waken you. And then when you're stretching, checking the world before letting it in, the reason you're still so happy is that there's an orchestra out there in the trees, already performing just for you, soothing your way into the trickle of the day. If only we could hear it better it might help us to decide what to keep out: the disappointment, the rage; and what to let in: the consolations of philosophy and the sound of the dew outside gathering up its skirts. I try that sometimes, hushing the sound of fury and listening to the birds instead. If only I could remember to do it more consistently. But I definitely do it in Australia; a body would be mad not to. Actually there is no choice really, because there's no tweeting there, it's a full-blown cymbal banging, lorikeet screeching, kookaburra laughing, raucous assault. But a good assault, if you know what I mean. And if you're careful in your listening you might hear, behind the tumult, the twinkle of the bell bird.

For our ears, trained to starlings, the sounds are just so extraordinary that you would be pied pipered out at dawn, and of course if you're in your first week there won't be any problem about that: you'll either be wide awake and have half your day over you or not have gone asleep yet. And when I think of the ancestors out there and their bewilderment I would like to believe that the birds, the cut and the colour of them, might be the thing that brought smiles to their faces, because there is no way of looking at an Eclectus parrot, a Sulphur-crested cockatoo or your run-of-the-mill galah without taking your hat off in salute. The golds, the sea-greens, blues and shocking reds flash about in a mad caper. And if those birds made them smile, what might the animals have done? No stand-up comic could beat a kangaroo as it deliberately bounds in front of you just to see your mesmerised stance collapse out of control. Kangaroos do not jump or hop, indeed bounding is only a minor part of the contortion of their movement; there is quite simply no word for what kangaroos do. And then they stop and confidently look back at you just to prove to themselves, once again, that yes that got you. And yes, I don't care where you come from, you'll remember me.

Back in Ireland, the morning pettifogging is replaced by our discreet melody makers, but the very uproar of their Australian relatives makes us more, not less, conscious of them. And bird-listening could put you searching for a bundle of poems.

SOMETHING OUT OF NOTHING SOUP

Catherine Ann Cullen

When you call from France
I say I'm writing about food
And you remind me of the soup I made
In our London bedsit.

While one of us cooked,
The other soaked in the big bath in the kitchen
Figuring out new ways to fool
The metre that gobbled our fifty pences.

Working yet another back week in the '80s,
Cash poor, dream rich,
We'd shop in Sainsbury's
Heaping our trolley with luxuries.

Your favourite was a steeply priced cheesecake,
The glossy fruit encased in a ruby jelly,
The cream cheese impossibly high and white,
The base pale as champagne.

Our mouths watered as you placed it
High at the front of the trolley
Where other people put small children.

As we nosed towards the checkout
Everything came out again:
Chocolate biscuits, ginger crackers, your father's favourite relishes,
Replaced on the reproachful shelves.

Last of all,
You'd bring the cheesecake carefully back to its fridge
As I crossed the last aisle.
Some day, you'd say.

At the checkout we'd pay for our bag of flour, our bread and porridge.
We lived on pancakes for a fortnight
When the eggs ran out, and then the milk,
We made them from flour and water.

And one evening for a change,
I decided to make soup.
There was nothing to make soup with
But I boiled water anyway,
Made a stock of salt and pepper
And dried herbs left by a previous tenant

It was delicious, savoury,
We relished its simplicity.
You said God was not the only one
Who could make something out of nothing.

When I got paid, I bought the cheesecake for you.
I carried it to the counter like an offertory gift.
It was the day you turned the telly on its side
So you could watch it lying on the sofa.

Side-by-side we bit into
The taste of disappointment:
The cream cheese stuck to the roofs of our mouths,
Its fruit artificially sweet, its base soft and sickly.

I thought we would treasure the time
We finally ate that cheesecake,
But on the phone from France
Your voice is warm with the memory of
Something out of nothing soup.

APRIL

THE CROSS ON THE HILL

Colette Olney

You could break a leg up there – at the site of the old cross. That's undoubtedly why the council put a metal fence across the foot of a dirt
track clawed out of the hill. The track slopes up and plateaus on a
windswept wasteland – a wasteland I do *not* remember. The track too, is
new.

I am loathe to break a bone, but I want to get up to where that cross
is looming against a midday sky swept clean of clouds. Rubble surrounds
it: bricks, bits of pipes, oil drums, rusting girders and the ubiquitous
ripped, flittering black plastic sacks – predictable detritus from our boom
time's construction-fest – blatant still, despite a soft, perforated blanket
of grasses, spreading season by season, growing over the mess.

The council fence is askew; warnings are fixed onto it. I tilt my head
and read: 'Danger' and 'Keep Out'. This is no kind of welcome, but I am
determined.

The cross soars skyward. I want to touch it, to stand on its plinth,
hear it speak to me of *my* days in 'Crosser': *Cross*haven.

My old homeplace! I expect the cross to *speak* to me!

As a child, I believed the place had taken its name from the cross; that
shape cresting the rugged hill over the village. Like Templebreedy or Gra-
ball Bay or Roche's Point or the Bull Rock out at Church Bay,
Crosshaven's holy cross was part of the landscape, and because it was
put there to mark a 'holy year', also the year of my birth, I felt some propriety towards it.

It was always off the beaten track, but when I was old enough to roam
with others of my age, the cross became a place of (totally *ir*reverent!)

pilgrimage. We scrambled uphill; stumbling, wrestling with brambles; weaving through thistles and prickly furze, seating ourselves for spells in small clearings; inhaling the nutty odours of gorse – and gleefully poking twigs into cowpats to repulse ourselves.

In those days, the cross caught the eye of home-comers or tourists turning the last bend into Crosshaven on their way south from Cork. In those days… Developments have since dwarfed it.

'Where's the holy cross?' I'm enquiring from the comfort of my car. The two girls looking back at me are aged about ten. They are the only ones out and about.

Moments earlier, they clipped past racing downhill on scooters – the toy-type you mount with both feet when you get up enough speed. Speed's no problem here. The now-paved hill winds around a clutter of housing estates. It's freewheeling territory. The girls now push uphill to repeat the thrill.

'Do you mean Ard Cross?' The taller girl asks. They are both wide-eyed, bemused.

'I don't know if I mean Ard Cross,' I say. 'Is there a cross there? There used to be a cross somewhere around here; a large holy cross.'

'Oh, that's in the dump,' the two say, almost in unison, breaking into giggles. Then they explain a route that leads to it.

The shorter girl tells me the cross was going to be knocked, but that there was a protest. I say I'm glad…I tell them the cross is as old as myself. 'We like it anyways – yeah, we like it,' they echo each other.

I follow their instructions: leave one housing estate, enter another. In a cul-de-sac I see the track, then the plain, austere, concrete cross – all thirty-odd feet of it – defiant above the rubble. I pick my way, goat-like, over the pitted terrain, over scrap metal and bricks, over carelessness, over neglect.

The cross, when I reach it, is stony silent.

I lay my hand against it and find it retaining some faint heat from the sun. I hear the faint grumble of a jet over the stiff breeze that is riffling plastic. On the hill opposite, I see my first home, its bay window, a green-house addition to its gable. I see pathways, steps, the church, the convent, and down almost at water level, the terrace that *was* shops and pubs. The deep silence of the cross is formidable.

Still, the view is panoramic: in Crosshaven's waters, hundreds of leisure craft sit like bored gulls. On the far shore, Currabinny's old trees mass darkly. Out in the inner harbour, tiny yellow sails cluster, fluttering like moths in distress. At my side, the old cross is mute. Below it, rooftops cascade in rows. With a lull in the breeze, I can hear, in the near distance, a sound that jumpstarts my heart – wild, mirthful screams. Those girls! Young things! Careering downhill. My guess is that they will climb up here later when they are tired of scootering. And because they will expect nothing from it, the cross will probably speak to them.

DAUB

Ted Sheehy

Daub is one of the great words. A dictionary will tell you it's a verb (from the old French *dauber* – to plaster) but up this end of the country it's a noun. If you look to your garden to grow things you pray you don't find it.

It's a perennially wet, sticky, anaerobic medium that a man with a spade – myself in this case – hopes to avoid when he entertains thoughts of growing food for the table.

The worst you might find is 'pure daub', a combination of words that must be uttered with resignation and hopelessness, a downcast expression, and a drooping of the shoulders.

All that'll grow on 'pure daub' is rushes and more rushes, and the occasional plant that prefers to swim shallow than to root. If daub was good for anything you could use it to throw pots, but I somehow doubt it has the right mix of minerals for firing.

To look at daub it is a wet, heavy, grey clay you can just about squeeze in your fist so that when you open your hand you've got a fat, rippled sausage that's forensically contoured with your palm and finger prints. I suppose it might have been used with straw and wattles to make walls in the long ago. A bit like Yeats's fantasy cabin in the bee-loud glade.

Back here in the real world, where people 'get up' rather than 'arise', you have to cross your fingers when you take a spade in your hand. And, as you might imagine, that doesn't make the digging any easier.

I had already chosen the bit of the acre for the vegetable patch. The soil seemed good – black, loamy and reasonably well drained. But you never really know what you'll find when you start to dig a little deeper and a little further.

I've been turning the ground over row by row, my slow process a form of pyrrhic victory for determination over experience. Lately it's a rear-guard action against scutch grass; the wizened, stubborn roots of thistle, dock, and dandelion, and the all-pervasive creeping buttercup.

But at least the soil *is* good – plenty of depth, lots of earthworms, and few enough stones to frustrate the spade.

It is ground, I am sure, that's been worked before, back in the day when a kitchen garden was a necessity rather than a lifestyle choice. Every now and then the spade throws up a fragment of pottery, a piece of old iron, a lid from a two-pound Fruitfield jam jar, or a chip from a willow-pattern plate – a shard of brilliant blue and white amid the black clay.

I was into the second last row and some ten inches down when the spade ran into an obstacle. A bit of leverage on the handle and up it came. It was a little white jar with a pale green metal lid, and on the lid a question printed in white script on an orange square. It asks, 'Have you tried Angel Face?'

The jar is reminiscent of the Pond's Cold Cream jars that used to sit on my mother's dressing table. I can smell their scent still. And this other jar from the past does say 'Pond's' underneath, but my mother's jars were curved whereas this one is shaped into corners at each side. And who or what was Angel Face?

A little research tells me that Angel Face was, well, that *other* sort of daub. It was an early form of cake-free foundation developed by Pond's in the 1940s. One of the faces used to market the product in America was that of an expatriate young Kildare woman, Sheila Connolly, who published her autobiography, *Angel Face – A Memoir*, back in 1999.

It's a curious turn of the world when an old jar in the vegetable patch leads you to the story of an Irish glamour girl in post-war Hollywood. On the off-chance that there are any archaeologists listening, eager to excavate a mid-twentieth-century midden, they'd better hurry up because the potatoes should be going in any day now.

But before I got to Sheila Connolly's days in showbiz, I rested my forearm on the handle of the spade and got to wondering how the little jar came to be buried 10 inches down in the soil, some fifty to sixty years before 'we're worth it' became a catchphrase.

Maybe it fell unseen from a pinafore pocket as the potatoes were picked. Or maybe it was thrown out into the ploughed field in an argument about how money was spent in hard times. Who knows? Perhaps when the jar was missed, it was hunted for by the woman of the house, or a daughter.

And when she came back in, the jar lost into the earth for all these years, did she catch her own glance in the looking glass? Did she draw a strand of hair from her face and see herself tired, a bit weathered, and aged before time by the work she was doing and the life she was living?

EASTER

Pat Boran

Easter morning, the first light
through the window, first second third fourth birds
already up and in place to sing their small
but crucial parts in the ongoing mystery.

Today, no distractions. Today
the observed routine of quiet.
The ticking clock given its stage,
the cold shock and sudden cascade
of water from the tap once again
miraculous. For the second time
I wash my face in its
cold shock, then, coffee in hand, slide back
the back door and step out
into existence, it feels like,
all the stars of the night
dimmed into second place
by our local wonder.

The coffee mug warm in my hands,
the sunlight warm on my face
but the air is still fresh, still sharp, still hard
with determination.
Beyond the cottage garden,
beyond the open fields and few bare trees,

the mountains seem to fall back into themselves
as if a circus master were folding up his tents
before moving on to the next too-busy town.

AN EASTER JOURNEY: 1916

Marguerite MacCurtin

The greatest journey of the heroic age of Antarctic Exploration began on Easter Monday, 24 April 1916, a date which for very different reasons is indelibly imprinted on the collective memory of the Irish people.

Half a world away from Dublin, on the edge of Antarctica, three Irishmen and three Englishmen set sail in a small open boat, called the *James Caird*, on an 800-mile journey to seek help for their twenty-two companions shipwrecked from Shackleton's Endurance expedition. For seventeen days they were blasted by the hurricane winds and 50-foot waves of the Southern Ocean as they battled for survival against towering icebergs, numbing cold, water saturation, sleep deprivation, hunger and thirst in their bid to reach the whaling stations at South Georgia.

Their combined talents as a crew, the mastery of Shackleton as skipper, the Herculean character of Crean and the incomparable skills of Worsley as navigator made this epic journey one of the greatest feats of seamanship ever recorded.

That was only half the story. They were forced by the elements and the fragility of their boat onto the wrong side of South Georgia, so it was necessary to cross the unmapped interior of the island on foot in order to reach the whaling station at Stromness. The three strongest men – Shackleton, Crean and Worsley – set out again, this time equipped only with a primus stove, two compasses, a pair of binoculars, fifty feet of rope, a box of matches and a few meagre rations of food.

They crossed icefields and crevasses, climbed peaks and glaciers, tobogganed down a 3,000-foot mountain slope, dragged Crean out of an icy inland lake and trudged ever onwards, thigh-high in snow, in the hope of finding life at the whaling station if Worsley's calculations proved to be correct. Finally, when they heard the siren in the distance calling the whalers to work, they threw caution and their primus stove to the winds, abseiled down a frozen waterfall into the valley, and staggered in rags, unwashed and unshaven, into Stromness.

Last year I followed their journey from Elephant Island to South Georgia and walked with a small group of people those last 6 kilometres of their epic 64-kilometre trek. At Elephant Island, the miserable stony spit 100 yards long by 40 yards wide, which was home to the twenty-two shipwrecked men for four and a half months, had not improved with time. It was so small, so bleak and so forbidding that I could only think that, apart from their inner strength, it must have been the tungsten-blue glow of the surrounding glaciers that enabled them to live in this hostile and wretched place.

The Southern Ocean was still as Shackleton described it: 'a seething chaos of tortured water' beaten by storms and giant waves and littered with sky-high tabular icebergs. South Georgia, by contrast, was now bathed in the light and heat of the Antarctic Summer. The sun shone in the cloudless sky and the luminous beauty of its mountains and its glaciers and its turquoise waters made it difficult to imagine the hardships, deprivations and attendant dangers of their epic winter trek. However, like other travellers before us, we discovered that it was the spirit of their journey that accompanied us and pervaded our every moment as we sailed in their wake and walked in their footsteps to Stromness.

Even in summer this is a shadowy place. Nestled beneath the dark, towering walls of the zigzag-shaped mountains, there is an eerie feeling of ghostly silhouettes lurking amongst the grey and gabled remnants of this long-abandoned whaling site. This eerie feeling is further compounded by the reflections of the sun's rays flickering through the dark shadows of the ruins. In such an isolated and rarefied environment it is easy to believe that Shackleton, Crean and Worsley discovered retrospectively that they each had experienced a strange sensation that a fourth person accompanied them on their odyssey across South Georgia to these shores at Stromness.

FOCLÓIR AN NUA-GHAEILGE

Cyril Kelly

In Yeats's poem, 'The Song Of The Happy Shepherd', there is a line, 'Words alone are certain good'. Well, that line came to me quite recently when I saw that the Royal Irish Academy is in the process of compiling *Foclóir an Nua-Ghaeilge*, a new Irish dictionary. But after thirty-four years of scholarship and endeavour, its enterprise has not progressed beyond words beginning with the letter 'A'; has not yet reached the letter 'B'. So the Royal Irish Academy obviously believes that Yeats's line, 'Words alone are certain good.'

This dictionary, however, is not going to be your common-or-garden compilation of words and meanings. Each entry is going to be the history of a particular word, the story of that word, if you like, from the present day back through its various nuances and shades of meaning, back to its earliest written citation. There are ten scholars working on this immense project. They have consulted a database that stretches as far back as 1600 and includes sources as diverse as *Agallamh na Seanórach* to the *Songs of Cathal Buí Mac Giolla Ghunna* and *Comhfhreagras Fileata ó Chontae an Chláir*, poetic correspondence of County Clare, if you don't mind.

Started, as I say, in 1976, and now in the year of the Lord, 2010, the work is only halfway through 'A'. Makes you think. And that was exactly what happened when I thought about it; it made me think. It made me think of those Irish words that were in common usage among the English-speaking people of sixty years ago.

I think for instance of the word *tomhaisín*. Its literal translation is 'a small measure'. But hidden beneath that bland fact, the word *tomhaisín* is a delight, evoking the senses of a 6-year-old. I am on my way back to school after the lunch break and I have a tanner. Eily Sheehy's is the last sweet shop before the grey craggy wall of the school. The shop is tiny. There is such a crush at the counter that I am afraid I will be late for Catechism, Bean Uí Chrúilí's first class after lunch. By the time I wriggle to the counter I am addled by the smells: black jacks, bulls' eyes, cough-no-mores, slab toffee. 'A *tomhaisín* of bon-bons please,' I blurt out at last. Slicing a small square from *The Kerryman*, Eily's hands disappear below the level of the counter. As if by magic, they suddenly reappear with a perfectly formed paper cone. Her fingers are smudged powdery white. What a treasure, that *tomhaisín*. I can still feel the hint of the bon-bon shapes as I waited for my change.

And all the other words in common currency at the time. The 1950s must have been a censorious time. Many of the words I remember were terms of castigation: *amadán, bastún, dulamú, gligín*. I am in class, in St Michael's College. I am standing up but unable to answer the questions on the Council of Trent. It started in December 1545, but when did it end? That was the rub. And what about Purgatory and the sale of Indulgences and Original Sin? You're a *pleidhce*, boy, the teacher informs me. What are you? I'm a *pleidhce*, Sir.

And then there's *smachtaín*, from the Irish *smacht*, meaning discipline. In today's parlance it would be The Enforcer. The *smachtaín* was a short wooden club, the head loaded with lead. I am on holidays outside Cappoquin. The widest part of the Blackwater. It is three nights before the fishing season opens. Afraid to say that I am afraid, I help the two local lads to slide the flat-bottomed boat along the slob, through the reeds and onto the river. The fog is thickening. Dipping oars hardly make a ripple. Rising oars hardly drip or trickle. One whopper of a cock salmon is caught in the trap. Landed into the bottom of the boat, the torch catches for a moment his winter brown and scarlet. But then we hear the bailiffs on the bank. I lean back, stretching out my hand to stifle the slapping of the fish. Just as the *smachtaín* comes swishing down to do the same. I'm not likely to forget that word.

All those Irish words that were at one time *fite fúite* in the weft and warp of the vernacular of my past. Words that in many cases hark back to antiquity. Their story is our story. Their changing usage reflects our changing circumstances. They are the rough diamonds of standard language, but they are cut and polished by dialect and district. They reflect our attitudes, our humour, our celebrations, our consolations. Just as the reliquaries of the ancient saints preserved sacred manuscripts, *Foclóir an Nua-Ghaeilge* will be a cornucopia, preserving the sometimes ephemeral existence of words so that their riches can be enjoyed by future generations.

REMEMBERING JOHN MCGAHERN

Dympna Murray Fennell

The twins were quiet girls, a little wary of others, serious and hard-working. They didn't join very much in the fun and games of a class of 12-year-olds; while most of the girls in the boarding school chattered and boasted about family and home, the twins were reserved about such matters. It was rumoured that their mother was dead and that their father was very strict, but he did take them out for tea most Sunday afternoons. Occasionally a rather handsome older brother was glimpsed; this made them quite interesting to a crowd of girls, who were beginning to fanta-sise about older boys. They dropped out of our school after a year; in later years as we reminisced about the early days, we often wondered 'what became of the twins'.

What became of them, and their whole family story, emerged a life-time later when the older brother wrote his *Memoir*. John McGahern un-veiled every detail of what made him and his siblings — a bitter-sweet account of traditional Irish rural life in the mid-twentieth century. Bitter, in that it depicted the dynamic of a family bereft of a much-loved mother and dominated by a tyrannical father; sweet, in his celebration of people and places, his appreciation of the fields and narrow lanes in which he grew up, and to which he returned after his wanderings.

He had a special love for the maze of lanes 'that wander into one an-other like streams until they meet the road, green tunnels pierced by vivid pinpoints of light'. In such a lane as a child he had walked with his adored mother, and absorbed her love of the hidden world of wild flowers and animals which permeates his writing. A memorable picture of the adult John shows him in such a lane, in a red jumper with his black and white collie dog, a contented countryman at home in his native place, observing the ordinary lives of ordinary people, which he enshrined in his extraordinary prose.

His father was not impressed by his son's choosing to settle down on a small farm in his native Leitrim. 'My son has bought a snipe-run behind the Ivy Leaf Ballroom.' But John loved the snipe and the herons and the quiet world of the small fields and lakes; he loved the expanse of Gloria Bog: 'an inland sea of heather and pale sedge, broken by stunted birch trees, and the dark gashes of the turf banks'. In this pastoral setting, like a latter-day Synge, he would record the closing chapters of the old rural way of life, the age-old rituals of birthing and dying, of sowing and reaping, of surviving – or not – in an often harsh world.

And McGahern was a survivor; his earliest memory was of his father roughly docking his childhood curls. A photograph from that time shows him with his three sisters, little chubby girls, solemn and rather scared-looking; John stands firmly as the leader of his little band, which in fact he was in later years when their father's draconian discipline became unbearable. A survivor too of the repressive climate of 1950s Ireland; maybe the skills he had learned in the harsh upbringing helped him to cope with the worst that the establishment of Church and State could do to him.

I never met John McGahern, but I feel I know him well; I can identify with the rural midland world that shaped him, a world of quiet lanes and quiet lives, of age-old customs and certainties, of darkness and light. At this time around the anniversary of his death, I especially remember him; I am eternally grateful to him for immortalising that almost lost culture with all its strengths and weaknesses.

SEAMUS HEANEY:
A LIVING VOICE IN KILKENNY

Cathy Power

In 1974 I had a broken heart. It is an indication of the woeful nature of my love life then and, indeed, now, that I cannot remember exactly who had broken it or by precisely what means.

What I do remember is that I was a miserable wreck and was doing what I have always done in those circumstances: running from place to place seeking solace from the pain in my heart and the knot in my stomach.

I would go to work and feel utterly miserable and long for getting-out time and home. I would arrive home to loneliness and misery and immediately run out again, usually to a pub and to the sympathetic ear of a friend. It was not very effective and so, in desperation, I ran further and left Dublin altogether for a break in Kilkenny.

My mother had a little house in Talbots Inch by the banks of the Nore for weekend purposes and it was there I took refuge in a high, soft double bed where I cried properly and privately, escaping into novels. There was a bike on hand and I used it to journey into Kilkenny for supplies and human contact.

On one such foray, I went to Don Roberts' bookshop on High Street to replenish my reading material, and discovered that there was an Arts Week going on: a rare event in mid-1970s Ireland.

I was fresh from the Leaving Cert and my experience of poetry up to then had been confined to my mother's repertoire and the exam syllabus, between the covers of the book *Soundings*. So, although I had not much by way of a track record, thanks to my mother and Gus Martin, I had no aversion to poetry, although I had never sought out poets either in print or in person.

So, perhaps it was my poor sore heart that directed me to Kytler's Inn and a poetry reading by someone of whom I had never heard: Seamus Heaney. I had no idea who he was or what he was to become. His first book of poetry was less than a decade old and his Nobel Prize no more than a twinkle in his eye.

The small room was packed, and when he read 'Limbo' I cried.

I was gobsmacked. Right there and then he almost knocked me off my feet. So began a love for his poetry that has endured for the past thirty-five years. It was only the second time that what is now the Kilkenny Arts Festival had taken place. Like all great events, it began with a group of passionate people getting up and just doing it. In 1974, the line-up of poets along with Heaney, all of them reading in a small room in Kytler's, was Ted Hughes, Michael Hartnett, John Montague, Thomas Kinsella, Anthony Cronin and Paul Muldoon. I don't know who devised that programme, but they certainly knew their onions and their poetry.

I saw Seamus Heaney in Kilkenny again ten years ago in St Canice's Cathedral with Liam O'Flynn, who had just dropped the *Óg*. Heaney read and O'Flynn played the uilleann pipes. As I filed into a pew I thought of the first time I heard Heaney and decided that this lofty venue would not suit him, but of course I was wrong. The combination of the music and poetry, not to mention the chat from both men, was wonderful.

In the intervening years, I have discovered artists and performers in Kilkenny to gladden my heart, but none have accompanied me like Seamus Heaney. I find his words come to mind in all sorts of situations and bring comfort or joy. When I stood on the side of a dusty road in Morazán, El Salvador and watched a miserable little procession pass with a small, blue-painted coffin, I thought of 'Mid-Term Break': 'a four-foot box, a foot for every year'.

After my mother died, his poem 'Clearances' brought my mother back to me.

When all the others were away at Mass
I was all hers as we peeled potatoes.

She was right there, standing at the sink in the basement kitchen in Dublin, a long ash developing on her cigarette as her wet hands deftly peeled and dipped spuds for dinner.

Seamus Heaney will be back again this year in Kilkenny, they say, and I will be there too. I can't wait.

SONATA ON A STOVE LID

John F. Deane

No man is an island, John Donne insists, yet we know that every man, every woman, is an island, a body occupying its own small space and surrounded by the vastness of the universe. I was born on an island and have been ever conscious of the implications of that word. *Island.* Yet the word brought richness with it, too; other words like 'home', like 'love', like 'family', like 'security'. Seamus Heaney began his conscious living in Mossbawn, a small farm, and what is such a place but its own island. He says of it, 'It sounds very idyllic, but it was a small, ordinary, nose-to-the-grindstone place.' And that is everyone's experience, for we all must live nose to the grindstone almost all the while. He speaks of the rainwater gathered in the water butt, just as we gathered it in Bunnacurry, Achill: 'The rainwater was prized because it was soft and made excellent suds. It was carried in from the barrel as needed, and heated in big pots and saucepans on the stove.' It is the love of home-place, of island. The glory of this is its ordinariness, its everyday familiarity and groundedness. In a Mossbawn poem he speaks of his aunt's apron dusted with flour:

'Now she dusts the board with a goose's wing…' while the scones are rising in the oven 'to the tick of two clocks'. And where does the ravaging wonder of this occur? Because the ordinary occurs in the overwhelming light of love:

> And here is love
> like a tinsmith's scoop
> sunk past its gleam
> in the meal-bin.

It is such vision, allied to the tangible, succulent words, that make sacraments of the ordinary. And Heaney's poetry has revelled in the ordinary, the shared, the recognisable. His poem 'The Forge' opens 'a door into the dark' where you hear 'the hiss when a new shoe toughens in water'. And the hammering is done by the smith at 'an altar / Where he expends himself in shape and music'. I often visited such a forge in Cashel, Achill Island, with my father and the recalcitrant mule that was our friend and servant. I loved the place, but where Heaney found the music of the anvil I found only school lessons; on our schoolroom wall was a coloured chart with pictures of bellows, anvil, rasp, and a great, brown, fetlocked carthorse with its trappings. I had to tell the process through, in Irish:

'The master curved his sally-rod about / to a horse-shoe shape: begin! *Boilg, inneoin, raspa.'* If my own memories were tainted with anxieties, Heaney's poem came to me as a redemption and suggested a revisitation of the words and the experience. Again, the ordinary become marvellous in his hands.

Seamus and Marie came to settle in Glanmore, Wicklow where, he says, he was walking one day and was confronted by a small herd of cattle galloping towards him, a distraught woman following behind. He knew the cattle had to be turned as they had broken out of somewhere, 'so I spread my arms,' Heaney writes, 'and let a shout out of me,' and he turned the cattle and became at once accepted in his new community. This, too, is a shared experience and makes writer and reader more part of the main – less islanded in the world.

I crept away, betimes, in Achill, to the old loft where my grandfather had erected a swing from the high rafters. It was a place to dream in the scent of hay-dust, in the dimness of the rafters, to savour one's isolation and silence, to have an opportunity to dream, to be… an island, safe, at home and, for the moment, master. Heaney has this in his poem 'The Swing':

> To start up by yourself, you hitched the rope
> Against your backside and backed on into it
> Until it tautened, then tiptoed and drove off
> As hard as possible. You hurled a gathered thing
> From the small of your back, into the air.
> Your head swept low, you heard the whole shed creak.

The accuracy of the language speaks directly to me and lifts my own life back out of the mists and into focus. And then there is the stove lid; we had an Aga which was one of the wonders of our island world. I toasted mushrooms with salt and butter on that stove lid; I poked the blackened iron lifter to drop stuff into the fire within; and forgot: but here is Heaney who can make a sonata out of such a thing:

> The mass and majesty of this world I bring you
> In the small compass of a cast-iron stove lid.
> I was the youngster in a Fair Isle jersey
> Who loved a lifter made of stainless steel,
> The way its stub claw found its clink-fast hold,
> The fit and weight and danger as it bore
> The red hot solidus to one side of the stove
> For the fire-fanged maw of the fire-box to be stoked,
> Then the gnashing bucket stowed.

The most ordinary becomes a marvel in Heaney's hands, and it resonates with the beauty and relevance of sacrament while your memory is lit with it forever. In gratitude for such gifts, I wrote the following piece for Seamus Heaney:

On Strand Road

Waves have been sweeping in over the sandflats
under a chilling breeze; there is a man
windsurfing, stooping like a steeplejack
into his task; the summer girls who ran

with long gandering strides over the sand
are ghosts within a book. The poet's window
looks out across the sea towards England
and the cold north; like his bird he has grown

fabulous, comes down at times to touch
the range wall for conviction. The man on the sea
relishes each crest and hollow, and each
bow bend starts out on another journey.

HIS ALMIGHTY BEST

Bernard Farrell

The first time I ever laid eyes on John B. Keane, I immediately betrayed him to the mob. This happened in the Gas Company Theatre in Dún Laoghaire – a compact little theatre that was tucked into the first floor of the building, above the showroom with its array of gas stoves, cookers and heaters. The year was 1961 and I was part of an enthusiastic audience that had just seen his play *The Highest House on the Mountain* and, coming down the stairs to exit through the showroom, we were all loudly discussing the drama and also speculating on the potential of this new playwright.

He was, at the time, not just a playwright who, in three years, had written three very successful plays – he was the man who, from the beginning, had to endure alienation by the theatrical establishment, find alternative ways to have his voice heard and, in so doing, had displayed a relentless determination to fight against the odds and to win. And at that time of my life, in my twenties and with only the vaguest intention of ever writing a play, I found myself drawn to the man as much as to his work and I followed his career and his theatrical survival with the greatest of interest.

I knew how his first play, *Sive*, couldn't find a home, was premiered in Walshe's Ballroom in Listowel by the local drama group, was then taken on the drama circuit where it began to attract some attention and eventually qualified for the All-Ireland Drama Finals in Athlone where, like the poor child at the party, it stood beside the more established, more celebrated productions to compete for the premiere award, the coveted Esso Trophy.

These finals have always been the Aintree Grand National of Irish amateur drama. To be just included in the line-up is, for any playwright, an honour and, for the performing drama group, a life-long achievement. To win it is a dream that, for most, will never come true. And, I have no doubt that on the night of 26 April 1959, when John B. sat in the auditorium of the Dean Crowe Hall for the performance of *Sive* and saw the lights dim and the curtain rise and the audience become silent in expectation, he knew that, within two hours, he would either be vindicated in his belief in the play, or he would have to concede victory to those he called the Doubting Thomases, those who questioned the worthiness of his work and who constantly forecast his theatrical demise.

But, against all opposition, critical and dramatic, *Sive* did win – and some say that the cheers that followed the adjudicator's verdict could be heard in the mountains of Kerry. John B. himself is on record as saying that this remains the happiest moment of his theatrical life. And I can understand why this is so – because in the mercurial world of theatre where success and stardom stand side by side with disappointment and despair, the most rewarding experience one can have is vindication. He knew that he had written a great play; others in power had disagreed, and it was only through the resources of the Amateur Drama Movement that he could actually show the world what had lived in his mind and his imagination…and then let the world decide.

And decide it did – and *Sive* has since become one of the most praised, the most enduring and the most performed plays that Ireland has ever seen. John B. then showed his versatility by following it with the wonderful *Sharon's Grave* – and then came *The Highest House on the Mountain* and my first sighting of the playwright himself in the Gas Company Theatre in Dún Laoghaire.

As we all walked through the showrooms to the exit that evening, I had turned and saw this tall, black-haired man desperately trying to be invisible as he pretended to examine a gas cooker in the corner. I immediately proclaimed, 'Look, there's John B. Keane', and a hundred people changed direction and swarmed towards him, pens and programmes at the ready, and I saw John B. look directly at me and, in that moment, I knew exactly how Jesus had looked at Judas in the Garden of Gethsemane.

Years later, I told him about that incident and, whether he remembered it or not, he certainly never allowed me to forget it. Thereafter, whenever we met, he would invariably greet me with the words, 'Well, if it isn't Judas Iscariot himself!'

But somehow I think he was still revelling in the memory of those years – when he was on the cusp of greatness with three plays written and even greater ones to come – and all just two years after that tide-turning night at the All-Ireland Finals in Athlone, when, in the words of the play itself, the Listowel Drama Group gave *Sive* 'their best, their almighty best' – and John B. Keane had finally arrived.

MEETING ON A TRAIN

Ciarán Folan

It was the Wednesday of Holy Week, or Spy Wednesday as people still called it then, and I was getting the Rosslare train from Connolly Station, Dublin.

I just made the train before it pulled out and I grabbed the first free seat available, opposite a handsome middle-aged couple. I was looking out the window as we crossed the Liffey when the man said something to his companion, and I recognised his mellifluous voice immediately. It was a voice I had heard many times on the radio over the years.

We soon got into conversation and I found out that he and his companion were also getting the ferry to France. We talked for a while – what about, I can't remember – as we travelled south along the Dublin and Wicklow coasts.

I had a copy of the *Selected Poems of Louis MacNeice*, which I'd just bought in Easons, and I asked him to sign it. I wasn't sure if he'd approve, but I thought it might be appropriate as he and MacNeice were both Ulstermen. Of course, he did sign it – in black biro on the inner back page: Benedict Kiely, 2 April 1980.

How was my French? Benedict Kiely might well have asked me, and, no doubt I might have told him it wasn't too bad. In fact, I hadn't much more than a few badly pronounced words, though the friend I was visiting was fluent. However, I felt I had prepared for the trip in more practical ways. For a week beforehand, I had been drinking Pernod every evening in the bar of the Railway Hotel in Ballinrobe, County Mayo, where I was staying at the time. Also, I had bought a second-hand copy of the first volume of George D. Painter's biography of Marcel Proust in Kenny's Bookshop in Galway. I hadn't read a word of the biography or of Proust's daunting masterpiece *In Search of Lost Time*, but I knew he was quite an important French writer. I had even seen the film *The Cars That Ate Paris* late one Sunday night in the cinema in Ballinrobe, though I was disappointed when I discovered early on that it was set in Paris, Australia, not Paris, France. And to top it all, I had bought a long dark Louis Féraud overcoat for £50 the previous Christmas.

Proust wrote that the images selected by memory are arbitrary and so it is with my trip to France. I can remember eating couscous for the first time in a restaurant in Rouen, but I can't remember seeing that city's famous cathedral. I remember walking through the countryside near Tours. We must have visited some of the famous chateaux in the area, but I have no recollection of it. I do remember that Good Friday in France did not have the same feel about it as Good Friday at home. I'm sure I drank Calvados, though I cannot remember doing so. I think I remember hearing 'Food for Thought' by UB40 coming from a jukebox in a café off the Boulevard Saint Germain. In the Luxembourg Gardens, I remember being surprised to see early apples and pears hanging from trees, each fruit with an individual paper wrapper to protect it from the frost – though that might have been during another visit. There are other aspects of the trip of which I have only a vague memory and there are many others which I've long forgotten.

But I have a clear recollection of how that trip ended – arriving back home in Ceannt Station, Galway the Friday of Easter Week; the shock and surprise I felt on seeing my mother walking ahead of me along the platform when I got off the train. We had both been on the same train all the way from Dublin and I hadn't known it. She had gone to see a specialist about her heart, she told me. Neither of us were to know then that in a few short years she would be dead from a massive heart attack. So, it is the start and the end of that trip to France that are clearest in my mind after thirty years. No doubt Proust would have something to say about that and so, too, I'm sure, would Benedict Kiely.

THE LOST HEIFER

Claire Coughlan

Nostalgia is, by its nature, always rosy hued. What else could explain the presence of a textbook in the Irish bestseller charts? *Soundings*, the Leaving Certificate poetry textbook, as used by thousands of Irish students from the late 1960s to the late 1990s, is certainly having another moment.

I should probably declare at this stage that I have bought two copies: one for my mother, who sat her Leaving in the early 1970s when Fleetwood Mac, The Carpenters and The Eagles ruled the airwaves, and one for myself.

I did mine in the late 1990s – a time when the bloom was beginning to fall off the rose for Brit Pop and conspiracy theories abounded about the death of Princess Diana.

Although our cultural references were dominated by icons across the water in the UK and the US, it's the Irish poets whom my mother and I remember most fondly – the 'Fab Four' as Joseph O'Connor refers to them in his foreword to the most recent edition. Yeats, Kavanagh, Kinsella and Clarke. 'No Second Troy', 'Stony Grey Soil', 'Another September', 'The Planter's Daughter'. They have lodged themselves in my brain, whether I wanted them to or not, like the murmur of half-remembered prayers, or the sweet mush of rice pudding.

They say that all memory is sensory – walk into your old school and the smell of the floor polish or the peal of a bell will deposit you back at your cramped desk quicker than a memory regression session with a therapist ever could.

For me, the feel on my face of that soft, misty rain that is peculiarly

Irish, will always remind me of 'The Lost Heifer', by Austin Clarke, my favourite poem in *Soundings*.

I didn't think much of it until the Easter holidays of my final year at school. I was ambivalent about *Soundings* and about school as a whole – I wanted to get it all done and be out of there as quickly as possible. Then I did a week-long revision course on the English syllabus, taught by a man I'll always remember fondly, even though I only knew him for a few days. He's dead now, I believe.

Women poets, he announced, in a booming voice that was somewhere between George Hook and David Norris, give me a pain in my left tit.

By rights, I should have 'felt a funeral in my brain' – I was a massive Emily Dickinson and Sylvia Plath fan. I should have felt outraged by this sentiment, but there was something so endearing about this pulsing figure striding around the room in his stockinged feet, spittle flying, blood pressure raised. I went home that night and announced with relish what he had said, hoping to shock my parents. They laughed and continued eating.

The next day I went back, intrigued, in spite of myself. There was more. He wanted to know what we thought about the poems, the thoughts that had been prescribed for us, like often bitter medicine that we had to swallow down. He thumped the blackboard and in a few short days instilled passion: for our convictions, for the book *Soundings* itself, for the notion that it was all right to express an opinion – that there wasn't necessarily a 'right' or a 'wrong' answer, although there could certainly be an unpopular one.

'The Lost Heifer' was, he said – well, what was it about? A cow, someone coughed. A lost cow, another wag shrugged. Ireland, a braver soul ventured. We were *all* right, of course. Well, according to him anyway.

Clarke was, he said, a consummate artificer of language. He rolled the words around on his tongue like they were 'the last honey by the water'. I was enchanted, and I'm guessing the rest of the class were too – the examiner probably got at least thirty exam scripts that year containing that exact phrase.

I never thought I'd get nostalgic for one of my textbooks. Which begs the question – what will we be all misty-eyed over in ten, twenty, thirty years from now? Bail-outs? Dole queues? Reality TV? Or maybe it'll be something we'd dismissed as insignificant in our lives, insignificant until one day you look back and remember how things weren't as bad as all that; in some small, indefinable way they were better.

MAY

QUEEN OF THE MAY

Catherine Ann Cullen

I won't wash my face in the dew at first light:
I never had that maiden skin, soft pink or hawthorn white.
Mine is oil and olive, the dawn water
would run off me like a mother's warning.

I won't heed my grandmother's *piseog*s,
the way she kept the may out of the house
and crossed herself if we came through the door
clutching its starry branches.

No, I'll cross the threshold of summer with a bold stride,
bringing in stars like a promise of harvest.
I'll close my eyes to the shadow of the scythe,
toss my hips at virgins and fairies,
and defy them to deny me
my blooming crown, my sweet bouquet, my *objets trouvés* of summer.

I'll heap clusters of flowers on my altar
and be my own Queen of the May,
and I won't believe in anything
except that summer is coming
and May needs nothing else to be magic.
I'll drink wine in the long twilight
with my love in the garden,
lie in the grass and love freckles on to his skin.

I'll dance at his maypole
with nothing to lose
but my chains of daisies that each say,
'He loves me.'

Oh you might as well talk to the wall
that's crawling with woodbine again
as lay down the law to me,
feckless and reckless with summer.

THE GHOSTS OF ST ENDA'S

Brian Crowley

St Enda's is haunted by the ghosts of the past. Pearse certainly thought so. In a lecture he gave at a Robert Emmet Commemoration in Brooklyn in 1914, he said that the spirits of Ireland's heroes 'dwell in the place where they lived'. He knew this because, as he said himself, he lived 'in a place full of heroic memories'.

The Hermitage, as St Enda's was originally known, was built in the late eighteenth century by a Dublin dentist, Edward Hudson, and, from the start, was designed to evoke a sense of the past. Hudson dotted the grounds with sham ruins and follies, inspired by the relics of ancient Irish history. These included a mock-ogham stone, cromlech and dolmen. To add credence to the estate's title, a hermit's cave was constructed, complete with a secluded seat for solitary contemplation. The wild, natural features of the landscape – the river valley, and granite outcrops – were tamed to create a parkland in tune with the sensibilities of the Romantic age. Legend has it that Hudson allowed Robert Emmet and his sweetheart Sarah Curran to meet secretly in the grounds when her disapproving father refused to allow them to see each other. The memory of Emmet clung to the place in the years that followed. The park still contains a path called Emmet's Walk and a fortress-like gate lodge is still known as Emmet's Fort.

It was these memories that drew Pearse out here in the summer of 1910. He had been reading Stephen Gwynn's book on Emmet and went to Rathfarnham to seek out places associated with him. He was so enchanted by what he found in the Hermitage that he decided to lease it and move his school there. St Enda's had been founded two years earlier in

1908, with the aim of providing a distinctly Irish education through the Irish language. This, however, was not the school's sole endeavour. Pearse sought to create an educational experience which would inspire the pupils under his care. Explaining the move to Rathfarnham in the school's magazine he wrote, 'Scoil Éanna had the highest aim in education of any school in Ireland: it must have the worthiest home.' The Hermitage certainly offered that, with its spare and elegant architecture, beautiful parkland and close proximity to the wild wastes of the Dublin Mountains. The grounds served as a backdrop to the open-air plays and pageants which Pearse wrote for the boys. With the boys dressed as ancient Gaelic warriors, St Enda's became something of a wonderland on these occasions, a place where the heroic past seemed real and manifest.

On a practical level the move to Rathfarnham was ill-conceived. It involved more expense, and pupil numbers dropped because its remoteness from the city meant that many of the day boys could not make the long journey out every day. Having found his ideal location, Pearse was never again free from money worries and the enterprise lurched from one financial crisis to the next. Yet the possibility of failure never deterred Pearse. 'A new heroic age may be a visionary's dream,' he wrote, 'our schools may pass away or degenerate: but at least this attempt has been made, this right thing has been striven after.'

The Hermitage was a place that fostered heroic aspirations, and Pearse drew sustenance from its history. One of his pupils said that sometimes it was as if Pearse could see the ghost of Emmet tap-tapping his cane along the roads of Rathfarnham. While many factors led to his involvement in the 1916 Rising, the memory of Emmet was certainly one. It is no coincidence that the Easter Rising had so many parallels with Emmet's rebellion of 1803. The issuing of a proclamation of independence, the emphasis on equality, and the commitment to a Republic – even the prospect of almost certain defeat – all had echoes in the rebellion Emmet had planned from his Rathfarnham home over 100 years earlier.

Ironically, it was the British authorities who ensured that Pearse would follow in the footsteps of Emmet to the very end; it was they who decided that Pearse's last hours on earth would be in the very place where Emmet had waited for his execution, Kilmainham Gaol. The journey in search of Emmet's ghost, which had begun six years earlier and which had led him to the splendours of the Hermitage, was now to end on 3 May 1916 in another grey eighteenth-century building that was also 'full of heroic memories'.

MISTER DOG

Elaine Sisson

It is probable that Mrs Pearse was not the only mother to lose two sons in the early summer of 1916. All across Europe death-edged telegrams arrived with their terrible news. Patrick, her eldest, died on 3 May and Willie, younger by two years, the next day. Described by friends as being 'mad with grief', for weeks she was seen wandering the streets calling for her boys by name.

In the months afterwards, Patrick the man slowly became replaced by Pádraig the revolutionary hero. When alive, he was known as Pat to his family and close friends; Patrick in an official capacity; and Pádraig when speaking and writing in Irish. The emergence of Pádraig Pearse, as the pre-eminent of the revolutionary leaders, is owed in part to the zeal with which Mrs Pearse elevated his reputation as the most devoted of sons.

It is a cruel irony that the passion with which Mrs Pearse sought to safeguard the position of Patrick has contributed to Willie's place in history as little more than a footnote. After all, there were two Pearse sons: two childhoods, two deaths, two losses. Willie is now the afterthought to Patrick, the trailing shadow, the pause between sentences. History remembers him as the lesser of the two brothers, a victim of circumstance rather than conviction: easily led, spectral. Photographs of his pale face, curved forehead and floppy hair have faded compared to the iconic profile images of his big brother. Yet if Willie has slowly been erased from public memory, he remains central to the life of Patrick. For who knows another better than a sibling? Brothers know things about each other that even mothers never learn.

Patrick describes the arrival of Willie as a day which marked the rest of his life for the better; the greatest thing that ever happened to him: the arrival of his true companion and most intimate friend.

Willie was artistic, a talent he inherited from his father, James. He studied art in the Dublin Metropolitan School under the tutelage of Oliver Sheppard, the sculptor, who was later commissioned to make the bronze statue of Cúchulainn now in the GPO. In the late 1890s Willie went to Paris and London to complete his studies and retained a *fin-de-siècle* bohemian style with his floppy hairstyle and neckties. Quite successful as a sculptor, some of his work can still be seen in Limerick Cathedral, St Eunan's Cathedral, Letterkenny, and in the Church of St Andrew, Westland Row, Dublin. The O'Mulrennan Memorial in Glasnevin and a Father Murphy Memorial in Wexford have also been attributed to him. When St Enda's School opened in 1908 he taught Art and Drawing, later becoming Assistant Head. He also was responsible for theatre and drama: designing sets, making costumes and sometimes acting in school productions.

The brothers' closeness provides a private glimpse of the Pearses. As children they had a cat called Minnie and a dog named Gyp, and neither could ever bear any kind of cruelty to animals. Patrick delighted in learning American slang, and as adults the brothers sometimes spoke to each other in a curious patois they had perfected since childhood. They loved practical jokes; once Willie dressed up as a beggar-woman and came calling to St Enda's seeking outrageous demands. Patrick enjoyed the trick enormously, laughing heartily when caught out and chuckling at the recall for days later. Willie was an avid handball player. Patrick had lovely teeth. Willie loved Chekhov and Ibsen and was a fine Shakespearean actor; Patrick an elegant ballroom dancer. Willie was Mister Dog, Pat's right-hand man.

After he was sentenced to death Patrick wrote a poem to Willie, afraid he might not see him again. The brothers did not meet; on his way to Patrick's cell Willie instead heard the volley of shots that took him, so Patrick's poem captures his last words to his little brother.

To My Brother

Oh Faithful!
Moulded in one womb.
We two have stood together all the years.
All the glad years and all the sorrowful years.

Own brothers through good repute and ill.
In direct peril true to me
Leaving all things for me, spending yourself
In the hard service I have taught to you.
Of all the men that I have known on earth
You only have been my familiar friend.
Nor needed I another.

FINDING THE DIVA:
MARGARET BURKE SHERIDAN

Anne Chambers

For decades the true story of Castlebar-born prima donna Margaret Burke Sheridan lay hidden beneath a layer of anecdotal stories, speculation and deliberate invention, some of it contributed to by the diva herself. She was an only child and an orphan, she implied. She was 'discovered' by Marconi. She had love affairs with Puccini and Toscanini. The pope wanted to make her a countess. An Italian aristocrat, whom she had rejected, shot himself in the opera house as she sang on stage. Melodramatic stuff: but what was truth and what was invention?

Her centenary in 1989 had brought her memory out of oblivion and I, a fellow townswoman, was asked to write 'something' to mark the event. That 'something' turned into a three-year marathon of travel and research in archives throughout Italy, in England and Ireland: trawling through operatic reviews of her performances; discussions with operatic critics far more qualified than I to evaluate her voice and her contribution to operatic history. But despite the copious records I garnered about her artistic career, the human story behind the voice remained illusive until Garech Browne solved my dilemma when he opened the door to a room in his house at Lugalla which was crammed with cardboard boxes containing the personal papers and effects of Maggie from Mayo. And what a treasure trove it turned out to be. Letters and telegrams from her school years in Eccles Street in the 1900s, to her final years in the Shelbourne Hotel in 1958.

Letters from her many mentors, such as the old Irish parliamentarian T.P. O'Connor, from Marconi, who was indeed instrumental in bringing her to Italy, from numerous admirers and friends, threw light on the path which had taken Margaret Burke Sheridan from the stage of the town hall in Castlebar to operatic glory. Invitations to 'at homes' from society hostesses such as Viscountess Hambleden, Rachel, Countess of Clonmel, the Courtaulds, the Cunards, Lady Howard de Walden, as well as dozens of calling cards from titled Italian admirers in Milan and Rome, confirmed her celebrity status. A 1921 New Year's Eve dinner menu from the Palace Hotel, Milan, which offered a desert named 'Fruits à la Sheridan' bore testimony to her nomadic lifestyle, as did the numerous hotel and restaurant bills she had accumulated over the space of forty years. From the age of eleven, when she left Castlebar, she was never to have a home of her own, which made sense of her comment to a friend: 'There's no place like home when you haven't one.'

One by one the cardboard boxes laid bare the intimate life of the diva – without her operatic costume and make-up. Numerous medical and pharmacy receipts, empty nasal sprays and decongestants, suggested a reason for the limited number of her operatic appearances; perhaps too, for her abrupt retirement from the stage. Receipts from haute couture salons in Milan, Paris and London confirmed the 'star' persona she presented off-stage. Contracts and agreements with agents, managers, opera houses and recording companies; telegrams and greeting cards from famous names in the world of opera; the tissue-paper theatre posters, one announcing her dramatic debut as Mimi in Rome in 1918; contracts with La Scala; her own stage directions for *Madama Butterfly* and *Andrea Chénier*; photographs of her as Butterfly, Mimi, Desdemona, Maddalena and the many other roles she made famous; photographs of happy interludes with friends in the lakeside paradise of Bellagio; on tour in Italy with operatic colleagues; a soft leather, mauve pouch (perhaps a stage prop) inside which lay a lucky rusty horseshoe nail.

Family photographs and letters from her brother Paddy, her nephews John and David in Ottowa, her sister Hester and her niece Moira in England, blew apart her assertion that as well as an orphan she was an only child. From their correspondence and her father's last will, it became apparent that bankruptcy and a family feud had made her choose to ignore her family connections during her career. A huge collection of 1920s postcards, mainly of the humorous variety, bore testimony to her own impish sense of fun, and her often acerbic wit (as when she referred to an Irish soprano, whom she felt had slighted her, as being just 'a Woolworths' soprano').

And the cardboard boxes revealed more. The names and rhymes of schoolfriends in Eccles Street in her 1909 autograph book. A rosary beads and a number of 'holy pictures'; numerous religious quotations copied in her florid handwriting, with which I was to become so familiar, confirmed the loneliness and lack of confidence that lay beneath the prima donna persona she presented in public, during her dreary retirement in Dublin.

Hidden deep in one of her handbags – genuine crocodile – perhaps the most poignant artefact of all: part of a telegram with the words '*ti adoro*' above the name of the one love in her life, Eustace Blois, Managing Director of the Royal Opera House, Convent Garden, as well as an anguished unsent letter telling him she could never become the lover of a married man. Face powder, rouge and sachets of shampoo made by long-gone Italian cosmetic companies; diaries (never completed); Christmas cards from friends such as Tallulah Bankhead, Marconi, Margaret Rutherford, Ivor Novello, Tosti, Lady Howard de Walden, from the owner of the famous Pagani's Restaurant in London, where she continued to be fêted as a celebrity long after her retirement. Star treatment in 1924 on the front page of the prestigious Italian arts newspaper *Melodrammatica*. In the carefully folded copy preserved among her papers, her photograph, dressed in the magnificent gown given to her by Puccini for her triumphant role as Manon, together with rave reviews by Italian opera critics, further confirmed the dizzy heights she had reached in her career. Her cheque book (Coutts on the Strand), bank statements, royalties from HMV, showed a modest income and confirmed the reason she needed the patronage of wealthy friends from the day she left Eccles Street to the day she died.

Her grave in Glasnevin, where, as she told a friend in 1958 as she lay dying in St Vincent's Nursing Home, 'I'll be tippy toes with Dev's secretary Kathleen O'Connell,' was paid for by the American millionairess, Ruth Haughton Axe, the last in a long line of benefactors.

Over the following months the contents of these cardboard boxes, as well as confirming the true extent of La Sheridan's artistic achievements, more significantly helped me complete the identikit of a wonderful, warm, witty, acerbic, complex woman and revealed the depth of loneliness, uncertainty and regret that lay hidden behind her brief but oh so bright time in the spotlight.

THIRTEEN

Conor O'Callaghan

I am nothing if not a child of the 1970s. Time was that fact, and all it entailed, would have been a source of mortification, like those wedding photos full of crinoline flares and paisley ties. Now I am at peace with the era of my provenance. I can openly admit, in company, to liking the Carpenters. It has silenced a few dinner parties, sure. But what the hell, I say. Lately, thanks to Youtube, I have persuaded my teenage son and daughter of the joys of Neil Sedaka. Some evenings, while I cook and they do homework, we sing 'Laughter in the Rain' together. Perhaps my favourite song of that decade is Big Star's 'Thirteen': a gorgeous, aching ballad of early adolescence and love I have been known to murder around the house. I even threatened to sing it to my daughter across the thirteen candles of her birthday last month.

My daughter is thirteen. Overnight, it seems, she has blossomed. Yesterday she was a slightly pudgy girl in mismatched tracksuit halves watching *Digimon* and thinking all boys revolting and eating for Ireland. Now she is taller than her mother and willowy and long-haired and obsessed with designer labels. Only last week she gave us a lecture on how your top and shoes should be really expensive, but how it was acceptable to accessorise with cheap bangles and the like. I sat there remembering holding her hand at the school gate. Now she asks me to park around the corner at bell time. Sometimes, to mortify her, I park front and centre and beep the horn of our ancient Skoda when she appears. She blushes, but I know she thinks it's funny too.

Her room, at the very top of the house, perpetually looks as if a herd of buffalo had passed through a little while before. All the wardrobe doors are dangling open and all manner of unwashed clothes are strewn around the floor. And yet, thanks to the array of perfumes she now gets for Christmas from aunties, it always smells of spring. There is a crystal disco ball dangling from the ceiling. On her unmade bed an iPod gets listened to in tandem with a ghettoblaster. She shuts the door and when dinnertime arrives you have to scream for all you are worth from the foot of the stairs. I have even been known to call her on the mobile, one end of the house to another, just to make a ripple in her world.

At thirteen she gets a £10 top-up every month. I suspect that's gone by the second weekend. But her room is also strewn with oodles of cash she refuses to spend except on phone credit. Her ringtone changes by the day. Her text alerts warble and vibrate and whistle at all hours like tropical wildlife. When all homework is done, she gets an hour on Facebook on my work laptop at the kitchen table. You clear around her and, thinking you're on the snoop, she minimises until you're back out of range. I've seen her profile and you'd think from it that she was Little Miss Activity. In truth, she loathes all physical exercise. Walk halfway up the street and she'll complain of sore legs. Bring her to badminton, just to make her feel included, and she'll refuse to change clothes. Instead, she'll stand there, rooted to centre court, in her jeans and her scarlet woollen scarf, saying, 'That's not fair!'

At thirteen she says her regimen of violin lessons is like being in a concentration camp. However tasteless the joke, it was the first evidence of historical awareness in her conversation, and something of a relief. She has taken up drums too, and goes to lessons with the drummer of the 1970s band Jilted John. She has a kit in the basement and doesn't need to be asked to practise. Last week Brian from next door called with a face like thunder to complain about her rhythmic pounding at ten to ten. He had a point. He stopped at the gate and turned back. 'What now?' I thought. He said, 'She's getting really good though, isn't she?' She is.

She talks boys with her friends, and feigns indifference otherwise. I grill her in the car home one day. What does she like in men? I throw out a few names and she seems about to wretch. Just when I'm getting nowhere, I run by her Liverpool's Spanish wonderboy, Fernando Torres. She smiles and looks off into the traffic and eventually says, 'Well, he's not number one…'. I might have guessed: the Latin looks. Her downloads feature lots of Enrique. Recently, a young Venetian waiter, long after meal and tip, stopped clearing and said in broken English, 'You have beautiful eyes.' The red of her face made their blue even brighter. A few minutes later he came back with a single gardenia for her. I told her to pay no attention to southern men with their olive skin and walnut eyes. What she wanted was a good Irish boy with roots in the local GAA *cumann* and legs like milk bottles. She said, 'Sure thing, Dad,' and laughed, and twiddled the gardenia in her place setting.

Thirteen. The number of place settings at the Last Supper, the tilly of a baker's dozen, unlucky for some. But not her. Hers is the generation fortune favours and the state, at long last, sees fit to protect. Where her father's school tours were games of 17-a-side on the Hill of Tara, hers are whole weeks in Andalusia. When, during one of our regular scraps, I clip her ear or kick her bum, she says, 'That's against the law... I'm taking legal action.' They deserve it. They deserve their affluence and safety.

I write this mid-May. It's just gone eight on a Saturday evening, and the sky is still blue. I can hear her with her friends out at the front wall, all thirteen beautiful years of her whispering and shrieking and whooping. I get up from the screen and go to the front window and watch her flick her fringe and sway in the summer wind like a sapling. She is so green. She is so becoming. That's the word, I think: *becoming*... In both senses. She is both so pretty and also already so close to the woman she will one day be.

CHAINIES

Hedy Gibbons Lynott

Those who built here understood the lie of the land. And the way of the sea.

This spring morning the air is calm, the waters of Dunbulcaun Bay, this inlet of Galway Bay, smooth and clear in the low morning light. Oyster boats rest on their moorings, raising barely a ripple against the incoming tide. The green one – my favourite – glitters, a half-submerged emerald against the dark inshore water.

The Burren lies south of this 'stony seaboard', – the poet John Betjeman's 'stony hills' still pouring 'over space', cool and grey and blue. Behind me – its 'grey-stoned shoulders saffron-spotted' – lies the village of Clarinbridge, wrapped in the largesse of its former owners, the Reddington family, its gaze firmly seaward. A pair of resident swans mooch along close to shore, disdaining Yeats's colony further south at Coole. They ignore me as I walk through the skeletons of sea-lavender and chamomile to reach the shore and a flat stone just made for sitting on.

Scanning the water for the cut stones that identify individual oyster beds for their owners, I realise that the tide is higher than I thought. Like the trestles on which the young oysters are grown, those markers are only visible at half-tide or lower, so I turn my attention inshore. It is only then that I notice another pattern of stones, different again from Burren flags or sea-bed markers.

The stones that are taking my attention this morning, were not, I think, placed by oyster-fishers. These stones outline the shape of a house. Sitting on my rock, I can make out the doorway, the living area, two rooms leading off it. In the 'kitchen', a small pile of stones forms a 'dresser'. This is someone's playhouse. And stacked on the 'dresser': chainies.

Chainies. It took me a few moments to find that word. I hadn't used it since I was a child. With little effort, it slid back into consciousness, turning up when I poked and prodded, just like those fragments of discarded china, when as children we turned the brown earth of new Dublin suburbs, and later scoured the shore of the River Lee at Passage West.

These chainies are different from the ones we found then. Instead of patterns of blue and gold, red and green laid on a background of white china, these come in opal overlaid with indigo, oyster sheened with palest mauve, a riot of periwinkle in purple, pink and lavender, the brown, cream and gold tiger-stripes of occasional razor shells. Here, in this house, rounded *edulis* – native Clarinbridge oyster shells – are stacked like dinner plates. The deep elongated shells of *gigas* – the Pacific oyster – will make good serving dishes. Those handfuls of mussels will be ideal as scoops, and the skeleton crab-claws will make useful tongs. And that crab shell can be the teapot. The one intact razor shell – a 'blow-in' from Island Eddy – that can be the bread knife. Those tiny periwinkles can be the fairy cakes we've just taken out of the lobster-pot oven!

The incoming tide spreads through the walls of this sea-house, lapping the stacks of chainies, and I find myself becoming anxious, wondering if I should move all this 'china' to higher ground. But as I watch, the shells scoop the salt water. Then hold it as the tide recedes.

These builders, daughters of the sea who made this house, knew where to build. Knew how high the tide would reach. Had already, perhaps even before they could read, learned their own story; a story left by those who built the shell middens, the *fodhlaíochta fiadh*, the stone forts, as well as grand houses like Tyrone and Kilcornan, and stone cottages hugging the shore at Ceibh. These builders are the keepers of the knowledge: for those who mark their oyster beds in stone; for who still moor their boats to invisible markers; for all of us, who are, in Betjaman's words, the 'last of Europe's stone-age race'.

SYNGESPEAK

Mary O'Malley

Growing up in Errismore, I believed, in common with many others, that of all the misfortunes visited on Connemara and the Aran Islands since Cromwell, *The Playboy of the Western World* was up there alongside the Cleggan Disaster and the Black and Tans.

Blame the letter famously sent to John Millington Synge by one W. B. Yeats, saying, in effect, go west young man, and saying also, in effect, you'll never cut it as a literary critic – and for one critic less in a genera-tion, we must be grateful.

It is almost universally acknowledged in literary circles that his deci-sion to take Yeats's advice was the making of Synge as a playwright. And so it was that the young man, driven into a frenzy of frustration by island girls, who doubtless thought it great sport to tease him 'in the long evenings after *Samhain'* introduced the Aran Islands and the Mayo coast to the literati of Dublin, whose thanks was, as we are endlessly reminded, to riot at the mention of a shift, while in the same play the bishop eats breast-fed lamb, a thing that certainly shocked me as a young woman when I first deciphered what was going on, sensing in his meat the ele-ments of a Christian, and no-one took a blind bit of notice.

So far so Myles na gCopaleen. But journalists are always shocked.

When we first read *The Playboy* in the Mercy Convent, it was obvious even to the nun that Christy Mahon was an eejit, and as for Shawneen Keogh… We assumed that Synge was taking the mickey out of us. So we did what schoolgirls do, and took the mickey out of him, talking in Syngespeak as naturally as we spoke bog Latin, giggling our way through the famous horse race, skitting at the Widow Quinn, thinking the nun wouldn't and couldn't imagine what any of this was about. Not knowing ourselves, but knowing that, unlike the nun, we would find out because we, unlike her, would get married and prance around in our own shifts in front of a man.

Did the nun, a woman of refinement and sense, shake her head in despair as much as foreknowledge, when she called one of us, in a tone of complete exasperation, 'You *goose*'?

There is a character in José Saramago's novel *The Stone Raft* who is accompanied by a cloud of starlings every time he ventures out. When I got to university, I felt like that man. Every time Connemara came up, someone mentioned Synge and I soon walked around with a cloud of phrases circling like gulls in my head, so that it was an effort not to be talking in soft whispers and knitting patterns into jumpers for my then boyfriend, whose only hope of being drownded was in the bath, or tripping into the river maybe from all the strong drink the students did be taking of a night as they would be walking home to be rolling a joint itself, maybe. Not that we would ever be inhaling, stranger.

Yeats, of course, knew we didn't talk like that exactly, and said as much when he defended Synge from accusations of being 'a faker of Irish peasant speech'.

'Perhaps,' he wrote, 'no Irish countryman had ever that exact rhythm in his voice, but if Mr Synge had been an Irish peasant, he would have spoken like that.'

Neatly put, Mr Yeats. The lives were lives imagined, not lives lived. Critics take note.

But the place is a different matter. That letter reached Synge in Paris, in a street a stone's throw from the Irish College, near the Luxembourg gardens where Synge walked daily, tortured between love and lust for two different women, and suffering from such paralysing stage fright that he could never realise his dream to be a great musician. He would head from there to invent a rich world, based loosely on the place I had grown up in. I had come to Paris for respite, to reflect that place, not to invent it.

I thought of him the day of a sudden spring, when blossoms appeared so impossibly fast on the black magnolia branches it seemed that gorgeous insects were resting there; thought how I was inventing my own Paris. Reflected too that Paris is too cool to care.

I was writing about a girl from my village, sixteen years old, of her six-week voyage beset by fog and bad weather.

She travelled the same ocean described by Synge in the Aran Islands, as he was leaving Aran for good:

> The slowness of the vessel and the lamentation of the cold sea about her sides became almost unendurable. Then the lights of Galway came in sight, and the crew appeared as we beat up slowly to the quay.

Except that his voyage lasted three hours and hers six weeks, and the quay she beat slowly up to was on Ellis Island. Slim, dark-haired Mary Conneely, ready, in her quiet, excited way, to take on America. She accompanied me in my walks along the Seine. She was a seamstress and she would have enjoyed the detail on the dresses in the little shops near St Germain, detail that would, without my grandmother's company, have escaped my notice.

THE LOST TRAIN

Peter Sirr

Five days a week, Michael Kiernan, fifty, a computer network administrator, makes the 90-minute commute home from the Bronx County Courthouse to suburban Long Beach on Long Island. Like a lot of New Yorkers, he has it down to a science. He leaves work at 4.45, walk-jogs across 161st Street, then hurries into the subway, where he gets into the first car on the D train. He stands by the door, riding two stops to 145th Street, then races up the stairs for the A train. Again he stands in the first car, by the third door, which at 34th Street opens at the stairs to the Long Island Rail Road. If all goes well, he catches the 5.20 home.

I'm reading this in the plane home from New York; the story of a man who collapses on the subway, having suffered a near-fatal loss of heartbeat. There happened to be a doctor in the same carriage, and the train happened to stop in one of the five stations out a total of 146 in Manhattan that have defibrillators. The story has a happy outcome, and the man is returned to the workforce and his fine-tuned commute after ten days.

A set of remarkable, almost incredible, coincidences, but also an example of the pure poetry of public transport – in this case of a system so regulated and reliable that you can plot a series of complex transfers, moving yourself around like a counter in a game so that you are always optimally positioned to advance to the next level. I'm reminded of a friend who always drank after work in Kennedy's pub beside Tara Street Dart station, pint in one hand and Dart schedule in the other, so that he could calculate with maximum efficiency the time between the last draught of Guinness and the next departing southbound train.

Transport systems take up residence in the mind and body of the city dweller. Imagine, though, as the systems become ever more complex, how the possibilities multiply, how, as a system makes more connections to other parts of itself, its connectivity increases exponentially until eventually it becomes infinite...

Last year I visited Buenos Aires and found myself one evening standing on a platform of line D of the subway system. The system is radial, much like Dublin's buses, so that if you need to get from a station on one line to a station on another you have to get back to the city centre first. This didn't prevent it from being used as the location for the film *Moebius*, a nervy mystery about the disappearance of a subway train and its passengers. It was made by a group of students from the city's film school under the direction of one of their professors, Gustavo Mosquera, and is based on a classic 1950s science fiction story by astronomer and writer A. J. Deutsch, and set in the Boston underground. A new tunnel means that all seven lines of the Boston subway system are connected. Now, a train on any line can travel to any station in the system, but this apparent perfection is exactly what triggers disaster, and on 4 March train number 86 disappears. The mathematician-hero tries to unravel the mystery by applying his understanding of topology. 'The system is a network of amazing topological complexity,' he explains to the distracted general manager. The new tunnel 'has made the connectivity of the whole system of an order so high that I don't know how to calculate it.'

The system has turned into a Moebius strip, along which the train hurtles eternally, occasionally heard but never seen. The starkly real and the nightmarish crash into each other. At one point the camera pans slowly over the station name 'BORGES' as the hero finds himself trapped in the missing train. There's another edge to the film, a darker resonance: the missing train is a clear allegory of the 30,000 'disappeared' during the days of the junta. The sinister group of men who gather to decide how to deal with the situation have no interest in the train or its passengers, but are anxious to sweep the problem aside. They refuse to listen to the driven young mathematician. 'It never happened,' one hisses menacingly at the general manager as the train eventually turns up empty. And we know the other trains that begin to disappear as the credits start to roll will equally be erased by the state.

Our train pulls in and bears us off safely. Hanging from my strap I think of Gustavo Mosquera hanging over the front of the train with his antique reconditioned 35-mm camera, riding back and forth for hours to capture menacing shots of tunnels, and of A. J. Deutsch, his name lodged in a battered copy of *Fantasia Mathematica*, and lodged too in the crater he discovered on the far side of the moon, heavily damaged along one side, as if maybe one of his lost trains had hurtled into it...

EDWARD VII AND IRELAND

Mary Kenny

The Edwardian age came to a close just about a hundred years ago, on 6 May 1910, when King Edward VII of Great Britain and Ireland died of bronchial emphysema.

His funeral would indeed mark the end of an era. So many of the crowned heads of Europe – the Hapsburgs and Romanovs and Hohenzollerns – would subsequently be swept away by the revolutionary impact of the First World War. English monarchs had seldom been lauded in nationalist Ireland but, at Edward's death, many messages of sympathy came from all over the country.

The *Nationalist and Leinster Times* remembered Edward as 'the first British sovereign to begin the work of reconciling the races which centuries of oppression, misgovernment and misunderstanding had well-nigh made impossible'. Former British sovereigns had passed away 'unwept, unhonoured and unsung', but in 1910, Ireland was 'sorrow-swept at the news of the death of England's king'.

At the Pro-Cathedral in Dublin, Archbishop Walsh took the unprecedented step of ordering a solemn votive Mass. Dr Walsh praised the late King as 'a great peacemaker and a sovereign better loved in Ireland than any before'. 'Veni Creator Spiritus' was sung for the widowed Queen Alexandra and the new King, George V. The Pro-Cathedral was crammed for the occasion. Not everyone joined in the mourning. Sinn Féin distanced itself from the rush of sentimental regard. Yeats and Lady Gregory decided to keep the Abbey Theatre open, when other Dublin theatres went dark as a mark of respect.

Yet most Irish people seemed sincerely sympathetic to the late King, who had been known as Bertie. He had the reputation of being a 'peace-maker' because he presided over the end of the bitter Boer War.

Constitutional monarchs have no power in ending – or beginning – wars, but Bertie was an amiable personality who could create a genial atmosphere, in the context of international diplomacy. He was adored in France and made friends with many an ardent French Republican.

And much liked in Ireland, too. On a famous occasion in 1903, when he arrived in Connemara he was greeted with a banner welcoming him as a 'Friend of our Pope'. When he visited Maynooth the assembled clergy flew his flags: not the Royal Standard, much less the Union Jack, but the King's racing colours of purple, scarlet and gold, alongside a venerated picture of – a horse: Bertie's grandest Derby winner, Persimmon.

It is well-recorded that Edward VII was a hedonist: he loved food, wines, cigars and a succession of mistresses. Yet he was more appreciated in Ireland for his love of the turf, and for his justified reputation for religious tolerance.

In a more sectarian age, when Roman Catholic religious processions were sometimes prohibited in London, religious bigotry was alien to him. His two best friends were Catholic – the magnate Ernest Cassel, a Jewish convert (and grandfather of Edwina Mountbatten), and the Portuguese diplomat, the Marquês de Soveral. Bertie was so religiously tolerant he was nicknamed 'Popish Ned' in Belfast.

Bertie's favourite spa was at Marienbad in Bohemia, a Marian shrine run by the monks of Tepl. He would sometimes attend a Catholic Mass at the monastery of Tepl, dressed in the uniform of an Austrian hussar – he adored dressing up. At Biarritz, another favourite resort, he was known to have visited the nearby shrine of Lourdes and spent some time at the grotto there, in contemplation, shortly before he died.

Although his official biographer called Bertie 'a cheerful Protestant', there were always rumours that he died a Catholic; the last person to visit him was his friend Cassel, said to have smuggled a priest into the King's death chamber. These rumours persist, and the priest has even been identified as Father Cyril Forster, chaplain to the Irish Guards.

Without documented historical evidence, I would not place serious credence on these claims, but I think it is evident that Edward was an ecumenist before his time, and, in his internationalism, a modernist.

Actually, there were a number of factors contributing to Edward's popularity in Ireland. The Edwardian age was an optimistic time. Prosperity was increasing. Home Rule was in sight, and the King was thought favourable to it. There was that flowering of the arts known as the Celtic Renaissance. My mother, born at the beginning of the century, recalled the atmosphere of her Galway childhood as 'a very happy and hopeful time'; and undoubtedly the amiable Bertie, Edward VII, benefited from the rosy glow of recollection that the Edwardian age came to represent.

THE STORY OF MICHAEL POWER, ARCHBISHOP OF TORONTO

Mark McGowan

They had barely known him. Yet hundreds of Toronto's citizens and newcomers stood in the ankle-deep muck of Queen Street enjoying a brief appearance of the noonday sun and a respite from the torrents of rain that had been falling since the previous evening. Those in the crowd who had read the newspapers leading up to 5 October 1847 or engaged in the gossip amidst the stalls of the St Lawrence Market would have known only the basics about the dead man for whom they waited. Michael Power was born in Halifax, Nova Scotia on 17 October 1804, the first of eight children to Mary Roach and Captain William Power, both natives of Waterford City. Because of the anti-Catholic penal laws in his home colony, he was educated primarily in Montreal, Lower Canada (now Quebec), where Catholics had enjoyed freedom of religion and full political rights for decades. He was ordained a priest for the diocese Montreal, spoke several languages fluently, and in 1841 was appointed the first Roman Catholic bishop of Toronto, a diocese that encompassed a geographic area almost four times the size of Ireland. Now just shy of his forty-third birthday, he was dead of the dreaded typhus fever, contracted as he cared for thousands of Irish immigrants who lay dying or convalescing in the Toronto emigrant hospital and its fever sheds.

Michael Power always had a special love for the land of his parents' birth and for its people, who came to Canada by the tens of thousands in the early nineteenth century. Even prior to the Famine, close to 450,000 Irish – Catholic and Protestant – had ventured to Britain's North

American Colonies, now called Canada. As a missionary priest Michael served Irish immigrants on the Canadian frontier; he baptised their young, cared for their sick, provided moral instruction, and buried their dead. As a bishop, he mediated disputes between Irish Catholics, their Scottish and French co-religionists, and members of other Christian faiths. As the chief pastor of Toronto he travelled hundreds of miles across his vast diocese and oversaw the creation of new parish communities that were primarily Irish in their composition.

Nothing, however, prepared him for the 109,000 Irish migrants who fled to Canada's shores during 'Black '47'. In that tragic year Michael Power saw the Famine first-hand. While travelling back to Canada from Rome he stopped in Ireland, where he recruited the Loretto Sisters to come to his diocese to open schools. While in Ireland he saw the torment and destruction wrought by the Famine among the Irish people. In June, having warned his own flock by pastoral letter about the horrific events in Ireland, he made a speedy return by steamship. Back in Toronto, he received the nearly 39,000 migrants that fled to the city, between June and November 1847, most of whom were Irish and many of whom carried typhus. These Irish had survived the six- to eight-week crossing of the Atlantic, essentially serving as ballast on ships converted from their primary use for timber, grain and cargo. These Irish had survived the quarantine station at Grosse-Île, near Quebec, where by season's end over 5,000 of their countrymen would find their eternal rest. These Irish had also weathered the fever sheds of Montreal and the week-long journey by open boat west to Toronto.

Working alongside his Protestant neighbours, Power helped mobilise the small city of 20,000. He cautioned local citizens not to blame the Irish for their condition but to work in the spirit of Christian charity to relieve them of their burdens. Thousands were stricken with typhus; 1,124 died. Daily he crossed the muddy street of this frontier community – which he once likened as being 'on the edge of civilization' – to anoint the sick, comfort families, and bury the Catholic dead, which accounted for three in every four of the human casualties in Toronto. When Power's own priests fell ill, it was he alone, in the late summer of 1847, who tended to the sick and dying in the fever sheds. His courageous and selfless work among the Irish caused him to contract typhus, which eventually took his life on 1 October 1847. He was buried in the crypt of his unfinished cathedral, after what had been recorded as the largest funeral cortège in the city's history. Despite all the work of his years as priest, pastor, and bishop, what has been remembered of Michael Power was that he was a 'martyr of charity; he died for his people.'

THE GREAT HUNGER ON CAPE CLEAR

Chuck Kruger

In the late 1980s, new to Cape Clear, my wife and I regularly explored the island. When we asked permission to wander through private property, we were often invited first to step in and have a cuppa by curious and friendly locals. Sadly, the eldest of them have now passed on, but I remember the stories they shared with us. And whenever I asked about the days of the Great Hunger on Cape, I heard how they had heard first-hand from grandparents who had survived the Famine that life had been much better here than on the mainland – those eight sometimes wild miles away. A common perspective indicated that, all considered, life was so much less threatening here that between two and five hundred people from the mainland moved to Cape, which had a permanent population of around 1,000 during those potato-less years. Here the newcomers could collect limpets and periwinkles, harvest edible seaweed, catch fish from the shore, and in general manage to eke out a way to stay alive.

Recognising that these stories could have been the consequence of an unconscious selective memory at work, I've since read many other bleak accounts of the Famine on Cape. Skibbereen Journalist Jeremiah O'Donovan Rossa wrote about a Cape woman to whom he personally delivered seven pounds of meal with the help of the island priest. He recalled, 'Father Collins took us to see the bedridden woman, Kittie O'Driscoll. He went on his hands and knees and crept into a hole in the side of a hill. I crept in after him, and there, stretched on the flag stones, with nothing between her and the flag stones but her shreds of body clothes and tufts of heath, was the poor bedridden woman. Leaving that place the priests took us into some cabins where children were lying dead – dead from hunger; took us into other cabins where the doors were flag stones – and things that were there in the shape of wooden doors having been burned for firing.'

One of the few statistics from Cape at that time indicates that fifty-two children were born on the island in 1845. In 1847 that figure dropped to nine. We can draw a tragic inference from such a decline.

Another journalist, Jeremiah O'Callaghan, who visited Cape in 1848, wrote for the *Cork Examiner* that he was met by 'moving skeletons with swollen legs and distorted features'. Yet in 1848 it is also noted that the Church of Ireland established a school and a church on Cape and, as Eamon Lankford writes in his book, *Cape Clear: Its People and Landscape*, 'Housing conditions … during this time were poor. Most families, many of whom had 10–15 children, lived in one- or two-roomed stone and mud cabins…. [But] The Minutes of the Island and Coast Society meetings of this time note the attendance of 70 pupils at the mission school and upwards of one hundred at church services. Given that soup, other food, blankets, clothing and fuel were distributed amongst the number, it is little wonder that deaths from starvation in Cléire after 1848 were few.'

And how do memories of the Great Hunger linger on in Cape – since the island has no special Famine cemeteries? As blow-ins, we've now learned that when a neighbour drops in, we don't ask 'would you like a cup of tea?' just once, as we used to, and then, when we heard the 'no', make tea for the two of us rather than all three. Now, with due respect to the Famine tradition, we have learned to ask three times, the first two questions the polite host's duty – and the refusals the polite guest's response. The third 'ask' meant that there was in fact enough tea for all of us in the house, so a 'yes' was not an imposition.

AUNT RITA

Nicola Lindsay

My husband's Aunt Rita died on Sunday 9 May and her funeral took place the following Thursday. She was well into her nineties and frail and confused at the end, so her death was not unexpected and, to her, it must have seemed a welcome letting go.

For a too-brief period in the 1970s she played an important role as the wife of Erskine Childers, President of Ireland, before his premature death while still in office. I remember seeing clips of her from old news-reels, well before I first met her and I thought how very slim and elegant she always looked in her Irish tweeds and her stylish haircut.

Her brother was my husband's father and the two of them shared a wicked sense of fun and the ability to see through any pretence or pom-posity. They both laughed at unnecessary red tape and long-winded jar-gon.

It was Rita who welcomed me into the family – literally with open arms – inviting me in and making me feel completely at home. When her nephew, Charles, and I married, she was delighted as she'd always had a special place for him in her heart and cared deeply about his well-being and happiness.

Her kindness was unlimited. My husband's older brother suffered ap-pallingly all his relatively short life from terrible epilepsy, but Rita and Erskine made sure that he didn't miss out on special events. He had pride of place with them at the Dublin Horse Show. Rita would often travel down to Camphill Village Community in Wexford in the presidential car to take Hugh out. She also organised regular visits to the Dáil and to Áras an Uachtaráin.

She was an avid reader and do-er of the crossword in *The Irish Times* and when we called in to see her, the kitchen table would be strewn with various articles she'd cut out from the paper with a pair of giant scissors. We would often be the recipients of cuttings she thought would be of interest to us. Because she suffered from a shaky hand, her handwriting was fairly disastrous and she eventually switched to typing out the accompanying messages.

When Rita lost her adored husband, life was far from easy. Apart from suffering the trauma of Erskine's sudden death, she had to leave the park and the staff with whom she had built close friendships. Past Irish Taoisigh keep their chauffer-driven limos. Erskine Childers' widow travelled by bus. She did learn to drive, somewhat haphazardly, and was much in demand as a speaker all over the country. She would set out in her small car, arriving home late at night and often exhausted.

In the nursing home where she died, her husband's portrait – the image of which was used as an Irish stamp for some time – hung opposite her bed. Suddenly lucid, she would point at it and say with a smile, 'He's watching me, you know.'

As we stood on the hummocky, gorse-strewn hillside at Derralossary, County Wickow, two blackbirds sang from a nearby tree, the liquid notes intermingling with the prayers as Rita's coffin was lowered into the grave to lie beside the husband she so loved.

I will never forget her warmth, her sense of fun, her Alice bands and clogs, her immense kindness and, above all, her generosity. We are going to miss her very much indeed.

SUNDAY MORNING, AWAY WEST

Peter Murphy

Sunday morning, forever ago. The smell of shoe polish. Hair fluffy as goose-down from the Saturday night bath. You had to eat breakfast as soon as you'd been rooted out of bed in order to fast for Holy Communion.

We gathered at the cathedral in the centre of Enniscorthy, a great looming neo-Gothic edifice designed by Augustus Welby Pugin and completed during the Famine. St Aidan's spoiled me for Mass anywhere else in the country. Other places of worship looked dingy by comparison.

My father stayed at the back of the church with the betting men and the horseshoe throwers and the Woodbine puffers who congregated by the holy-water font, all the better to bail out at half-time when the Eucharistic bell sounded the signal for an early escape.

I accompanied my mother to her usual pew about halfway up the aisle. Although she never said as much, I got the impression she considered it unseemly to hug the altar railings. That was for people who wanted to be seen to be seen – merchants and moneychangers who'd say their prayers to the high rafters of a Sunday, and rob you blind during the week. So we kept a healthy distance from the tabernacle until it was time to queue for Communion, rows of us kneeling like blindfolded prisoners of war or gangster's marks awaiting execution.

This was when you got to see the cut of the town's tongues. Fellow Enniscorthy man Colm Tóibín served as an altar boy in St Aidan's and once described to me the Francis Bacon-esque panorama of oral protuberances that assaulted his eyes every Sunday morning as he helped the priest dispense Holy Communion. 'Little ones with glasses and knitted caps with these big muscular tongues,' he said. 'You got to know people gynaecologically, without understanding that it was gynaecology you were looking at.'

We returned to our seats after receiving the sacrament, my mother upright and dutiful, perfume wafting, me weak and wet-eyed with boredom trying to remember the correct protocol of what points in the service one should stand or kneel or sit. Some prayers were burned into memory from repetition, others remained forever evasive and you had to murmur or lip-sync the words. *It was never the same since they did away with the Latin.*

Always it seemed, the mind wandered westward. To pass the time, I retold myself Stephen King stories. The inner eye re-ran every reel of *The Omega Man* or *The Thing.* The inner ear replayed albums by Alice Cooper or The Doors. As I write, I think of 'Sunday Morning', the first track on *The Velvet Underground and Nico*, a song that seems light as a feather, with its prettified melodies, wispy voice and celeste sounds, but the lyric is freighted with a terrible weight. 'Watch out, the world's behind you,' Lou Reed sighed, and I wondered what he meant.

Or 'Sunday Morning, Coming Down' by Kris Kristofferson, perhaps the saddest song ever written, the words and melody enlaced with the ache of the drunk who is exiled from the paradise of family, his heart caught by the smell of frying chicken and the sight of a father swinging his child in the park. Long before I came to know the sickly guilt of the Sunday-morning hangover, Kris Kristofferson's words allowed a small boy's mind to apprehend the awful sorrow of the lost soul, the outcast, the addict, the social leper, the irredeemable.

I started skipping Mass about the same time I began to go to rock concerts. Different forms of worship; same impulse, same search for something that might give shape or meaning to the whole shebang. To this day some of my favourite things invoke the high drama of the Catholic Mass, the fire of religion, the mythic, the epic, the art that is more important than life or death. The music of Bob Dylan and Johnny Cash and Nick Cave and Bruce Springsteen. The words of Flannery O'Connor and Harper Lee and Herman Melville and John Steinbeck and Ray Bradbury. Robert Mitchum in *Night of the Hunter.* Robert DeNiro in *Cape Fear.* Rutger Hauer in *Blade Runner.* The heavens over the *Old, Weird America*, the hell beyond Connacht. Sunday morning, away west.

MARRIAGE IN ITS ELEVENTH YEAR

Joseph O'Neill

It is what it is,
Id est (i.e. i.e.),
It isn't what it isn't.

Thus it is not what it was
Was is not what is, is
What is, is, is what it is,

Thus what it is, is it
What it isn't is fair,
Or enough, or done.

Fair's fair; enough is enough.
What's done is done.

I.e. it is what it is
Is what it is.
That being said, and so,
So be it, so be, that is,
What it was, is, will be.

JUNE

THE NIGHT SKY AND MARY BRUCK

Colette Olney

In the recent good weather, I was in the garden, after dark, putting a pile of washing out to hang in the night air. This, for me, is a pleasurable household chore, particularly if, for instance, the night is mild, or if the stars are out.

The stars were out.

I saw them twinkling away in great numbers. They made me think of Mary Bruck. Although I never met her, Mary Bruck often comes to mind when I find myself under a velvety, star-speckled sky. I think of her sometimes, too, under the moon, if it's full, and if the man up there (the one in the moon?!) is wearing his usual grimace.

Also known as Máire from her birth in 1925 in Ballivor, County Meath, Dr Mary Bruck passed away in 2008 at the age of eighty-three, having acquitted herself with great distinction in the field of astronomy and as a prolific writer on the role of women in science. Her best-known book is probably *Agnes Mary Clerke and the Rise of Astrophysics*.

It was fitting, if not inevitable, that Mary Bruck should write the story of that nineteenth-century Skibbereen-born chronicler of astrophysical discovery. Mary Bruck was herself, in a manner of speaking, the twentieth century's answer to Agnes Mary Clerke: Mary Bruck followed the Skibbereen woman's example – immersing herself in the field of astronomy and contributing hugely to the international scientific and literary world.

You might imagine such lofty scholarship would transport a person into a realm apart – detach them from others – maybe even make them crazy. But Mary Bruck was as sane and rounded an individual as one might hope to meet.

Here's how I know: when I was a jobbing substitute teacher at primary level, my fastidious principal offered me a box of bedraggled books from the school library – some of them pulverised from years of page-turning. Surplus to requirements, the books were to be replaced by new stock. I could do what I liked with them – use them to start a fire; distribute them to friends with small children who wouldn't mind their grubbiness; or slip them into one of those doorstep bags for collection. In sorting them, I found a few to keep – pocket-sized early Ladybird books from the 1960s and, among these, I discovered *The Night Sky* by Mary T. Bruck Ph.D. (no less) of the Royal Observatory, Edinburgh.

From it I quote: 'The Earth from which we view the world around us is a large ball about eight thousand miles across.' Now *there* was a fact I'd never fully registered. Mary Bruck's telling it was pure child's play! Her trawl through galaxies is similarly distilled into language that bridges gaps not just between ignorance and information, but between the world of a pensive, knowledgeable adult and the real curiosity of a child … or indeed any reader.

Satisfying the tallest order, however, is the relationship Mary Bruck posits between mere mortals and the solar system. She does so in one fell swoop with a breathtaking sentence that reads: 'There is nothing special about the Earth.' This statement is subsequently qualified with an explanation of Earth's place in a family of nine planets, but the impact has been made; our imagination appealed to directly, and we are obliged as Earthlings to graciously accept our precarious predicament.

What makes someone devote their life's work to astrophysics? Mary Bruck said her interest in the stars stemmed from her childhood fascination with the man in the moon. It's more than a little ironic that she wrote extensively on the role of *women* in science.

Mary Bruck was born to schoolteachers Thomas and Margaret Conway; the eldest of eight, she attended St Louis convent in Monaghan, sat for her Leaving Certificate aged sixteen and earned a physics degree from UCD. Later obtaining a doctorate from the university of Edinburgh in the field of solar spectroscopy, she proceeded into research and a post at the Dunsink Observatory where she met her husband, astronomer Herman Bruck, and started a family.

Now, when *The Night Sky* was published in 1965, man had not yet put a foot on the moon. 'The moon has already been reached by rockets from the earth,' Mary Bruck touchingly observes – dating (irredeemably) the little book, and giving any busy primary-school principal reason to chuck it out in favour of some other, newer book containing up-to-the-minute rocket science.

But because I'm not so busy, to me the book is valuable and timeless: that 1969 moonwalk – a mere blip on the radar.

And, because of Mary Bruck, I, for one, with no studying to speak of, understand, for instance, that on late spring and early summer evenings, the constellation known as The Lion stands in the south and right in front of us.

And that's what has me out in the dark, hanging up washing, dilly-dallying in the garden, saluting astronomer Mary Bruck … and stargazing.

SERENDIPITY

Maurice Cashell

Her name was Dorothy. Her father had the bakery in our town and, some summers ago, when we were both twenty, we had a steamy affair when her boyfriend, a medical student, was working abroad to finance his studies. I was on a scholarship, bright but penniless, feckless and fancy-free. It came as no surprise that, when he returned, she dropped me like a stone. What did surprise was the pain, the emptiness, the extent to which I was prepared to grovel and to plead.

Advice poured in. My mother said that faint heart never won fair lady. My sisters talked about there being plenty of fish in the sea. In our house, in matters of the heart, there is a cliché for every occasion.

Fate intervened in the form of a maiden aunt who needed company on a pilgrimage to Rome. Her interest was in a papal audience, prayer and absolution. For me the attraction – and distraction – was subsidised travel and the completion of a minor thesis on Raphael Sanzio of Urbino. When my aunt took to her rooms to rest from the intense midday heat, I spent hours in the Pantheon, the Vatican Museums and the Borghese and Doria Pamphilj galleries. My thesis was to critique what Joshua Reynolds described as 'the propriety, beauty, and majesty of Raphael's characters, his judicious contrivance of his composition, correctness of drawing, purity of taste, and the skilful accommodation of other men's conceptions to his own purpose'.

Absorbing, and eminently satisfying given the abundance of Raphaels on view, but for all that I missed the distant Dorothy. However, some vicarious pleasure was provided by the story of Margherita Luti. Better known as *La Fornarina*, she and Raphael were an item, despite his being engaged to Maria, the niece of Cardinal Medici Bibbiena. According to sources, Raphael's premature death on Good Friday, 1520, at the age of thirty-seven, was caused by a night of excessive zeal with Luti, after which he fell into a fever. Not revealing to his doctors what was its cause, he was given the wrong cure, and he got progressively worse. My aunt would have approved of what happened next: Raphael was composed enough to receive the last rites and to put his affairs in order. He left sufficient funds for his mistress's care and she betook herself to a convent.

On her last night I took my aunt to Trastevere. For me there was the Villa Farnesina, a small two-storey palace where Raphael was commissioned to do the fresco decoration. I then took her to the Basilica of Santa Maria in Trastevere, one of the oldest churches in Rome. Outside in the Piazza, with its elegant raised fountain and sidewalk cafés, a woman was playing haunting tunes on a viola amid the comings and goings of tourists and locals. My aunt ordered what was for her a rare sherry and talked excitedly at her proximity to the Holy Father during that day's audience. Seeing a neon sign at the end of the street, and thinking it the perfect coincidence, she suggested dinner at a restaurant called Romulus. I went along with the idea, half wondering if there was a Remus. I was amused when I saw on the menu that the full title was *Romolo nel Giardino della Fornarina*, but dinner with my aunt didn't seem the right occasion on which to pontificate on the subject of the mistress of the great artist of the Vatican.

My heart lurched, however, when the waiter translated the term. *La Fornarina* was the baker's daughter. The restaurant was in the very house and garden that Raphael had provided for his mistress. But my heartbeat really took off when we emerged and I turned to see where we had been. The restaurant is at 20 Via de Santa Dorotea. Significant coincidence? Or was I just fantasising?

On the plane on the way home to Dublin my aunt slept and I spoke at length of my experiences to the philosophy student from Trinity College who was in Rome to research the origin, history, domains, traditions, and patterns of serendipity.

She and I are, as my mother would say, still seeing each other.

THE DRINKS CABINET

Sheila Maher

There was a time when very little alcohol was consumed in our house. My mother used to pour herself a solitary glass of sherry while preparing the Sunday roast. This tiny glass she kept by her side, moving it with her as she stirred from surface to surface around the kitchen. No other alcoholic beverage was consumed most weeks.

The drinks cabinet was a press in a unit that Dad built. This unit fitted precisely into the alcove in our sitting room. On the bottom shelf was our set of encyclopaedia. A to Z aligned across the width of the unit with just enough room for a *Philip's Atlas*. I was encouraged – forced – to use these books whenever I had a geography, nature, science or music question. 'You'll remember it better if you look it up yourself,' was the annoying mantra Mum and Dad singsonged if I moaned at the prospect of having to work for the answer myself. It never occurred to me that they might not know the answer. On the next shelf up were some old novels by A. J. Cronin, Daphne du Maurier and a few John F. Kennedy biographies. This is where our *Oxford English Dictionary* and our *English–Irish Dictionary* by Tomás de Bhaldraithe sat. Above this to the left was open shelving filled with photos of our extended family and us as even smaller children, and to the right sat the drinks cabinet.

When visitors called for supper or a party, once greetings were over and they were seated, the door to the drinks cabinet was let down – it was like a drawbridge over a castle moat. It was the only door in the house that opened like that. All of the drinks and glasses were on display, so guests could take their pick. There were large bottles of Paddy's Irish whiskey, Martini, Harvey's Bristol Cream and Gordon's gin. A bottle of Baileys was added at Christmas time in later years.

Never one to let anything go to waste, my Dad made several lamp shades from empty whiskey bottles of curious shapes. A Dimple Scottish whisky bottle sat in my bedroom for years. Through the clear glass I could see the wire enter from a tiny bored hole in the base of the bottle and travel on up through the main cavity into the lightbulb. I thought my dad was a genius to invent such a lamp.

Around the large bottles of alcohol, like small children clustered at their parents' feet, were fitted numerous toy-like bottles: rum, Cointreau, Curaçao, and other odd-sounding potions in bottles shaped like musical instruments and churches that Mum and Dad received as gifts from well-travelled relatives. These bottles were never opened. On a shelf above all the alcohol sat the glassware. There was a muddle of mismatched Waterford Crystal glasses – these were wedding presents for my parents but there was no longer a complete set. An assortment of odd tumblers made up the shortfall.

When they had visitors in, Mum would have a Martini, or maybe two. She liked it mixed with TK white lemonade and ice. Some guests went straight for the whiskey and water, while our sophisticated relatives from London asked for a G&T. Dad never drank. He was a proud pioneer his entire life. So just as the occasional Martini and sherry were a treat for Mum, the odd glass of 'mineral' did for Dad. Of course we children benefited from Dad's abstinence. At Christmas time or special occasions huge bottles of Cidona, Club Orange and red lemonade arrived into the house. They were lined up high on a shelf in the cold garage until guests arrived.

A glass of Cidona made me feel so grown up. There was something mature about the look and taste of it. It smelt like alcohol, it looked as if it was something I should not be drinking and it definitely did not taste like other kids' drinks. It was the fizzy drink of choice for the child with discernment.

Over the course of the following decades, with the arrival of wine, the drinks cabinet lost its usefulness. The bottles inside grew sticky and grubby as dust crept in and clung to them. The whiskey and sherry stood unopened for years, relegated to ingredients in trifle and Christmas cake, while our guests sipped Blue Nun and Black Tower. The surviving Waterford Crystal tumblers and sherry glasses remained safe, tucked away in the back of the cabinet, as Mum and her guests plumped for clear wine goblets. The wine was stored instead in tight cubby holes cleverly designed into our new fitted kitchen. The previous pivotal role of the drinks cabinet at all social gatherings has long been forgotten. Now its drop-down door creaks and screeches loudly on the rare occasion it is opened in the frantic search for a corkscrew.

WEATHERING EXAMS

Sile Agnew

God doesn't listen to major sinners like me. When I need divine inspiration I light a candle. Sometimes I get results, sometimes I don't. I light a candle if someone is dying, so the children ask, 'Who's dead?' They know the candle doesn't really work. 'No one is dead,' I answer confidently. 'Well who is nearly dead?' they ask as they look into the fridge packed with food and complain, 'There is never any *food* in this house.' 'That mysterious Mr Nobody probably ate it,' I tell them.

Mr Nobody lives with us and will frequently put empty cartons back in the fridge, use the last tea bag, won't replace the toilet roll when it runs out, leaves the freezer door open, drops wet towels on the floor, never turns off the immersion after a shower, leaves lights on in every room, eats all the biscuits and goodies, but is never caught in the act.

I also light a candle if anyone is doing an exam, and today my son is sitting a paper in economics. The sun is beaming and it is 25 degrees – authentic exam weather – and two candles burn since midday on the kitchen table to be sure to be sure he will get divine inspiration.

I go outside to the backyard to enjoy the exam weather. My daughter is already soaking up the sun and my husband arrives home from work early and we sit around chatting and marvelling at the sunshine. Summer has come at last after floods and snow. We discuss the news of the day: Naomi Campbell returning diamonds she doesn't have; the recession; the guy who collected his dead pal's pension for twenty-three years and only got caught when the president wanted to give the corpse a cheque on his hundredth birthday.

Throughout our conversation a small distant beep can be heard. The chat goes on. 'What is that beeping?' I ask.

'Oh, it's probably a truck reversing on the road,' they answer. We chat on, oblivious. We discuss the UK election; Rihanna's concert in the O_2; the art raid in Paris; clampers; Bono's back pain – and the beep goes on.

'That truck is reversing for an awfully long time. Are you sure it's on the road?' My daughter looks towards the house: 'THE KITCHEN TABLE IS ON FIRE!' We all stand up and look through the window as flames lick through newspapers, a plastic bag, and a canvas shopping bag. A bonfire is raging on the wooden table top. Hallowe'en comes early in June. We rush into the kitchen to see the last letters on the bag melt away 'better value beats them all'. My husband transforms into Fireman Sam and throws a newspaper – not an ideal choice of extinguisher – onto the flammability zone. The edges of the paper ignite. From the smouldering mess we lift the soot and debris. Icelandic ash clouds fill the air. We have a kitchen table that resembles a prop from *The Exorcist*. I wait for the dog's head to spin right around. 'Gosh is it ominous?' I ask. 'I wonder how the exam is going: do ye think is he on fire and knows the answers to all the questions?' They nod in hope and say, 'Maybe it's the exam paper from hell?' The smell of burnt pinewood fills our nostrils. They *all* now declare they knew it was the smoke alarm all along; they *never* thought it was a reversing truck.

CSI Family establish that Mr Nobody put the newspapers and the shopping bags on the table beside the two candles. The glare from the sunshine rendered the tiny naked flames invisible. It was the exam weather that ultimately caused the fire.

Everyone agrees the table is a unique charred work of art. The economics exam wasn't cost-effective for the household; if we keep this up we won't have any furniture left by the time the exams are finished. The following morning, he sits his next exam and I light a candle safely in a glass hurricane candleholder.

Exam weather can cause fires and exams are stressful, very stressful if you have a kitchen table that is set alight by Mr Nobody.

GRACIOUS LIVING

Claire Kilroy

It was Dessie's idea that we sit outside and keep an eye on the Portakabin – I mean, the sales suite – from a discreet distance. He'd had the interior designer mock up a sort of bistro affair to give an impression of... he couldn't think of the word. 'What's it?' he asked me, clicking his fingers, '*genteel* living?', but genteel wasn't quite it. 'What's the word I'm looking for, Tristram? Begins with a "G".' 'Dunno,' I replied. 'Anyway,' he continued, 'it's a lifestyle we're selling here, is my point.'

We couldn't have asked for better weather; the first proper summer's day of the year. The apartments glinted just as they glinted on the plans. The flags lining the avenue fluttered in the light sea breeze; the foliage of the brand-new plants shimmered lime green. The rental garden had been unloaded the morning before from the back of a truck. As had the sales suite, the bistro, and even the lawn. Yesterday this had all been a patch of scrubland. It was, by any standards, an elaborate scam.

Dessie put his sunglasses on and contemplated the sales queue with satisfaction. The punters had been waiting for three days by then, and were dazed, dehydrated and desperate. The taxi-drivers, their wives, anxious young couples, solicitous parents – all of them transfixed by the desire to acquire 'luxury apartments' in an 'exclusive development' along 'Dublin's sought-after coast'. They were studying the brochures and price lists, doing the sums in their heads, sizing up the people ahead of them in the queue, worrying that they had their eye on the same apartment, the bastards, and so discussing their second choice, and their third. Plan B, Plan C and Plan D. They muttered to their partners, they muttered into their mobile phones. So preoccupied were they with their quarry that they didn't register Dessie and I trained on them. They didn't register that *they* were the quarry.

That's when Maura approached with her clipboard. I checked my watch. The apartments had been on sale for forty-five minutes. Dessie removed his sunglasses. 'Here she comes.'

'Well?' he said when she drew up. 'Are we in business?'

'We are, Mr Hickey. Just to inform you that the first fifty units are now sold.'

Dessie brought his fist down hard on the bistro table. 'Yes!' His teaspoon bounced and landed on the gravel. Maura stooped to pick it up. 'Good girl. Right. Withdraw the final 105 units from sale.'

'What?' I said, sitting up in my chair, but Maura had already Yes-Mr-Hickeyed him and was marching back to the Portakabin – I mean, the sales suite. I turned to face Dessie. 'Run that past me.'

He punched a number into his phone and raised it to his ear before cocking an eyebrow my way. 'We decided that if they sold briskly, we'd release ninety-eight apartments today and call it Phase One, and hold back the others, add 30 per cent to the price, and call them Phase Two. We'll launch Phase Two at the end of the summer. Hello, Michael? D. Hickey here. Good news, good news.'

I stared at Dessie in his suit. He never looked right in a suit, same as I never looked right in jeans. A tuft of black bristles protruded from his ear, the match of the bristles sprouting from his nostrils, as if something were growing inside him, forcing its way out. He was a coarse man, a crude one, a few stages behind on the evolutionary ladder – or perhaps a few stages ahead on the evolutionary ladder; or on some as yet undocumented section of the ladder which had forked and gone off on a tangent, so he was not quite a man but instead something hybrid, something wolfish, something that wore its pelt on the inside; because they were a new breed, weren't they, these developers? And their development was escalating, and the country was facilitating it, an Ireland-shaped Petri dish of ideal conditions. Soon they would take over altogether. They would enslave us. In fact, they already had. A commotion had broken out in the queue. Maura had placed a sign in the window: 'Phase One Sold Out'. Voices were raised, fingers were pointed, faces were covered with hands. A small child wailed in fright. Security was standing by.

Dessie clapped his phone shut and turned to me. '*Gracious,*' he said.

'That's the word I'm looking for. Isn't that what we're selling here, Tristram? *Gracious* living.'

Yes, I'm angry. Of course I'm angry, but anger is not a policy.

THE CLOUD ON MOUNT OLYMPUS

John Banville

I have come to realise at last that it was all my fault. For it all began with a piece of writing, and did not end until I had made my peace with the jealous gods.

In 2008, just as I was finishing my novel, *The Infinities*, the international financial order collapsed after the failure of Lehman Brothers. I should have heeded the portent. My fictional setting in the book is a house in the Irish countryside one Midsummer Day vaguely in the present. The head of the Godley family, old Adam, a world-famous mathematician, has suffered a stroke and is in a coma and dying, although his mind is still in perfect working order. Around him the family members have gathered, including his son, young Adam, and young Adam's young wife Helen. The main narrator of this minor midsummer dream is the god Hermes, whose father Zeus has fallen for the beautiful Helen and has come speeding down to earth to spend a night of love with her in the form of her husband. In this case, heaven cannot wait. Pan, too, is on the scene, and the mischievous fun is perfectly divine, with the gods behaving as they always have: impishly, childishly, foolishly.

The book was duly published, first in London and later in New York. The reviews, I am told – I never read them – were excellent, and all seemed set fair for success. Came the autumn, though, and with it the long- and shortlists for the major literary prizes, with nary a mention of *The Infinities*. Surely some jury would recognise the book's merits? One did. On the day that it was announced that Colum McCann had won the American National Book Award, word came to me that *The Infinities* had been shortlisted for the London *Literary Review*'s Bad Sex Award.

The passage in my book that the *Review*'s tribunal had settled on, like blowflies settling on something putrid, was a brief and, so it seemed to me, perfectly innocuous description of a tryst in Venice between old Adam when he was young and a somewhat vaporous prostitute going by the lovely name of Alba. The other shortlisted scenes, I should say, were far more graphic than my delicate dalliance, including, for instance, Philip Roth's voyeuristic description of a scene of rampant lesbian love-making, and an even more extreme encounter, I think, in a novel by Nick Cave, involving a guillotine and a young woman's defenceless bottom.

I am happy to report that I did not win the award, and I do not know who did. A lucky escape – but still.

Thinking the immortal ones would consider this humiliation sufficient revenge on me for my irreverence in portraying them in all their concupiscence and pettiness, I went ahead with preparations for an American book tour. I felt doubly safe in that the book I was promoting was a crime novel, *Elegy for April*, written by my pseudonymous dark brother, Benjamin Black. The gods, however, were not to be diverted by a mere pen-name. Just as I was due to fly out to New York, Vulcan the fire-god got busy up in Iceland and stuck his poker into the seething innards of the Eyjafjallajökull volcano – yes, that one – and within days an ash cloud had spread over western Europe and all airline flights were grounded.

Of course, I recognised at once the part I had played in this disaster. The gods will not be mocked, and I would have to make amends. A pilgrimage, a journey of supplication, was surely required of me. So I went to Greece – yes, I did, I went to Greece and scrambled up the hill of Delphi, on the flanks of Mount Parnassus, and there, in the Temple of Apollo, abased myself on those rough stones and begged that the curse be lifted. And lo! the volcano stopped erupting, flights are flying, and I have won the Kerry Group Award at the Listowel Writers' Festival. But I have learned my lesson, and from now on will stick to earthbound fictions.

THE COLOUR OF WORDS

Cyril Kelly

Language is, quintessentially, feminine. Words have female propensities. You know the way a woman can highlight her hair or change her lipstick, and, hey presto, there she is, redefined. So too with words. Take the word 'pot'. Forty years ago, you could 'boil the pot' or even 'burn the backside off a pot', but then, the word had a makeover; 'pot' could be grown, even smoked; it was liberated from its dowdy, domesticated image and began to appear in *Cosmopolitan*.

And what about 'brown'? Every mortal house had a 'brown habit' in some mothballed drawer. But that was before 'brown' began to frequent late-night, speak-easy sort of joints, where consultants and councillors hung out, and then she emerged, like a caucus call girl, hand in hand with politicos and, henceforth, entered the vernacular as the notorious 'brown envelope'.

So too with place names. When Writers' Week was born forty years ago, it was destined to give the name Listowel a makeover. But, luckily for me, the colour of the town in 1970 was created by the annual Listowel Races. That was the year I gave up the permanent pensionable job in Dublin and came back here for a while to live. My father had died suddenly and I wanted to carry on his small sawmill, a naive urge to give some posthumous life to his dream. The consolation of labouring away while he ghosted among timber stacks, or, evoked by resinous scents his spirit shuffled through shavings. But the nightly ledger was cold comfort, tracing his flowing script through pages of credit which he had, somehow, doled out.

And so I found myself, one June evening, driving through an avenue of poplars into the ostentatious domain of Pheasant Hall. Mr Pheasant

Hall Esq owed us a substantial sum of money. Dressed in cavalry twills and riding boots, he – as they say – saw me coming. After a grandiloquent tour of his new farm buildings, slatted unit, milking parlour, etc., he assured me that he would be paying off every farthing, but the government was refusing to give him the grant until he finished pebble-dashing this concrete empire. His problem, he bewailed, was the ongoing cement strike; two more hundredweight was all he needed to complete the job; no cement, no pebble-dash; no pebble-dash, no cash.

You could argue that the solution which suggested itself to me during the following days was a felony. So, I reasoned, if one is intent on compromising one's integrity, it might be prudent to have a lady by one's side; the female of the species lends an air of respectability to the dodgiest undertakings, even smuggling, and, at the time, cement was top-notch contraband. Sitting into my late father's VW Fastback, I hit for Dublin one fine morning, collected a dark-eyed damsel and was crossing the border at noon. In Newry, cement was being flogged by the ton; I was nearly ashamed to buy three paltry hundredweight. And then, rather than return by the main road with my loot, I swung westward, past signposts that were primed to explode onto national and international consciousness: Cullyhanna, Crossmaglen, Cullaville. Speculatively, I swerved southwards, onto a byroad, past narrow fields bordered by hawthorn, where furze on drumlin slopes was a resplendent dialect of whins. Suddenly this customs officer sprang from a roadside caravan like a zany zealot. 'Nothing to declare,' I blurted but, as if I hadn't heard his curt command: 'Open the boot, front and rear.'

Here memory jerks into grainy staccato motion; he is groping in the black maw above the engine; my mother's picnic rug is yanked from its widowed pining; three furtive bags of cement surrender themselves. As if he despised my ineptitude, he grimaced at me to follow him. In the caravan, while I was filling in some incriminating document, he outlined dire consequences; the car would be impounded – forthwith. Smuggling carried a lengthy sentence. And so on and so forth until my knees knocked and my stomach was doing bile green summersaults. Eventually, taking the form, he began to peruse my details, sizing me up from time to time. 'Ever hear of Razor's Edge?' he enquired. I shook my head. And then, slowly, he ripped the page in shreds. 'Big win on Razor's Edge last year at Listowel Races,' he said. Now, like a good lad, go home with your cement … before I change my mind. In my haste to escape, I almost tripped over myself. And I was still fumbling with the ignition, when he was by my side again. 'A red-hot tip for Listowel this year,' he wheezed. 'Say Nothing, first race, first day.' With that he slammed the door.

Sure enough, on the opening day of the Harvest Festival, 1970, Say Nothing obliged, at a handy 20–1. And my companion, the dark-eyed filly, she proved a good ante-post wager in the Maiden Hurdle. But, even to this very day, it grieves me to relate that Pebble Dash, carrying a three hundredweight. handicap, with Pheasant Hall Esq on board, was a non-runner in the Debtors' Credibility Chase.

IN MY FATHER'S HELL

Trish Long

In my father's heaven there is an amazing bar. It stocks all sorts of wondrous things including the danger of spirits but, vitally, it has *the* most wonderful Guinness.

He can hear the low companionable silence of men who know each other's lacks so well – but each other's essence so little – as they sit in their lonely togetherness and reverently anticipate that most satisfying slaker of all kinds of Irish thirsts. It's so quiet he can hear the slurping gassy topping up of the head and then those settling sacred silent seconds before the unrepeatable, indescribable release that comes from that first pint of the day.

In my father's hell, there is the most amazing bar, which he suspects is filled with all his cronies…. He is pretty sure he can hear the voices of his drinking buddies as they go again. He is definite he heard Lama or Christy starting a round of Vaughn Monroe's 'Ghost Riders in the Sky' or Norman Wisdom's 'Don't Laugh at Me 'Cos I'm a fool'.

Yes, in my father's hell, there is an amazing local…. But no matter how far he walks or how many corners he turns, it's always just out of reach.

In my father's hell, I'm there – with all my back-answering, contradicting and generally just-getting-above-myself ways; he feels like I've invaded his snug in Dick Devane's and I just won't stop talking to him and asking him why he told me I was never wanted, or had been nothing but trouble since the day I was born.

In my father's hell Star Rovers never wins and Garryowen is certainly never in Glory.

There are no matches, no removals and no funerals, so he has no excuses to sneak out. There's *no* sorry-for-your-troubles deadhouse forays with their promise of a free-drinks passport or going on the batter with the lads.

It's always Lent and there's no St Patrick's Day to break the 'drinkfast' with.

There are no walls to hold him up as he slaps and stumbles from side to side on the way home from the Ramble Inn (and stagger out).

In my father's hell he has no friends. It makes hell even more hellish that some of his buttys made it into heaven. He doesn't understand that at all, and will not figure it out for all eternity. He knows some of the rest of the band of house devils/street angels are in limbo and that some haven't popped their clogs yet. After all, he was only fifty-six when he learned, on earth, that hell can take many shapes, including a poky one-bedroomed Thomondgate bungalow where you drink yourself to death a whole year and two weeks after cancer did something you could never do ... quench my mother, Bernie. Where you finally lose the woman you couldn't live with – but find to your soberly drunken horror that you couldn't live without.

When I was a smally – while I was still 'Daddy's little girl' and before I somehow became the 'cause of all our troubles', I asked him, what is hell like?

'Hell is when nobody knows you and you know no one,' he said.

And perhaps because it was one of those rare summer days, when his 11-year-old walked like the big girl she was, the whole ways through town, past Cannock's and down the docks to present her proud sunburnt eldest daughtery self on the new grain trawler in Ranks docks that was *her* daddy's job, he added, Hell is hot. Scorchingly screamingly hot. Hot like the inside of a Russian grain boat on the hottest day of the summer. So hot no matter what you drink you will never slake your thirst.

So, in *my* father's hell, there's no cold fizzing Andrews liver salts, or thirst-quenching mugs of scald, lovingly made by Bernie or one of the kids. There's no salty baconed cabbage water that fools you into thinking you'll live to drink another day.

There's no full-to-the-brim Sam Maguire to wet your sipping lips and slake your gulping gullet – where for a heart-stopping, laughter-filled happy minute, surrounded by t'boys – all is right with the world.

There are no saunters down Cruises' Street where everyone knows Patrick Joseph Francis to a backdrop of 'Great singsong last night Pa' or 'how's it going PaJo'?

There are no big-hearted grandchildren who surprise you with their strangley chubby-armed hugs as you are setting the winter's day fire and sneak under your skin with their 'stop smoking Granga – I don't want you to get a black heart and die like on telly'. As he did.

In my father's hell there are no children who somehow find it in their hearts to forgive you – and to accept you probably were all you could be. And – a testament to their survival skills? – instead try to remember the briby Nash's red lemonade when you tried to make it up to us, or the perfect Cidona-filled day when you hired a horse and cart for the Killaloe picnic where even soggy cottage bread tomato sandwiches and cold hard-boiled eggs tasted great, because belts were for holding up trousers and blackthorns were sticks for walking.

There is no wife to take you back again and again and again; no matter how many times you blacken her eye, throw her out on the street or drink *her* wages so she has nothing to feed the kids but prairie sandwiches.

In my father's hell, that ever-elusive perfect pub is not the worst thing, and this truly makes him gasp.

In my father's hell he can *never* find my mother.

TWENTY YEARS AGO WE WENT TO THE WORLD CUP

Joe Horgan

Twenty years ago I went to the World Cup. I went to the World Cup. It feels great just saying it and I literally do tell everyone I meet at some stage. Okay, it was only the one match and then our money and travel plans went astray and we watched games in bars instead, travelling back through Europe in the old car we'd come in. But still. I went to the World Cup. They can't take that away from me. I saw Ireland's first ever game in the World Cup finals. Some commentators called it a terrible game of football, but I can tell you that standing in that stadium, in Cagliari, Stadio Sant'Elia on the 11 June 1990 – I have the ticket here on my wall – watching Ireland play England, with a thunderstorm breaking around the ground, was the best football match I've ever been to.

Of course I'd go back to those days if I could. Who wouldn't want to wander through their youth again? I remember too the day we came back. We were driving back through England on the day Ireland were playing Holland to get through to the next round. We got to the pub just before Quinn equalised. Romania, Italy in the quarter finals, it was all still ahead of us. Okay, we hadn't been out there for long and money was as short in those days as it ever was, but we were back now and we had been. I'd even phoned my mum and dad from halfway up the Eiffel Tower before we headed off to Italy just so they didn't think we were in a pub in Kilburn. I remember it all so well.

Apart from sentimentality and self-indulgence and the air of another World Cup in the air, even though we're not in it, the reason I'm writing this is because of the peculiar feeling I have living here in Ireland and so often missing that Ireland in Britain I come from. I miss my Ireland. My own Irishness. The one made by British streets and British cities. The one said in a British accent. I miss those redbrick streets and those back-street pubs. I miss those dirty old football grounds that have all been replaced by what look like supermarket extensions. I miss the pubs on a Friday night in a British city where all the customers spoke with local British accents, had spent the day working in British cities doing the same things as everyone else, but who still congregated together at night in the same places as other people who shared one thing with them that the rest of the city didn't. They had been brought up in an Irish family. They had an Irish mom and dad.

When we were kids growing up and we came back to Ireland for the summer holidays, our parents always called it going 'home'. Now that in itself has quite a psychological effect on a child. The idea that somewhere else is home is a pretty profound one. It is no wonder then that there is some kind of conflict at the heart of our Irishness. Even then we would have known that our cousins in Ireland thought of us as the English cousins and yet our parents said we were going home. How could we be going home if when we got there we were foreigners? How could our Irishness define us in Britain and our perceived Englishness define us in Ireland?

So when someone like me, someone like that, brought up in that Ireland in Britain, that Ireland abroad, comes to live in Ireland, a whole flock of conflicting identities comes too. And after eleven years, when most of them have settled down and there is a kind of psychological peace, the oddest thing starts to happen here amongst the rolling hills and the dreamscapes of rural Ireland. You find that, more than anything, one quiet Sunday afternoon you want to walk down that redbrick British street in that British city, listening to the traffic and the noises of the place and walk into an old-fashioned, back-street city pub and order a pint and listen to the local city accents around you and recognise the Irish faces and take a sip and think, ah, I'm home.

THAT SILENT STONE

Louise Lyons

The Old Hag of Beara is a lump of rock overlooking Caulagh Bay. She's not that big – maybe about four feet high, and three feet long and two feet wide. With a pointy top. Her surface isn't smooth at all, but jagged and ridgy and full of cracks. This stone holds the secrets of the souls of countless pilgrims. And in her cracks their offerings. Coins, hairslides, balls of silver paper. Pebbles, rags, a silk hanky. A lump of coal, a little bottle of perfume. And notes.

Loads and loads of notes. Faded, folded, yellowing pieces of paper that must have got wet and dried out over and over again. All stuffed into the cracks or weighed down with stones. What did they wish for, these nameless, faceless people who travelled the back road, came through the little gate and crossed the steep field that runs down to the sea? Was it love, or health, or wealth? What troubled them?

Was it a sick child, a broken heart, an ailing cow? Was it loneliness for family in far-off places? Was it uncertainty about a planning application? Was it a simple wish that the sun would shine on their wedding day?

Maybe not all the offerings are in hope. Maybe some are in thanksgiving. Maybe the shiny 20 cent was left by the girl who waited for the guy with the blue eyes to phone her. And he did! Maybe the big black bead was left by the woman who prayed her husband would get through his operation. And he did! Maybe that rusty nail was left by the lad who hoped the uncle would leave him the farm. And he did! We'll never know. For the silent stone holds her secrets.

The Old Hag of Beara is just off the back road from Eyries to Ardgroom. It's a hilly road. A narrow, twisty road. A magical road. The best way to travel it is by bike. There's nothing like whizzing along between ditches bursting with blood-red fuchsia, and the pointy leaves of montbretia promising their fiery blooms to come. Beara in June is grand. Everything is new and fresh and full of hope. Beara by bike in June is special. What a way to shake off the woes of winter, cast away the cobwebs of life and lose yourself in its magic.

Beara is full of surprises around every corner. There's the petrol station in Ardgroom with great coffee and loads of space outside for the bikes. And Mrs Murphy's post office in Urhan where you can buy just about everything: cooked ham, hardboiled sweets, woolly socks. Whatever you need is there. And no matter how tired you are after the bike, the dance in the pub in Eyries on Sunday night will revive you. Locals, tourists, blow-ins for the weekend like ourselves, all waltzing, jiving, military two-stepping together, as the sun sets out at sea.

There's something about Beara by bike. In June. With life bursting out all over the place and magic in the air. It's great for the spirit. It's great for the psyche. It's great for the soul. Beara. Mystical Beara. And her Old Hag.

What are your plans for this June weekend? Maybe you too will cycle the byways of Beara and feel the wind in your ears and the sun on your back. Maybe you will open that gate and cross the sloping field where the Old Hag sits mute, watching eternally over land and sea. And tell her your story. And walk around her three times. And leave *your* offering on her ancient flank.

Like the thousands who came before you, and the thousands who will come after.

That lump of rock has heard the woes and worries of generations of passers-by. She's waiting there for you, quietly and calmly, waiting to unburden you. And your story will be safe with the Old Hag of Beara, for that silent stone holds her secrets.

JULY

GALILEO: THE YEAR OF ASTRONOMY

Éamonn Ó hUallacháin

On a recent visit to majestic, glorious Florence, we walked down along the Arno River, across the lively Piazza Santa Croce and into the vast and magnificent interior of the Franciscan Church of the same name. Along the walls of the nave are the tombs of the greats who flourished in the rich cultural life of Florence: Michelangelo, Machiavelli, Dante, Galileo. Galileo's tomb depicts the great scientist with a telescope in his right hand and his left hand resting on a globe of our planet, testimony to the mind-blowing discoveries that he made about our galaxy and universe. On each side of him stand the muses of Geometry and Astronomy, whose truths he endeavoured to honour throughout his seventy-seven years.

In the summer of 1609, exactly 400 years ago this July, Galileo heard rumours about a new instrument from Holland that could enable you 'see faraway objects as though nearby'. He immediately went to work on replicating this device and later that year he demonstrated his first tele-scope to the leaders of Venice from the top of their tallest bell-tower. All were utterly amazed at the eight-fold magnification of everything. Ships out at sea, way beyond the lagoon, were clearly visible long before they came into harbour. It is due to his efforts that summer that the United Nations have made this year, 2009, International Year of Astronomy and thousands of events throughout the world will keep alive the memory of the courageous seeker of truth from Tuscany.

And he certainly needed to be brave to express what he did in those less enlightened days. With his observations of the planets in particular, he quickly realised that this Earth was not the centre of the universe as was believed by people at the time, in that self-important way that is our wont.

He confirmed and popularised what a few others before him had suspected: that our planet was but a relatively small, circular object flying around the sun at 1,000 miles a minute. This idea flew in the face of common sense that clearly sees the sun rising and setting, it flew in the face of the accepted wisdom going back to Aristotle, and, more dangerously still, it went against the 'divinely inspired' Bible. Did it not say in the Book of Joshua that 'the sun stood still'? If it 'stood still', it must previously have been moving. *Quod erat demonstrandum*, no further argument or doubt about it.

For Galileo, all hell broke loose, emanating mainly from Pope Urban and the authorities in the Church of Rome, and troubles by the score poured down upon him. His books were banned and remained so for 200 years. He was sentenced to jail in a Roman dungeon for an indefinite period and eventually kept under house arrest until he died in 1642. He had been a university professor but was now forbidden to teach or discuss his ideas with anybody, even in the privacy of his own home. He had chosen the heavens before Heaven and thus he had to be punished as a heretic.

His greatest source of consolation and strength in those most difficult days was his oldest daughter Virginia. As a young girl she had become a Poor Clare nun, taking the name 'Maria Celeste' in recognition of her father's fascination with the stars. She wrote to him constantly, was always solicitous for his health, encouraged him to battle on: 'Guard your good spirits and don't jeopardise your health with excessive worry.' And when part of his punishment was to recite the Psalms once a week for three years, she offered to do that penance for him. 'Father,' she wrote, 'I have begun to fulfil that requirement with great zest, to relieve you of this care.'

When she died at the young age of thirty-three, he was laid low with an overwhelming grief. He wrote to a friend: 'With all my mourning, a perpetual sleeplessness leaves me in a state of fear.' He himself died just a few short years after his daughter, blind, fevered, arthritic and virtually alone. A contemporary wrote prophetically of his passing: 'The sublimity of intellect of that divine man will one day come to be known more widely and will serve all posterity as a guide in the search of truth.'

And guide he has undoubtedly been. He saw further into space than any human being before him had ever seen. He saw more clearly than anyone had ever done before, the mountains of the Moon, the rings of Saturn, the moons of Jupiter, and Venus 'the mother of lovers, waxing and waning like the Moon', as he eloquently described it himself. And if thousands, all around this country and throughout the world, have in recent months enjoyed these wonders of the night sky, it is thanks to Galileo's pioneering work and courage. Thanks to him also, it is now impossible for us to look again on ourselves and our Earth as the centre of the universe. We are only a medium-sized planet, orbiting around an average star in the outer suburbs of an ordinary galaxy, which is itself only one of a million, million galaxies in the universe. Yet in our arrogance we had claimed that this vast construction existed simply for our sakes, and we condemned to death and isolation those who thought otherwise.

But, as we saw, he paid dearly for his insights. Even in death he was denied the simplest of respect. He had hoped to be buried next to his father in the main Basilica of Santa Croce, but Pope Urban prohibited this wish and made it clear that any fuss over the dead body of Galileo would be deemed an offence against papal authority. He was put in an unmarked grave near the novices' chapel and there he remained, hidden away for ninety-five years, until a small group of Florentines decided that he deserved a more worthy burial place. Permission was obtained and, late one night, when the Basilica was closed, they opened the grave of Galileo Galilei. To their amazement it contained within it not one but two bodies; one was, as they expected, that of an old man, but the second was a young woman – the loving daughter who had been his most loyal supporter during his life. Both were removed with dignity and respect to the newly built monument, and there she has remained by his side ever since, unbeknownst to the visiting throngs, but surely not to the teeming heavens above.

WILLIAM LOBB:
MESSENGER OF THE BIG TREE

Megan O'Beirne

'The object of the journey is to collect a quantity of seeds of a plant ... this is the object, do not dissipate time, energy or money on anything else.' Such were the uncompromising demands made by the successful Victorian nurseryman James Veitch of one of his young gardeners before he embarked on a plant-hunting expedition to China.

In those times there was intense competition among nurseries for plant novelties from the prospering colonies. Into this race James Veitch and Sons plunged with urgency and determination. However, rather than depend on missionaries and diplomats to source new and exotic plants from abroad, Veitch calculated that it would pay in prestige and plants to send out his own collector.

Furthermore, Sir William Jackson Hooker, director of Kew Gardens, would identify the new plants and subsequently describe them in the prestigious *Botanical Magazine*. Immediately, updated listings would appear in his own catalogues to tempt his wealthy land-owning clients.

William Lobb was the first to be entrusted with a plant-hunting mission by the Veitch nurseries, and for fourteen years in the continent of America he didn't spare himself in their service. Though not formally trained, he had a vast botanical knowledge and a thirst for adventure. These qualities, plus his diligence and trustworthiness, made him the ideal plant-hunter. The dizzily angled verticals of his handwriting in his only extant letter to his employer illustrate his earnest, even dogged, sense of purpose. The flourish of the signature, too, suggests the extravagance of the risk-taker.

Conditions during such trips, which usually lasted three years, tested the mental and physical mettle of the plant-hunters. They worked in extremely isolated places, climbed mountains often as high as 7,000 feet, in severe weather conditions, were exposed to diseases such as the plague and dysentery and had to cope with the anti-foreign feeling and suspicion resulting from colonial activity.

Veitch's faith in William Lobb was rewarded by the quality of his work, illustrated by the only other extant document of his, dated July 1843. It is a list of 138 plant specimens from South America which he sent by ship to Veitch. Against the name of each specimen, information is given on the size of the plant, the locality, the colour and elevation at which it was found. This meticulously tabulated document is a model of its kind. Such was Lobb's dedication to duty that not even the contagious excitement of the gold rush in San Francisco distracted his gaze from the task at hand. While countless ships lay at anchor in the bay, most abandoned by their prospecting crew, Lobb continued his gruelling prospecting for plants.

Lobb's loyalty to Veitch embroiled him in controversy in the notorious Big Tree incident. Normally secretive in their quest for novelties, plant-hunters and botanical scientists were sometimes prompted by a certain zeal to share information. Dr Albert Kellogg, an American botanist, naively, in hindsight, showed Lobb specimens of the Big Tree in the Californian Academy of Sciences. Kellogg had patriotically named it the Washington Cedar before he actually ever saw the tree. While he and fellow American botanists dithered over the taxonomic position of the tree among the conifers, Lobb, with a lynx-like instinct for a sensational and lucrative find, hurried to the Calaveras Grove, where the big tree had first been sighted.

He collected seeds and living material, allegedly from a fallen specimen of the giant tree, and immediately hightailed it to England. There, Professor John Lindley of the University of London published the description of *Wellingtonia Gigantea* in the *Gardeners' Chronicle*, thereby honouring the British war hero. Soon after, the biggest tree known to man had its commercial launch, a scoop attributable to Lobb's loyalty to his employer and to the quality of his herbarium specimens.

Unsurprisingly, the American botanists, who reasonably claimed first discovery of the tree, were incensed but fumed to no avail. The ensuing hostility across the Atlantic lasted for decades, with mutterings of the almost criminal nature of Lobb's actions. It is little wonder that the episode earned Lobb the sobriquet 'Messenger of the Big Tree'. Did this make Lobb *persona non grata* in San Francisco? Given his sad and friendless death and burial in the public plot there some years later, it is a reasonable surmise.

In 1853 the big tree was definitively named *Sequoiadendron* – by an American!

DROWNED WORLDS

Gemma Tipton

In Venice, when the floods are coming, sirens sound across the city. These are followed by musical notes that let the initiated know what heights (or should that be depths?) of water to expect. The floods in Venice, known there as *acqua alta*, don't sweep in from the sea, or surge across burst river banks; instead they bubble up, at first almost imperceptibly, through the stone flags of the pavements. While tourists scurry for the raised walkways, or tie themselves into the ludicrous-looking temporary wellies, which suddenly appear for sale, the locals are better prepared. You'll see handsome men wearing suits from the waist up, and waders from the belt down. Glamorous women stand in their wet shops, selling jewellery and Murano glass, and managing to make their rubber boots look like the most desirable of accessories.

Splashing through the waters in my own temporary wellies, I experience a strange sort of pre-nostalgia, for although Venice floats on, there is a sense that all this stone, and the glittering mix of shadows and light, can't survive the force of the waters forever, so I wade on, missing what hasn't yet gone.

If Venice does one day disappear, it won't be alone – instead it will become one of the untold numbers of buildings, towns and even cities that lie under the waters that cover 70 per cent of the earth. And even though floods themselves are deeply unpleasant catastrophes for anyone who has experienced them (especially if sewage is involved), I find I'm drawn to the idea of drowned cities, drowned worlds.

Some are fictional – like that described in J. G. Ballard's haunting novel, *The Drowned World*, written presciently in the 1960s and set in a future where an overheating planet has seen rising sea levels and the flooding of the world's great cities, and where the lagoons that cover London are home to lush tropical flora and exotic fauna.

Others are mythological, like the lost island of Atlantis, whose location has been claimed all over the globe, including Antarctica, the Bermuda Triangle, and, yes, even off the coast of Ireland. Some are awesomely real – like the city of Alexander the Great, off the coast of Alexandria, believed to have been submerged by a tidal wave over 1,600 years ago. Granite columns, a sphinx and the remains of a palace lie beneath the sea. Off the coast of Jamaica – and more biblically perhaps – the remains of what was once called 'the world's wickedest city' lie, like a warning and a punishment. Port Royal, Jamaica, once a haven for pirates, privateers and prostitutes, collapsed into the sea after an earthquake in the seventeenth century. Part turned into rubble, but a whole section of the city collapsed vertically, and is remarkably preserved.

There are also submerged cities and temples off the coast of Turkey, Peru, Japan, Greece and Cuba, now lived in by fish and visited only by intrepid divers. We are said to have our own drowned villages, under the waters of Lough Neagh and Lough Ree, and in England and Wales a number were more recently submerged by dam- and reservoir-building projects.

Places like Derwent and Ashopton, Llanwddyn and Mardale were lost, and their histories slid into legends of still-tolling bells and haunting wisps of smoke coming from long submerged chimneys. Dry summers and droughts occasionally bring their watery walls to the surface, although, even in the wettest of times, their lure is so compelling that at Derwent they went back in 1959 and destroyed the church spire, to discourage people from trying to peer too deeply at what lies beneath.

I think one of the reasons these sites are so beguiling is that they are so utterly lost and also so purposeless. Everything that they were meant for has been taken away. In the case of other drowned things, like warships and fighter planes – those things that were built to kill – there's a restfulness to the idea of their lying at peace below the sea. And listening to divers describing things that I, as a non-diver, will never experience; or seeing underwater photographs, they seem a little like those tiny creatures preserved in amber, dimly visible, not gone, but just tantalisingly out of reach – like those bits of dreams you wake up with, or memories evoked by a scent or a taste.

The oxygen that sustains our lives on dry land slowly destroys artefacts – but not underwater. Underwater, everything is preserved, and the mud at the sea or water bed can be the most preservative of all. When, in Venice, the Campanile at the entrance to St Mark's Square collapsed in 1902, they discovered that the wooden foundations, driven into the mud of the lagoon, were still in near-perfect condition, one thousand years later. We live in an uneasy compromise with water. All these places were once people's homes, and all have their histories of catastrophe, but these drowned worlds are still haunting, poetic, compelling – until it may happen to us.

ALEXANDER SELKIRK

Vona Groarke

It begins with salt water. His younger brother has, for a good trick, filled his cup with it. There are words and there is a fight that spills over into the street: the town elders of Fife judge that he must stand in church for six Sundays to be lectured on his temper by the clergy. He obeys, but the day after his punishment expires he runs away to sea. He is nineteen. It is 1695.

Here he is, nine years later, arguing with his ship's captain off the coast of Chile. The ship, he says, is unseaworthy: they must put ashore and mend it or they will all be drowned. The captain does not lightly heed advice from subordinates. His first mate is stubborn, hot-headed: he says he'll not sail another day on such a dangerous ship. To oblige him, his captain has him taken to the nearest land, an uninhabited island called Juan Fernández. It is 1704.

Here he is, Alexander Selkirk, being rowed ashore with a sea-chest packed with the bits and pieces granted to him from the ship. He has a firelock rifle, bullets and gunpowder, a kettle, a cup, a hatchet, a knife, a Bible, some tobacco, a flask of rum. And under them, secretly, are the tools of his navigational trade he has filched from on board. And here he is, left alone on the beach, wondering what dividers or compass will spirit him to Valparaiso, the nearest inhabited land to him, 600 miles to the north. He has changed his mind: he is calling the rowboat to turn back for him. He is shouting an apology, but either they hear and ignore him or his words are scattered like spindrift by the wind.

Here he is, sleeping his first night on the beach, hoping against hope to be rescued, waking to spy his familiar world sailing further and further away.

He keeps a fire on the go on the beach in the hopes of attracting help. It dawns on him that he will not be rescued, at least not in the short term. He begins to explore his island and discovers fresh water, wild goats, legions of wild cats and rats, and plum trees planted, improbably, by temporary Spanish settlers many years before. He knows that he will live, at least, that he has at his disposal the means to survive.

He sets about filling his days. There is food to be organised and kindling to be gathered. He gets into the habit of maiming the legs of young goats with his knife so they wouldn't out-run him later on when he might be ailing himself.

He builds himself a home; a hut made from pimento trees and lined inside with goatskins. Rats are a bother: they come at him while he's sleeping and nibble on his feet and clothes. He learns to attract the wild cats with meat from goats he's killed, and they clear the rats away. He makes clothes for himself of goatskins stitched with a nail and wool thread he pulls from the pair of socks he wore when he put ashore.

He cuts his name into the bark of trees. He tries to keep count of the passing days. And then there are the nights: fifteen hundred of them to be filled howsoever he might. He has one book, his Bible. No doubt, he has his dreams.

Later he will say that he'd been in the habit of dancing around the fire at night with his tamed cats and his wild goats. He will call it 'company'.

At some stage, he stops talking. There is no one to talk to, and his cats and goats he can communicate with without recourse to words. When he is eventually rescued, Captain Rogers of *The Duke* will write that Selkirk has lost the power of language but seems to have retained his mind.

He returns to Fife to visit his family, bringing with him his sea-chest and the cup made from a coconut that he had drunk from on the island. It is 1712. He stays with them for nine months only and then he is off seafaring again. In 1720, he dies of fever off the coast of Africa. He is buried at sea. It began and ended with salt water. Salt water and words.

We could leave him there in Africa, but we can get him a bit closer to home – all the way, in fact, to Inniskeen Road in land-locked Monaghan, where he fetched up as the King of Loneliness in Patrick Kavanagh's poem, 'Inniskeen Road: July Evening'. It is July and there's a dance in Billy Brennan's barn which the poet foregoes to write a sonnet about the curse of isolation.

Perhaps it's a fine enough line after all between Juan Fernández and Inniskeen; between the writing of sonnets and the two-step of a wild-haired man with his half-tamed goats, keeping loneliness at bay. As fine a line, perhaps, as the letter 'l' at the heart of the word 'loneliness' or at the centre of this poem's last word that returns us to the touchstone facts of the real, known world.

Oh, Alexander Selkirk knew the plight
Of being king and government and nation.
A road, a mile of kingdom, I am king
Of banks and stones and every blooming thing.

SACRED SPACE

Mary O'Malley

Young death is a savage thing, like an act of war. The mind, rightly, refuses at first to accept it.

A year and a half ago, there was a car accident – doubtless one of many that night – in the city of Chicago. Over several days, a thread slowly and inevitably pulled from a tapestry, tearing my world, and the world of my family. Time began to behave erratically and people repeated phrases as if words might somehow help.

Solvitur ambulando, walking solves it, is one of the few dictums I have generally found to be true. This time walking will not solve it, but walking is all I can do.

I walk the town and, tired, find myself in Middle Street.

The Augustinian Church is quiet. A man sits on a chair. A woman prays, seeming agitated. This is no Saint-Sulpice, with its dark lowering Delacroix painting of a desperate Jacob wrestling with the angel, whose face is that of someone everyone would love, if only they could meet him. This is neither Old Testament nor enslavement to the functional. White statues, white altar, white faces of the little corner angel shaped like a capricious heart. This is sacred space, the trick of stone and geometry made light, drawing the eye upwards, through the arches poised elegantly along both sides, echoed in the high windows where the late evening is lined up, like so many packets of blue.

I go to the small side chapel. Our Lady of Good Counsel, drawn by a glint of gold, needing the lustre of those remnants from an older church. I miss the candles, but I make my offering and make do with their poor electric shadows.

This alchemy is not, of course, purely architectural, but this is what Philip Larkin calls 'a serious house on serious earth' in his poem about an unbeliever's compulsion to seek out churches. Reading it brings a shock of recognition. The need for churches has not left us with the departure of both faith and superstition. They were where people congregated, where communities worshipped and wept, where some still do.

They are what all good civic space should be – for everyone, of any creed and none. This church stands the test of time. Here, the tabernacle, the nave and the apse allow the idea of values beyond concrete. They legislate for the sacramental. They provide little chapels of adoration, nooks and crannies of comfort in an age of nihilism and brutalist design.

Four men, one of whom may be a priest, enter and recite a short liturgy, then leave. Paul Walsh's stained glass windows, situated behind the altars and in the side chapels, fill with the cold intense light of approaching night. They have a wintery beauty, in this stark hour. Glass is my favourite medium, the only art I saw as a child. I wait as the light drains from the glass, keeping as best I can a silent vigil with my sister in Chicago.

I am grateful for this building's vast spaces, towards the end of a hard, bright day. The streets are streaked with light as I make my way back across the river, to wait.

So much of our lives are lived Elsewhere. In Boston and Chicago and San Francisco, in Paris and Beijing. We inhabit them in our imagination, whenever our loved ones come to mind. Or if we have visited, we can see the kitchen, the street, smell the asphalt.

Papers are written and conferences held on concepts such as 'place', but when we hear 'they are bringing him home' – hear it with a physical relief – each knows the exact road we will all travel, through the Twelve Bens, past which lakes, where the land will open out into the sea. We know where that journey will begin, and where, exactly, it ends. And hope that there is peace there.

THE CHARMER

Mariad Whisker

I first fell for Dominick Dunne, the writer, back in 1985. I was a bit of a literary philistine, with my tastes leaning towards true-crime magazines and the like. A friend recommended *The Two Mrs. Grenvilles* – an account of an American high-society murder, fictionalised by Dominick Dunne. I read it in one sitting and was hooked instantly on his work. This was long before the eyes of America became glued to his constant presence on CourtTV – the channel that televises criminal trials and is notorious for Dunne's running commentary on the O. J. Simpson murder case.

I've entertained a whole string of literary crushes since then, from Raymond Carver to Truman Capote to Richard Ford, but Dominick Dunne has a special place because he only took up writing after he turned fifty. I can relate to that. I also like that his novels tend to be thinly veiled gawks into other people's chaos. Rubber-necking at its purest – it appeals to my baser reading instincts.

Dunne's writing career had its roots in personal tragedy: the death of his only daughter, Dominique, murdered by her boyfriend. He attended her killer's trial and, at the urging of the editor of *Vanity Fair*, wrote an account of the experience. That article kick-started his career in journalism. Over the years, his regular contributions of voyeuristic anecdotes, trial observations and social diatribes added hundreds of column inches to my bedside tower of *Vanity Fair* magazines.

I would have given anything to be a guest at his table, or at least a fly on his wall.

I came close to that in 2008 – while having afternoon tea at Claridge's Hotel. Not a regular habit, I hasten to add. I was in London on business and had some time to kill. As I mooched around Oxford Street, I was reminded of my student days in the West End. On work experience in the rag trade, I was always penniless but perpetually in awe of the fashionable swells I would see from the top deck of the bus, sweeping in through the doors of those fancy hotels.

So, when I found myself outside one of them, Claridge's, I thought – why not?

I was shown to a small table in the centre of the art-deco lounge and served, not only with the menu, but with a fresh copy of the *Herald Tribune*. The table afforded me an enviable view of my surroundings and I was soon far too busy checking them out to concentrate on reading.

Beyond the lounge, across the black-and-white chequered foyer, I noticed a gentleman sitting at another small table. He was wearing tasselled loafers and had silver hair, but the rest of him was hidden behind his newspaper. I wondered why he chose not to sit by the cosy fire.

It soon became obvious. Discreetly placed as it was, his armchair offered a bird's-eye view of anyone entering or leaving the foyer. He was gawking – just like me, dipping his newspaper now and then, not to miss anything. Peeking over my own newspaper, I glimpsed his face. Round tortoise-shell spectacles. Very distinctive. Very familiar.

It was Dominick Dunne. Not ten yards away. All by himself. I was rooted to my chair, china tea cup fixed in mid-air. But not for long. I stood up, brushed the shortcake crumbs from my skirt, and strode off in his direction. Not of my own accord though. Approaching strangers is as foreign a habit to me as having afternoon tea in Claridge's. Nevertheless, propelled by this force beyond my control, I found myself in front of the man himself. I was vaguely aware of the ever-watchful eye of the concierge – on full alert.

'Mr Dunne, I presume?'

He lowered his newspaper and looked up. Then he cocked his head a little to one side and gave me a wonderful smile.

'And you are?' he asked.

'I'm a big fan,' I said.

I know we talked for quite some time, because my peppermint tea was cold when I returned to my table. I remember that he had liver spots on his forehead and behind the trademark glasses, his eyes were rheumy.

He told me that he came to London often and that he was a big fan too – of Claridge's. He said it was the perfect hotel for people-watching. He said its charm was legendary.

I was glad I was so uncharacteristically forward, for he died a short time later.

Now I can say his charm was legendary also.

GROOME'S HOTEL: WHERE POLITICS NEARLY MET THEATRE

Emer O'Kelly

There was a disco in Dublin in the 1970s called Zhivago's with the sub-
title 'where love stories begin', with little strip ads on the buses trumpet-
ing the slogan. Nobody at the time seemed to think that a name like that
would suggest that love stories beginning there were liable to be fairly
doomed, given what happened Pasternak's original lovers. But there were
other places, less ostensibly glamorous and trendy, where love stories definitely did begin. One of them was Groome's Hotel on Cavendish Row,
right opposite the Gate Theatre. Theatrical lovers met there, and you
could trace the rise and fall of relationships as ardent glances and wandering hands at three in the morning were replaced after months, or
sometimes, more hopefully, after a couple of years, by studied indifference and turned backs. The breakdown of a romance didn't mean that
one of the parties would desert Groome's: there was nowhere else to go
if you were 'a theatrical' who had to do your drinking after the curtain
came down. Not merely were licence extensions rare, and granted only
for individual events, nightclubs were an exotic new breed of venue, and
aimed at and limited to a clientele of the young intent on wrecking their
eardrums to the insistent disco beat. Groome's was for conversation.
Sometimes it was argumentative conversation; there was the occasional
fight, but even fights in those days were a more innocent affair than they
are now. Music was limited to the odd semi-sober regular tinkling on the
ancient piano.

Nor was Groome's Hotel frequented only by members of the theatre.

Joe Groome, who owned it with his wife Patty, was a stalwart official and supporter of the Fianna Fáil party, and half the cabinet could sometimes be found in his establishment. But there was no mixing of the two professions: the politicians gathered in the front bar, the actors in the back. The drinks were dispensed (literally) through a hatch, presumably in nodding deference to the hour that was in it. I don't think Groome's was ever raided in the long years it operated. The late Brian Lenihan was a frequent genial presence, and I remember talking to him about having had my name taken. I had been clocked driving at 36 miles an hour in a 30-mile limit, and warned there might be a summons. It was amazing that I had even reached such an exotic speed, since 'car' was a fairly loose description of the vehicle I possessed at the age of twenty-two. There were eight previous owners listed in the log book; I can't remember the age of the little sewing machine on wheels, but it was mine, all mine. Horrified at my fall from driving grace, I was boring the eminent minister when he whipped out a notebook, demanded the details, noted them, and told me not to worry. Those were the days when things were 'no problem' in the minister's catchphrase. Actually, it made me feel worse: I'd been reared to take my medicine for wrongdoing. Whether he acted on it, or I was merely deemed by the vigilant garda to be not worth taking trouble over, nothing further happened.

Groome's was a far cry from that even earlier era so naughtily caught by the painter Muriel Brandt in her portrait (now hanging in the Gate Theatre bar) of Hilton Edwards and Micheál Mac Liammóir in full conversational cry in Jammet's restaurant, in the presence of Christine, Lady Longford. That is very definitely a *recherche* in the best sense of café society, limited in Dublin, but still there if you looked for it. The great days of Groome's came later, and were more a haunt for midnight's children. They were best summed up by the languidly mordant Patrick Bedford when Patty Groome finally decided to call it a day. Her faithful clientele decided to make a presentation to her in memory of their long years of illicit consumption on her premises. The great and the good were approached, as were even the lowly. And it was Paddy, among the greatest of them all, who raised one of his always expressive eyebrows so high it almost disappeared into his still luxuriant hair: 'A present?' he inhaled, rather in the manner of Dame Edith Evans as Lady Bracknell. 'A present for Patty?' Eloquent pause, to allow for the pained quivering of closed eyelids. 'Ye gods, she's had me wages for thirty years. What more does she want? Blood?' Suffice it to say, having had his moment, like so many of the devotees of Groome's, the wonderful Paddy paid up.

MATTY MCGOONA

John MacKenna

It was a warm summer afternoon in 1980 and I took the road from Slane, back towards Navan, leaving behind the birthplace of Francis Ledwidge; leaving his nephew, Joe; leaving the cowshed with its early Ledwidge doggerel on the whitewashed wall; leaving the Cunningham Arms where Ledwidge had danced and chatted; leaving the shadow of Slane Castle where he had discussed his poems with Lord Dunsany.

A couple of miles along the road I swung onto a narrow lane in the townland of Donoghmore and drove slowly beneath the overhanging bushes, briars knocking on the car doors. At the top of the lane I found the house I was looking for and the woman I wanted to meet: Winnie McGoona, sister of Matty McGoona, Francis Ledwidge's best friend.

Winnie's sight was failing, but she still lived in the family home and she welcomed me with a smile and a promise of tea and homemade bread. But first, she said, we'd walk in her garden, in the shadow of the orchard about which Ledwidge had written and dreamed during his time at the front during the Great War.

Later, as the sun began to slip down the back of the sky, we went inside the house and she made tea, cut the bread and urged me to eat up. And she chatted about 'Frank' and what he was like and how he and Matty had been inseparable.

'More like brothers than friends,' she said. And then she paused. 'Or maybe more like friends than brothers.'

While she poured the tea, I listened to the ticking clock, the singing birds outside and I listened most particularly for some echo of the poet's voice.

'Frank used to sit on that form that you're sitting on now,' Winnie laughed, as if she had read my mind. 'That was his chair. He'd settle himself in there of a wet night and he'd be hard put to move out of it into the rain and the miles home.'

I remained silent, overpowered by the fact that I was sitting on the seat Frank Ledwidge had sat on, listening to a woman he had often listened to, talking about a man who was the angel on his shoulder for much of his short life.

To say Frank and Matty were best friends is like saying Lennon and McCartney dabbled in songwriting – it does no justice to how things truly were. Frank and Matty played football together, acted together, cycled together, sat in McGoona's orchard together watching the drunken bees fall from the plum trees, they discussed the vagaries of Ledwidge's relationship with Ellie Vaughey and it was Matty who reassured Frank when the affair crumbled and she started going out with John O'Neill – the man she would marry.

Matty was one of the first to learn that Frank had decided to join the British Army – partly as a response to a broken heart and partly because, as he said himself, he 'wouldn't have it said of us that we stood by and did nothing while others fought for the rights of small nations'.

And Matty it was, according to his sister Winnie, who was one of the first people to learn of what had happened to Frank Ledwidge at the front. Not that he knew at the time but, in the days afterwards Matty would realise that he should not have seen what he saw in Navan in the late hours of 31 July 1917.

In those days, Matty was working as a printer in the town and Frank was close to the front line of battle.

On that summer evening, as Matty was locking up at the print works, he saw Frank passing further up the street. He called Ledwidge's name but his friend kept walking. Presuming Frank to be home on leave and assuming he hadn't heard his call, Matty went about his business, cycling back home and only commenting on the fact of Ledwidge's return the following morning over breakfast.

'He said he'd seen Frank, that he must be home on leave,' Winnie told me. 'He said he must cycle over and see him. He was all excited to think Frank was back again, that they could catch up on all the news about everything that had been happening, here and in the war.'

But, as Matty would soon discover, whatever he had seen on that street in Navan it should not have been his friend Frank Ledwidge or, if it was – and Matty was adamant that he had seen Frank though he would never comfortably discuss it afterwards – then it was a ghost soldier, for by then Frank Ledwidge was dead, killed by a stray shell while he worked on building a road at Ypres.

'Do you believe he saw Frank?' I asked Winnie.

'I do, why wouldn't he? Weren't they as close as brothers, closer even.'

Why wouldn't he indeed? If anyone should see him it was Matty McGoona.

And why, in his hour of greatest need, wouldn't Frank come looking for the man whose company he had always sought in times of happiness and times of sadness, the person in whom he confided; the person to whom he wrote of his longing to be back on the bog at Wilkinstown, listening to the cuckoo, smelling the bluebells; the man who was his brother and his friend – the closest comrade he had ever found.

EFFIN' SONGS

Brendan Graham

'How did you write the effin' song?' the man in the small, country-town supermarket demanded more than asked.

He had cornered me between the Flahavan's Oats and the Jacob's Fig Rolls.

'Are you goin' to tell me – how did you write the effin' song?' as if there was only the one 'effin' song' I had ever written.

'Which one?' I countered, protective of my poor level of output.

'You know effin' well which one. Sure didn't we see you on RTÉ walking the mountain road – and then you disappeared, and we didn't see you again, till you came out the far side . . . a million euro later!'

'I don't really know how I wrote it,' I answered.

'You know effin' well,' he said, and in disgust turned on his heel and walked out the door.

Mostly we songwriters don't. Or, should I say, we don't know how we write the effin' songs; those few, half-decent scratchings that catch the public ear. Mostly it is a fumbling for the light; a desperate hoping that 'something will happen'. It is an unbiddable thing.

To start out I need a geography of place; 'the room where you can do no wrong', as 'MacArthur Park' songwriter Jimmy Webb calls it.

For co-writing, ego must be left outside the door. The writing itself is a swinging pendulum – blind panic, even blinder optimism

Then there is scraping the meat off the bone: the losing of that utterly brilliant line you love, but of which they say in Nashville, 'That dog won't hunt.'

But all this is merely the bricks and mortar of songwriting. What we seek is to go beyond; into that twilight between self and other self where things happen, things which later you don't ever remember writing. Often the effin' songs live in that twilight place.

A day, a week, a month, a year later, you have what you think is a song.

Already you are seeing the 'pension-song' possibilities of your newest creation, but you have been here before. You think of the large sign over your London publisher's door: 'Don't Bore Us – Get to the Chorus!' Now you are afraid to leave 'the room where you can do no wrong'. However you know something is stirrin' when Walmart want to use your wonderful creation as the song in a 'singing flower'!

Of course if your song is parodied then you know it has truly 'arrived'.

I never knew I had written a song called 'Salute to the Underwired Bra' until American comedienne Anita Renfroe alerted me with lines that went:

'You Raise Me Up … and make my molehills mountains,

You Raise Me Up … and change my Bs to Cs...'

You get the idea: it left my own lyrics looking rather tired; needing a lift.

Sometimes a song comes where you know it is destined for no such high calling as Walmart or in praise of underwire, where the song's only impulse is to answer its own call.

Such a song was 'Crucán na bPáiste'.

'Crucán na bPáiste' ('The Burial Place of the Children') sits atop *Bóithrín a' tSléibhe*, the mountain pass road between Finny and Maamtrasna. High, lonesome, looking down on Loughnafooey and Lough Mask, it is a place above the world – hung between Heaven and Earth.

Here lies the graves of unbaptised children from other, darker days. Here there are no names on tombstones. Bare boulders mark the final resting spot of each holy innocent.

I have always been drawn to this place of unparalleled beauty filled as it also is with an emptying *uaigneas*.

Now 'Crucán na bPáiste' had become a claw in my gut, and my pilgrimage. Over many months it inched out in me its cry – *focal* by *focal*, line by line – until I was set free and it had found its epiphany.

On the journey there, I had learned a valuable lesson: to keep out of the way; to let the song write itself.

This, I suppose, is the real answer to the question with which we started. The truly special songs write us, *we* don't write them; we don't find them, *they* find us.

How else is it explained? How a song can seep out of the wilderness, out of rocks and streams and the deep pools, out of its own dark history; and how a remote place in the Mayo mountains can, of its own volition, send out its story to the world.

I am grateful to be merely the conduit, an accident of time and place through which something I don't fully understand is given voice and is heard.

AUGUST

THE LAMP

in memory of Rosaleen Melvin

Gerald Dawe

The scene would be something like this –
ducks in the yard gargle at a muddy pool,
a horse walking on its own rope
and, within, the pyramid of an open fire.

Would it be late evening, summer or autumn?
I cannot remember. Let's say, near spring.
You at any rate would be fixing the dinner
for the family and whoever else may call.

On the wall the gracious clock,
and hardy armchairs, a good deal table,
the practical accoutrements to cook and feed
circle the glimmering jug of spring water.

There would be brothers and sisters,
one already off in England, another to follow,
father and mother, and maybe a newspaper
headlines the latest political meeting.

The room would fill with darkness
until the lighting of the lamp.
It stands now on the fine ledge
of our living-room window rarely lit.

But the light of its globe shines
nevertheless, along with the dent
in its copper side where the Tans
burst in after some men on the run

and struck the lamp a blow.
When I married your daughter
it became your present
from an unforgettable past,

so fooster away there in the presses
and see what else you can find,
bring back to life the love
that was always on your mind.

SWIMMING

Julie Parsons

I'm standing at the edge of the swimming pool wearing my new black togs. I'm clutching my swimming hat and my brand-new goggles. It's a Tuesday evening in summer and I've come along to my first lesson in the improvers' class at a swanky gym and pool in Dublin 4. Suddenly I can't think what I'm doing here. A few days ago it seemed like a great idea. I was bringing Emily, my 4-year-old granddaughter, to her weekly lesson. And I noticed. The other swimmers. Grown-ups like me. Up and down, up and down, up and down: swimming lengths. Breast stroke, front crawl, even butterfly and backstroke. And I was suddenly overwhelmed with the notion that I, too, could do that. Of course I could swim. I'd grown up by the sea in New Zealand. I'd taught myself. I could do what might be called a variation on the theme of breast stroke. Head above the water, chin elongated, legs doing a passable imitation of a frog. But now watching these aquatic paragons it occurred to me that I could learn to do it properly. Head in the water instead of sticking out. Arms and legs moving together in perfect synchronisation. And, why not, the front crawl, the gold standard of swimming strokes? It had always been a mystery how you could keep your head down, keep your arms moving, keep breathing and not splutter, choke, stop and sink to the bottom. So, of course, what I needed were lessons. Just like Emily. And as I watched her brave little face, her oversized goggles giving her an Amelia Earhart look, her determination to make it across the pool, I resolved. I would join a class. I would be her swimming granny.

So here I am. I look around at the others and I realise I am years older than they are. I cast a surreptitious glance downwards over my body.

I look OK with my clothes on, but squished into my black lycra? I cringe. And grin feebly. My fellow students have put on their goggles. I fiddle with mine. Suddenly they seem much too small. And I can see nothing through the opaque lenses. I fumble down the steps and into the water. It's cold. I try to look calm. The girl standing next to me smiles.

'Your goggles,' she says. 'I think you need to take that bit of paper off them.'

'What?' I pull them over my head. There's a label of sorts stuck over each lens. I peel it off. Oh dear, this is bad.

Our teacher is called Marianna. She is South American with an enviable body. She refers to each length as a 'swimming pool'. We are expected to swim many swimming pools. I take a deep breath and lunge forward. 'Head down, head down,' she shouts. I keep my head down, and gingerly open my eyes. I can see. I breathe out. My breath becomes bubbles. I can breathe. I kick my legs behind me and move my arms in a circular motion.

'No, no, not that way,' I hear Marianna's voice faintly above me. She demonstrates. The breast stroke is an exercise in minimalism. Your arms move out only as wide as your shoulders. They never go behind your shoulders. As you bring them forward you scoop the water out like scooping flour out of a bowl. You breathe in as you lift yourself up. You breathe out as you sink back again. I gasp, I splutter, my heart pounds. But I understand. I may be years older than the others in the class, but age counts for something in the swimming pool. I am determined to do it.

And afterwards in the dressing room I feel so good. They say you can't teach an old dog new tricks. They also say you're never too old to learn. My skin tingles. My heart has settled down into a new rhythm. And as, weeks later, I watch the Olympic swimmers, I am as one with them. The underwater camera reveals their technique. They do the front crawl the same way I do. Head down, turn to the side of the extended arm. Lift your head every third stroke. Suck in air. Then head down again. I marvel at their skill and strength. The water binds us together. Water babies, water grannies. Together as we breathe and move and swim. And sometimes win.

READING THE RIVER

Michael Coady

In the lost world of my schooldays they taught me many things by heart, from Shakespeare, Wordsworth and Yeats to the Theorem of Pythagoras. Like most others, even by the end of primary school I knew many poems by heart, along with a wide repertoire of songs in English and Irish, and Gregorian chant in Latin. I'm grateful for such enduring cultural transmission, even if there was in my time a lack of continental languages and science, and a particular blank in the curriculum that I'd have to fill in for myself.

For all that they taught me in school, there was virtually nothing about the place in which I was born and actually living, and where, as things turned out, I would continue to live. Formal schooling didn't concern itself with what was local. The unexamined implication was that such little places as ours were of no significance. The poet Kavanagh would not have agreed.

Local in my case meant the lower Suir Valley, with the fabled *Sliabh na mBan* to my back, and across the river to the south, the Comeragh Mountains and their mysterious lakes left by the glaciers, only six or seven miles from the Main Street of our town, with its west gate and town clock tower, and the bronze salmon over that to oversee us all and show us which way the wind was blowing.

My place was and is the small town of Carrick-on-Suir, *Carraig na Siúire*, in the south-east of Tipperary and touching the borders of Waterford and south Kilkenny. We spoke of the familiar southern hinterland across the river as 'out in the County Waterford', implying some significant frontier otherness, though we too were part of the tribal territory of the *Déise*.

The heart and soul of my place was the river that gave the town identity and name. No one at school had ever pointed out that the river name, *Siúir*, meant sister, one of the three of Suir, Nore and Barrow, umbilically linked from the Silvermine and Slieve Bloom mountains. According to the ancient *Dinnseanchas*, all three rivers sprang up on the same night that Conn of the Hundred Battles, High King of Ireland, was born.

Those three riverine sisters diverge to find their individual life courses until, with a beautiful cyclical symmetry, at long and at last they meet again and become one at *cumar na dtrí n-uisce* in Waterford Harbour.

They didn't tell me at school that the town had grown where it is because that was as far as the upcoming tide reached on the Suir, and so was a significant point for navigation between Waterford City, downriver, and Clonmel, upriver. The tide was an abiding and recurrent transfiguration that brought the original settlement into being.

Twice with every global turn through light and dark that cosmic shift occurred; the river transformed by sun and moon before our eyes, flooding and ebbing again and again at the old stone bridge – that bridge itself the first above the estuary for centuries, and built before Columbus. Upstream landscape was pastoral, changing to estuarial immediately below the town.

As boy and man I'd learn to swim in that mature river and fish for eel and trout and salmon, and learn of floods and tides and drownings, of people and their destinies across the generations and the mist and flux of centuries. River skills and lore came from tradition bearers, men whose school and script had been the river. I learned to handle a river cot with pole and paddle, discovered I had ancestors who were boatmen, and found migration links with America and Newfoundland.

My first poem to be published by David Marcus was about refurbishing a boat, and when it appeared I had an encouraging note from Hubert Butler in Bennetsbridge, who didn't yet know me from Adam, but who took care to notice such things. I was a novice with the pen, but I was launched.

All rivers are one. If I'm blessed or lucky I may see the gleam of rising sun through the eye socket of the salmon over our town clock at the west gate, and know that time and tide attend upon us all, and bear us to the delta.

TWO WORDS

Mark Roper

Recently, I was asked what my favourite word was. My immediate thought was that I hadn't really got one – surely there are far too many to choose from. But, in time, I did come up with a couple of words I have long relished, both for their sound and their meaning. The two words are 'pond' and '*chelidonias*', *chelidonias* being a Greek word apparently meaning 'swallow-bearing wind'.

'Pond' is a pretty obvious word, but that's exactly what I like about it. It's a satisfying word to say, from the lip-opening 'p' to the tongue touching the roof of the mouth on the 'd'. There's a weight in the syllable, a gravity, a sense of something dropping down, dropping shut. Strictly, 'pond' means a fairly small body of water. But it carries the connotation of something manmade. The cognate word 'pool' suggests something more ethereal: you might expect a maiden or a hand clutching a sword to arise from a pool, which might well be a mist-covered pool. In a pond you'd be more likely to find broken glass, bits of concrete, a traffic cone. Industries have tailing ponds, to soak up wastes and poisons from their workings. Pond life is not pleasant. Where you might happily go to a swimming pool, you'd be less keen to go to a swimming pond. And where the English might be happy to have the Channel renamed the Anglo-French Pond, you could imagine the French might prefer the Franco-English Pool.

Pond is a Middle-English word, as you might expect from the sound. In its etymology it carries traces of 'pound', as in a cattle pound, a place of confinement, and also as in 'to pound', to crush or hammer. The word is freighted with centuries of human intervention in nature – it's a word which refutes the idea of natural purity.

If pond suggests earth and water and human presence, the five light syllables of *chelidonias* suggest something much more airy. The word comes from *chelidon*, the Greek word for the bird, the swallow. We all know what a swallow-bearing wind is: one of those light, mild breezes which come like a blessing in March, carrying a warm balm, the first trace of spring. Such soft winds make you realise the earth is starting to wake up after the winter, starting to stretch and breathe again. Very soon, the first swallow will appear: as the English poet Ted Hughes wrote, in one of his many poems about swallows, 'flicking past' and 'twinkling away'.

The Greek word *chelidon* is also at the root of the word 'celandine', the flower. The lesser celandine is the simple, round, shining yellow flower which appears in February, rising from a flat clutch of shiny marbled leaves. It's the first flower of the new year. One idea for the name celandine is that the flower was the vegetable equivalent of a swallow, signalling the arrival of spring with its appearance from the earth, just as a swallow does with its arrival through the air.

The sixteenth-century herbalist Henry Lyte, quoted in Richard Mabey's *Flora Britannica*, suggests the name came about because the flower 'beginneth to springe and to floure at the comming of the swallows'. But strictly, this isn't so. Celandines are in flower long before swallows arrive. The lesser celandine belongs to the buttercup family. There is also a greater celandine, *chelidonium majus*, which has softer, non-shining flowers and leaves. The lesser and the greater are not related. The greater celandine belongs to the poppy family. In parts of North America, it is known as the swallow-wort. If you cut the stalk or leaves, the plant exudes an orange latex. Somehow the myth arose that swallows used this latex as a restorer of eyesight.

So the exact reasons for the word celandine's association with swallows remain a mystery. Still, we have *chelidonias*, a swallow-bearing wind: a wonderful concept, even more wonderful for being expressed in a single word. When you see a swallow arrive, you can think about the amazing journey it will have made, all the way from Africa. You can also think how deeply its presence has become entwined in the roots of human language. You might even see the first one skimming over a man made pond.

PICNIC IN AHOURA

Anne Le Marquand Hartigan

A few days after our arrival in Ahoura, New Zealand, we were called on by one of the ministers of a local church. This minister invited us to join him the next Sunday on a farm picnic. My daughter-in-law was delighted, and we agreed to go. I don't know what picture comes to your mind when you think of a farm picnic, but I think of rugs on the grass in fields; sandwiches; a thermos of tea; maybe cows. We were told we did not have to bring anything.

I had travelled with my son and daughter-in-law and their two very small children downcountry from Auckland to live in a tiny village of 300 people, called Ahoura.

My son had taken a job in the local secondary school in order to work as a teacher so that he could get his New Zealand residency. When he had got his residency he was going to start up his own business. I was there for a month or so and no one in Ireland answered my letters. This was the late 1980s (pre-email time) and they did not believe my address: Anne Hartigan, Ahoura, New Zealand.

Off we went to the picnic in my car on Sunday, driving out the village, leaving behind the tarmac road and on to the metal roads. These are roads with just stones and dust when the weather is fine, and stones and mud in the rain. They have no timbre at all and it is very easy to skid, whatever way the weather is. I skidded off the road into the grass at least once during this journey and the weather was dry and sunny.

Out we went into the open country: fields and hills into wild bush country. After some miles we came to our destination. To our surprise there was a respectable, rather formal brick gatepost such as you would see in any suburban housing estate. A tidy drive curved upwards with geraniums on either side. At the top a little brick bungalow, neatly planted flower beds, a wrought-iron fence and gate. We park and get out and walk through the gate and come to a welcome of mowed lawn. Small tables with parasols overhead and all laid out with china cups, sandwiches and tea. Seated there were ladies in large hats and flowery dresses waving and calling out a welcome. This was a farm picnic, yes it was.

I felt I had stepped back in time and this was a garden party in the 1930s. There was a swimming pool, of course, and the children were encouraged to swim.

So over we went to the waving ladies and sat and had tea, and met these friendly New Zealanders. As I sat sipping tea from a china cup I noticed odd men, mostly young, standing rather alone drinking tea, but somehow rather isolated. Some of them were Islanders. By that I mean from Samoa, Tonga, Honolulu. I was keen to meet people so I went and spoke to one of them. I discovered they were all from a local open prison, invited as we were to take part in the Church farm picnic. This open prison was for drug offenders. The young man with whom I spoke was from Tonga. He was going to go back to Tonga, he told me, when he had served his time. He wanted to join his father and brother when he got home again. He said he wanted to build a hotel, that there was no hotel in Tonga and he had ambitions to change this. He gave me the impression there was very little in Tonga.

Because of the strangeness of this picnic I have often thought of him since, and hope he has built that hotel, and one day soon I want to go to Tonga, and it would seem to me now with the huge spread in tourism maybe there would be plenty of hotels in Tonga, and I just hope one of them belongs to him.

THOMAS FOLEY: A SOUND MAN

Sean Moffatt

In 1872 a 24-year-old Irishman called Thomas Foley arrived in America, hoping, like so many others before and after him, to make his fortune. Thomas Foley did indeed prosper because there he is in the 1900 census, all of twenty-eight years later, living in Queens, New York – a contractor, a home owner, married to Margaret, a woman born in New York, but herself of Irish parents. And the Foleys have two children, James and Margaret.

James is just nine years old. And what his parents don't know, and never will, is that one day their only son (or Jack as he came to be known) will give their surname to a brand new art form that is still practised the world over and experienced by millions of moviegoers every year.

The intriguing 'art of Foley', or adding sounds to movies after they have been shot, is an essential part of the film-making process. A meaningful soundtrack can often be just as complicated as the image on the screen. Way back in 1929, Jack Foley was the pioneer.

It was a case of the right man in the right place at the right time. Namely, the high desert town of Bishop in California in 1914 to where Jack had moved from New York with his wife, Beatrice. Before the move he'd had a number of odd jobs, but, like his father, Thomas, he packed his bags and set off to make his fortune.

Jack found himself making ends meet in a local hardware store at a bleak time for the general population of Bishop as the farmers had sold their land to the City of Los Angeles for water rights. But fortune did eventually smile on Jack when some Hollywood producers came calling in search of locations to shoot westerns. Jack initiated a campaign to attract the studios to the area. It worked, and before long he was in the pay of Universal Pictures, working for over a decade as a jack-of-all-trades: from stuntman to double, scouting for locations and even a little directing.

It was during the making of *Showboat* in 1929 that Jack showed just how inventive he could be. The problem for Universal Pictures was that while *Showboat* was initially filmed as a silent movie, Warner Brothers had just released the hugely successful *The Jazz Singer* with sound. Jack hit on the idea of recording a soundtrack for *Showboat* – everything from dialogue to footsteps, opening doors or a slap in the face – live while watching the projected film: and it worked!

And Jack proved to be a wizard in this department. Like a strangely choreographed dancer, he shuffled or tiptoed about the studio reproducing footsteps on different surfaces, creaking cell doors, leaves rustling in a soft breeze, lace being unpacked from folds of tissue paper.

Jack gained a reputation for being able to imitate the walks of famous actors. 'Rock Hudson is a solid stepper,' Jack once said. 'Tony Curtis has a brisk foot; Audie Murphy is springy; James Cagney is clipped; Marlon Brando soft.' And of the women he said, 'Their steps are quicker and closer together. I get winded doing ladies. Jean Simmons is almost, not quite, the fastest. June Allyson: I can't keep up with her at all.' Jack estimated he covered 5,000 miles 'walking actors'.

Jack's final triumph was probably his greatest. In 1959 Stanley Kubrick was working on *Spartacus*. He needed something special to convey the sounds of the entire Roman Army marching into battle decked out with swords, shields and chain mail. Kubrick was set to return to Italy for a complete reshoot. To Kubrick's astonishment an assortment of keys on a metal ring was all Jack needed to create the all-too-convincing sounds of this marching juggernaut.

But by the late 1950s Universal Pictures was bought out by Review Pictures. The scene was set for modern corporations to take over. As an old timer with over forty years' service behind him, Jack knew it was time to go.

Jack's name was finally officially linked to this whole process when Desi Arnaz and Lucille Ball's production company built their own 'direct-to-picture' sound stage and named it the 'Foley Stage'.

In 1962 Jack was awarded an honorary membership from the Motion Picture Sound Editors. He died in 1967, and in 1997 they further recognised his contribution to motion picture sound with a Lifetime Achievement Award.

Jack never once had a single on-screen credit and, probably the saddest irony of all, no recording of his voice exists.

AUNT ESS

Margaret Hawkins

She didn't look like a woman who needed a corset. Stick thin and almost ninety, she wrapped the salmon coloured foundation garment round her body, fastening the hooks and eyes with great difficulty because of her arthritic hands.

Was it more out of habit than need that she wore it at that stage, the steel stays providing some kind of definition and restriction that she was comfortable with? Whatever the reason, she wore it into old age.

Dressing was quite a ritual – interlock underwear then corset and slip and, one by one, the thick lisle stockings held up with bands of elastic, then the pink blouse and the gun barrel grey skirt with the concertina pleats that was hitched high under her chest. Next the navy cardigan and then it was the turn of her hair – long and fine and white and twisted into some kind of bun with what looked like a pipe-cleaner, then a black velvet hairband added as a final touch. With shoes and glasses on and stick in hand, she was finally ready, at around 11 a.m., to make the 6-yard trek to the kitchen in search of liveliness and heat.

We called her Aunt Ess – never Essie, as visitors did, and definitely not Esther, the name she was baptised in Kilpipe church in 1881. Somehow names didn't stay stretched out in those days of land wars and civil war and world wars on the double. She became Ess, one of six tall, angular and sallow-skinned sisters – Elizabeth, Mary Ann, Suzanna, Sarah Jane, Esther and Matilda who, over time, became Lizzie, Mynie, Anna, Jane, Ess and Tilly.

She was a grandaunt, of course, but life was also too short for that kind of appendage. Aunt Ess was seventy-nine when I was born and I was thirteen when she died on 10 April 1973 and it was early morning and the cows were being milked and I had to do a maths test and I didn't care what answer 'pi r squared' gave me that day.

She was the sister who stayed at home. The 1911 census shows her living in the house in Loggan, near Gorey, County Wexford, aged twenty-nine, with her father then aged eighty and her younger brother Thomas, my grandfather, who was then twenty. One of thirteen children, she'd been the one to mind him after their mother died when he was only nine. The second youngest girl; I wonder exactly why she was the one who remained behind to keep the brown bread made.

Why didn't she fly the coop and make a home for herself in somewhere like New Zealand or Canada or Dublin like her sisters did? Did she make that decision because she was a natural-born homemaker, or were fear of change and a sense of duty the psychological stays that kept her within the radius of home and gave her life the definition that she needed?

In later years she went to live with my grandparents, where she helped out in the house and saw their children and some of their grandchildren grow. My childhood memories of Aunt Ess are mostly of a silent, background presence. In her old age and deafness she didn't move or talk a lot, but mostly sat on the bench beside the fire, on frosty days jigging her leg up and down as if to shake the pain out of it or, on better days, dandling the baby in the house on her good knee and singing in her now creaky voice:

Jobby, jobby, little horse, how many miles to Dublin?
Three score and ten, sir, to bring me back again, sir.

Thirty years she'd been crippled with arthritis and I can see her hands still, knuckles knobbled by the joint damage and the skin mottled with age. Thinking of her, and all the other elderly aunts who lived in our locality, I don't think their lives could have been that easy – single sisters living on the circumference of relatives' lives, women who probably knew no regular income until they got the pension but who, in their day, were major picker-uppers of domestic slack in homes around the country.

Rumour has it that Aunt Ess's tongue wasn't always quiet, but even if it was sharp on occasion was that sharpness born of disappointment at the straw she'd drawn in life, not to mention the frustration of immobility and pain from an early age?

I wonder, too, if she ever dreamed of marrying and rocking her own children to sleep. There are no stories of romance for Aunt Ess that I know of, but she was young once and human and could have harboured such desires. There aren't that many photographs of her, but in those we have she often looks a bit sad or downcast or slightly startled in the light of the lens.

There's one photograph that's different, though. She is in her forties and wearing a check-patterned apron over a dress and standing in front of the whitewashed house in the Milland. It's a warm working day and wisps of hair have escaped from her bun and she is smiling broadly, her eyes crinkled up and her teeth joyfully on show.

I don't know who made her laugh that day or who took the photograph, but I'm glad that someone did for, in that one photograph, my aunt Ess's face is a face transformed.

BULLS' WOOL, KILTS AND SWORDS

Michael Fewer

The fiftieth anniversary of the Irish Army UN Mission to the Congo has been in the news recently, and it prompted me to unearth a piece of 8-mm film taken by my father of the 33rd Infantry Battalion's departure from the Irish Air Corps station at Baldonnel in August of 1960. I was with him that warm but cloudy day, and the flickering, grainy images brought me back to another age, showing how far our peace-keeping forces have come from that modest, almost naïve beginning in 1960.

When the First Republic of the Congo gained its independence from Belgium on 30 June 1960 the region swiftly fell into chaos and the UN was requested to send a force of peace-keepers to assist the Congolese army. The Irish government was invited to supply a contingent of troops, and in less than two weeks the 32nd Infantry Battalion had been hastily put together and was on its way to Africa. Within another few weeks the 33rd Battalion had been assembled to reinforce the 32nd, and it was the embarkation of this force that I was fortunate enough to attend.

It was an unforgettable experience for me as a 14-year-old to stand out in the middle of the airfield at Baldonnel, watching a huge US Airforce Globemaster coming in to land. It taxied in – a white, silver and orange monster towering as high as a four-storey building – to join the other two planes that had arrived earlier, and as it came to a halt before the little brick buildings of the Air Corps control tower, two vast doors in its nose began to open, and two ramps, like robot arms, extended towards the ground. It reminded me of a movie I had seen not long before called *It Came from Outer Space*.

Today no one would be allowed anywhere near the planes, but in those days it seemed there was little concern about security other than to keep the general public well back behind barriers. As soon as the plane stopped, the deafening roar of its engines had ceased and the propellers stopped windmilling, it was surrounded by army officers, newspaper men, Air Corps personnel and eager young soldiers, much to the bemusement of the US Airforce ground staff who were there to organise the loading. The Americans looked like film stars with their neatly cut bomber jackets and tight, light slacks, and they watched, with barely concealed amazement, members of the army pipe band who were shortly to embark for Africa and a civil war, strolling around the planes in their saffron kilts, saffron plaids draped over their shoulders, each man wearing a tam-o'-shanter sporting a large feather. While the Irish officers had respectable lightweight uniforms, some wore riding boots and cavalry twill jodhpurs, and the ordinary soldiers were dressed in forage caps, dull green, thick bulls' wool uniforms with hastily made-up tricolour armbands, brown puttees and boots.

Many of the soldiers were not much older than I was, rosy-cheeked country boys, some wearing their caps at a rakish angle, and they were all clearly excited, if a little overawed, at the turn their lives in the quiet Irish Army had taken.

An hour later the whole force of over 700 men paraded out from a hangar, fully equipped with their packs on their backs and rifles at the slope. At the head of the parade was an officer in jodhpurs and boots, sporting a sword and a pistol at his waist and carrying a large gold-tassled tricolour. The force formed up in front of the viewing platform, where an Taoiseach Seán Lemass, flanked by Kevin Boland and Frank Aiken, were joined by the British and US military attachés. I remember the brightly braided and decorated uniforms of the attachés looking garish in contrast to the dark suits and hats worn by our ministers. After an inspection by an Taoiseach, the whole force knelt for a blessing by John Charles McQuaid, the Catholic Archbishop of Dublin. Then, after a brief period saying goodbye to their families, they were back on the tarmac again, boarding the aircraft, marching up the ramps into their cavernous holds. In addition to their backpacks and their World-War-II vintage rifles slung from their shoulders, each man carried his rations for the flight of 4,500 miles: a plastic bag that contained fruit, sandwiches and a drink. The army pipe band boarded, carrying their bagpipes and drums and their leader his conducting staff, waving farewell in the general direction of the crowd as they disappeared into the planes. There was a poignant scene as one man's elderly parents, who had arrived late, were brought out onto the tarmac by the Minister of Defence to hug and wish their son bon voyage amidst the flashing of press cameras.

Finally the great doors closed, and the planes lined up to take off. Each one was watched carefully as, engines roaring, it lifted ponderously into the air, seeming to barely clear the trees to the west, and disappeared into the clouds, taking the Irish Army into a new age.

ALEX HIGGINS: THE ENTERTAINER

Joe Ó Muircheartaigh

It was love, love at first sight. A first love. Mano-a-mano, but such is life. Anyway, I wasn't the only one. Alex Higgins was the object of our desires. The *enfant terrible* of the green baize, but one who always inspired devotion, never-say-die awe and respect. Through good and bad, thick, thin and very thin.

It was one fine day in 1980. I wasn't quite in short trousers, but still not yet a teenager, and holding out for a hero. And he came like a comet from the Crucible Theatre in Sheffield right into my living room. We'd just got a colour telly, and it had a remote control, and I hogged it.

David Vine was the BBC's master of ceremonies – introducing the Hurricane onto the grand stage of the world championship final. But it was no ordinary intro, no ordinary entry either. My new hero had Scott Joplin's *The Entertainer* blaring out as his backing track. He wore a trilby and spats, threw away his tie, smoked cigarettes, drank beer and potted balls for fun and at breathtaking speed.

Snooker's rebel with a cause. A Georgie Best! A Jack Doyle! A genius! He was up against Cliff Thorburn in that final – the Canadian was a great player too, but hey, he was boring. After all, they called him The Grinder.

And guess what happened? He ground down my hero all those thirty years ago, suffocated his spirit and beat him. How I cried, but not for long, because *bheadh lá eile*. There had to be. *Mé féin* and my band of brothers wanted it so much and were in it for the long haul, with Scott Joplin's arrangement ringing in our ears at the mere mention of his name and the hurricanes he whipped up on and off the table.

Yeah, he was a kaleidoscope of different personas and split personalities. The good, the bad and the ugly was in him, but when he was good, he was great – not a force of nature, but something else out there that's unexplained. Above all he was an emotional soul and a softie who yearned to be loved and loved to please.

So it was that my generation, or more parochially, the first-year class of 1980 in Coláiste Mhuire on Parnell Square in Dublin, seemed to hit every ball with the Hurricane. Win with him too – his Masters triumph at Wembley in '81, this long overdue second world title in '82, coming from 7–0 down to beat Steve Davis in the UK final in '83.

We mitched the odd class because of him, left exams early even – misspending some of our youth by tearing down Parnell Square on to the O'Connell Street drag, hanging a right down Henry Street, and another sharp right down a laneway to a small snooker hall. We were twelve, we should have been eighteen; we still got to play.

We chalked our cues like him; we played at the same speed to get as much value out of our harvest of 10p coins; we didn't pot balls like him, but were Alex Higgins in our own minds.

And he was our little industry too. Higgins made snooker and made us – budding some entrepreneurship in us. It was a tentative thing at first on the part of me and my pal Cillian Ó Conaill – a few betting slips were acquired from the office of the old Black & Tan, William Hill, down the road, and we opened up a book on all the big snooker competitions for the chosen few.

But word got out and got as far as *seomra na múinteoirí* – or *Seomra* 1916 as we called it – the room where Pearse, Plunkett, Clarke, Connolly *et al.* met to finalise their grand plans.

We feared the worst, but not for long, because word slowly and quietly came back that some of the teachers, lay and Christian Brother, wanted a slice of the action. You see, they loved their snooker and loved Alex Higgins too. Maybe that's why Higgins came to Coláiste Mhuire one day around 1984 – hard to believe, but it happened when he swaggered into Halla an Choláiste to play an exhibition against fellow pro Eugene Hughes. The Brothers were there and so was I – the highlight of the night coming when Higgins played a few shots with our *príomhoide*, An Bráthair McCraith, and the two of them then posing for a photo for *The Irish Press*.

He was all I expected and hoped – the People's Champion was a man of the people. And that never really changed, even when next we met some twenty-five years later when he came to the West County Hotel in Ennis last year. He was frail, thin and a sorry sight, but still fighting, still entertaining, still inspiring devotion amongst his flock. I was a journalist now, out for a story from my hero.

'Do you remember that night in the Mhuire?' I asked hopefully.

'What about a great night you had in Durty Nellies in Bunratty after an exhibition in Shannon?'

Neither registered! How could they after so many frames and so many years?

'What about your old friend Oliver Reed – did you ever make him off when he lived in Kilrush?'

At last there's a spark. 'Myself and Ollie,' he croaked. 'I loved him. He was like me. We were brothers. I'm not sure about Kilrush, but maybe…' and his voice trailed off.

It was enough. I had my story. Maybe he was with Oliver Reed in Kilrush, maybe he was there the same time Richard Burton called by. What a party to be at! Hellraisers all holed up in Crotty's Pub in the town square – sure, when Burton was there, when told by some local wag that Burton Street across the road was named after him, he promptly bought drinks for the house. Oliver Reed would do the same; it's what hellraisers do as they live for the moment. Alex Higgins did just that.

It's why Scott Joplin's ragtime classic will always ring in the ears.

PILGRIMAGE TO VENTRY

Grace Wells

I have begun to think of our annual holiday in Ventry as a sort of pilgrimage. It doesn't look like one, what with its buckets and spades, and burying uncles up to their necks. Mostly we laze on a beach three miles long. At night as the moon crests mountains, there is sand in the shower, sand in the sheets, and the good towels stolen by children who have wrecked theirs with sand earlier in the day.

We stay in a small wooden cottage that reminds me of a polar explorer's hut. I expect to round a corner and come upon Tom Crean in a handknit jumper, smoking a pipe. Elsewhere families are hiring cottages with dishwashers and wide-screen televisions, but I love the simplicity of the wooden house. It was once the summer home of Michael Joseph O'Rahilly, known as The O'Rahilly, one of the leaders of 1916. During King George's visit of 1911, he hung a banner across Grafton Street that read, 'Thou are not conquered yet, dear land.' I like to imagine The O'Rahilly walking Ventry Strand at dusk, dreaming of a free Ireland. He died in the fighting of Easter 1916 as the rebels left the GPO in search of shelter, and a distilled sense of idealism and courage linger on in the cottage like a small steady note beneath our noise and laughter, our music and poker rivalry, with its shrieks of 'liar', and 'cheat' and 'it's not fair'.

All week we flop between the beach and the house in our happy round, and in the long evenings, the adults stir themselves out into the landscape. We drive down small roads lined with fuchsia and bright montbretia, their pink and orange flares guiding us to dolmens and passage graves, to standing stones dense with silent secrets. We visit the Galarus Oratory, the beehive huts, the ogham stone at Kilmalkedar. Often it rains;

sudden squalls thrown in off the Atlantic. Deep in heather, stones and moss, we are porous to the elements as they sweep in off the ocean. Every small sign of human life speaks of survival against all odds. And everywhere there are records of injustice. We have been to Smerwick's *Gort a Ghearradh*, the Field of the Cutting, where 600 Spanish and Italian men were beheaded alongside the local Irish. We have driven to Kinard and seen the monument to Thomas Ashe who died on hunger strike in 1917, arrested for making 'seditious' speeches alongside Michael Collins. And though all our journeys spill us back onto the Dunquin road, weaving us between tour buses and backpack-laden tourists seeking the dolphin, the *craic*, the effervescent joy of Dingle, it is the sense of human endurance that speaks to me most loudly.

Every year within my pilgrimage holiday I take a deeper personal voyage, not to stones and history, but to the café called Tigh Áine out at the far end of Slea Head. From there the view is endless; the Atlantic stretches as far as America. Clouds pass shadows over a sea that is turquoise, grey-green, a bewitching silver-blue. Seagulls provide their white circus. It is possible to glimpse seals and dolphins. The waves move constantly, the water soothes, and the world stops spinning on its axis. My past busy year and the busy year ahead meet in a moment of stillness.

Eventually my trance of ocean and thought ceases, the eye returns to the land, the cragged shoreline of dark cliffs, the green of grass, purple of heather. My glance harbours on the small cove across the bay. I love the miniature cars parked in the field car park, the minute figures on the beach. One year I saw a woman emerge from the sea to wrap around her shoulders a huge black towel that suddenly billowed behind her like a sail. It flashed at me like a sign and I thought at once of Aegeus waiting on the cliffs for sight of the boat that would bring home his son, Theseus. There had been a promise made, that if Theseus lived he would hoist a white sail at the mast, but the promise had been forgotten and the hero returned beneath black sails. Aegeus, thinking his son dead, plunged from the cliffs into a sea ever after called the Aegean.

I think I go back to Tigh Áine each year not just because it is one of the most beautiful places I know, but because I want to see again that same black towel; for when it moved, it flapped over centuries, it spoke of human pain and the fact that we have always lived in incomprehensible times. But the black towel does not come again; I am only offered its ghost shimmering on the Kerry air. And that is enough. My moment of pilgrimage passes. I pick up my possessions, and willingly let the arc of another hectic year commence. I drive back from the most South-Western tip of the country, back into Ireland with The O'Rahilly's words in my ears, 'Thou art not conquered yet, dear land.'

TWO MEN IN A BOAT

Gerry Moran

It was the summer of 1970 and I had just finished my first year in college, or 'uni', as we called it. There was no such thing as inter-railing or J1s to the States back then, or at least not for me. Summer was about finding a job, any kind of job that would pay a few bob and go towards my keep the following academic year.

The job I found that summer, or rather the job that found me, was cutting rushes on the River Barrow. The job found me because my employer, an entrepreneur of sorts, though he was called a businessman back then, happened to be married to my sister. He manufactured coffins for a living, and when the coffin factory closed for the summer holidays in August he, along with his workers, took to the river, in boats, to cut rushes – and this particular summer, he took me with him.

My mother, I must confess, was reluctant to let me go. Would I be safe on the river, she worried, sure the chap can hardly swim, which was true, but my brother-in-law, who made up in charm what he lacked in stature, smiled at my mother, saying: 'Arrah, we'll make a man of him yet, Mam'.

Actually my mother had every right to be worried as the boats in question were made of soft obeche timber by the workers in the coffin factory and would most certainly not meet the health and safety specifications of today.

My brother-in-law cut rushes because his father before him cut them and sold them to Guinness's, I believe, where the coopers used them for insulation in the wooden beer barrels. The use of rushes, however, was in sharp decline back in 1970 as aluminium barrels began to replace the old timber ones. Yet my brother-in-law continued the practice, having sourced a market for them with some basket-maker in Holland.

There were maybe eight of us in all, cutting the rushes, and we worked two to a boat: one cutting the rushes with a scythe while the other, positioned directly behind, stacked them, tying them into neat bundles until such time as the boat could hold no more, when we'd offload them on the river bank.

I worked with Martin who was not just the rush-cutter but the captain, as it were, of my boat. Standing directly behind him, I neatly stacked the rushes that he smartly and swiftly cut and swung back to me by the fistful. Because we were paid by the bundle, those rushes came thick and heavy and it took everything in my power to stack and tie them neatly with the lengths of baling twine dangling from my trouser belt, all the while wary that I might lose my balance and fall headlong into the river. When the boat was full, Martin rowed to the bank where we stacked the bundled rushes in rows, leaving them to dry for a week or so, before they were stored in some central depot – a disused shed or hay barn that my brother-in-law had rented from some local farmer.

Martin and myself became good buddies over the course of the summer. Come lunchtime, Martin would light a fire on the river bank, place the kettle on top, but not before tossing in a few fresh eggs to boil, which we'd later devour with slices of thick brown bread and the reddest, ripest tomatoes I had ever seen.

When we had finished for the day, we piled into the back of my brother-in-law's pick-up truck as he drove to the local village for some well-earned minerals, ale shandies and maybe a game of darts. And afterwards the *craic* was mighty in the back of that truck, speeding towards home, singing at the top of our lungs the huge hit of the summer, Mungo Jerry's 'In the Summertime'.

I don't know if my brother-in-law 'made a man of me' that summer, but here's what I learned that August of 1970. I learned, not least from Martin the captain of my boat, how to boil an egg in a teapot. I learned that tomatoes taste better with a pinch of pepper and, above all, I learned that whatever it was I learned in my first year in university it was of no consequence whatsoever in a boat for two, cutting rushes on the river Barrow.

UNDER THE KIRSCHBAUM IN GRAZ

Andrew McKimm

We take our ability to communicate for granted. Frequently, it is only when abroad, with a scant knowledge of a local language, that one learns to appreciate the power of one's domestic fluency. Not being able to speak meaningfully to others, spending hours present at conversations with little knowledge of what's going on, is crushingly claustrophobic. It is, mostly, isolating.

I found myself once again cursing my own lack of linguistic skills while visiting my girlfriend's parents in Austria during the last days of August. My copy of *Instant German* lay open for days on my bed, one quarter read. Every other day I'd give it another go, but unhappy memories of my loathing of learning off pages of vocabulary when I was at school kept drowning my progress. I was painstakingly working my way through the section 'How often do the Germans go out?', wondering how words like *das kino* or *der biergarten* were ever going to lead to anything.

School was also on my mind for a completely different reason. There were only six days and twenty-two hours left before I would resume my duties as a maths teacher. The nightmares of being back had already started – the usual ones where I'd stumble into the wrong group of students, looking stupid, or where I'd run around the school looking for a classroom that no longer existed. People think that back-to-school trauma is only the province of students, but it's a feeling that never leaves most teachers. It's probably nature's silent revenge for having such long holidays.

The programme for the day was to drive from Vienna to Graz with my girlfriend's family and to visit her ageing great aunts, both of whom were retired nuns.

I was facing yet another day of polite *ja*s, *nein danke*s and *guten tag*s.

With so little to think about, the encroaching inevitability of the start of the school year loomed ever more grotesquely in my mind. The shimmering heat of the drive to Graz, a day warmer and more sumptuous than I could ever dream of in Ireland, quietly reminded me that my teacher's delusion of an eternal summer would shortly cease.

Both of my girlfriend's great aunts were elderly and ailing. Rosi, thin-faced and alert, a former teacher herself, was the younger. She had been quietly fighting cancer for many years and had defied medical predictions by still being around. Liesi, serene and more heavy-set, was a year older. She had been a former nurse and was now coping with encroaching deafness. Their almost beatific smiles betrayed no hint of the suffering their frail ninety-something bodies were enduring. The tranquillity of both their expressions yielded no trace of regret for lives spent serving others.

On hearing their ages, I did my customary uncontrollable calculation to determine their ages during World War II. Both aunts had seen the war through the eyes of twenty-year-old girls. I shuddered to think of what horrors they had lived through and how it contrasted strikingly with my own war-free youth. As I thought of the carnage that lay buried behind the hills of Graz, with their almost womb-like sense of serenity, the beyond-perfect weather of that late-August day flickered briefly in my imagination and darkened fractionally.

I maintained a frustrated silence for most of the visit, trying to catch the odd word and smiling respectfully as I was gestured to. Occasionally, I met Rosi's watchful teacher's gaze. Liesi, a prisoner of her partial deafness, tuned out of the conversation and stared ahead of her, as if into another world.

Later we moved our visit from the stuffy confines of the insipid convent rooms to sit under the stillness of the cherry tree, or *kirschbaum*, in the back garden. The light daggered through the shade of the cherry tree in sultry, sinuous lines. Rosie and Liesi crept haltingly from their wheelchairs, an age passing before their enfeebled bodies made it to the garden seat, their daily quota of residual energy almost spent.

I sat down beside my partner-in-isolation, Liesi, as she returned to her invigilation of the eternal, whilst my girlfriend continued to translate.

On hearing English being spoken, Liesi abruptly broke her reverie, her face creased with agitation. She pointed at me, saying that she hadn't understood foreign languages either when she had been stationed as a young nurse in Klagenfurt during the war. All she had comprehended were the screams of the young Italian and Russian soldiers whilst she fought to discover exactly where their pain was. Mostly she could do no more than hold them as the life ebbed from their wretched bodies.

Despite the breathless quiet of the afternoon, I too could almost hear the soldiers' screams as I pursued Liesi's thoughts back into the hospitals of World War II. By now the soft atmosphere of the summer afternoon became brittle as everyone focused on Liesi. The calm authority of her days as a head nurse returned to her face and she seemed younger. Tears formed slowly in her eyes.

She felt most sorry for the young Russians. When the war was over, all the recovering soldiers from all the other countries were overjoyed. But the Russians wanted to stay in the hospital. They cried like babies with the knowledge that they would be executed as soon as they re-crossed the border into Russia. Liesi, unable to reassure them with words, could only continue to hold and pray for them.

Silence descended. The invisible clock, with its countdown to the beginning of school, that I could hear ticking ponderously in my mind, suddenly halted. Liesi peacefully sank back out of the conversation and resumed her invigilation of the infinite.

That night I didn't dream of school. I fell asleep thinking of Liesi's serene countenance, realising that I had spent the afternoon gazing at the same kindly face which was the last image that so many men, of all languages, had seen before they breathed their last breath in this world.

SEPTEMBER

A SAINT AND SCHOLAR FOR OUR TIME

Pádraic Conway

John Henry Newman's time in Dublin was among the most benign of all the failed interventions on the part of prominent Englishmen in the affairs of Ireland. As we anticipate his beatification on Sunday, 19 September, it is no harm to remind ourselves that, despite failing to achieve many of his objectives, his time among us has left a lasting legacy to Dublin and to the world.

Before he ever came near Ireland, Newman had a number of experiences that might resonate with us today. He experienced the raw reality of a banking crisis when, aged 15, his father's bank collapsed in the aftermath of the Napoleonic wars; his father subsequently made the rather dramatic career shift from merchant banker to brewery manager.

And for all his undoubted brilliance, Newman made a mess of his final undergraduate examinations and ended up with a pass degree. 'Crisis? What crisis?' you might well reply and having been myself, for a time, of the view in relation to university examinations that 'anything more than 35 per cent = wasted energy', I might smile in recognition. Yet we should deny no man his pain and Newman surely suffered deeply in the let-down of this moment. Both the cross of his disappointment and the resurrection of his subsequent brilliant career will strike a chord with many a student and parent listening as we begin a new academic year.

The trajectory of his career in Dublin began with a visit to Newman's Birmingham Oratory in July 1851 by Paul Cullen, then Archbishop of Armagh. Fearing that the recent establishment of the Queen's Colleges would be a force for liberalism and secularisation, Cullen asked Newman to become Rector of the proposed Catholic University of Ireland.

By the time he delivered his first five *Discourses on the Scope and Nature of University Education* in 1852, however, Newman was acutely aware of the difficulties involved in leading the mooted university, not least that many of the Irish bishops were opposed to the venture.

Newman finally arrived in Dublin on 7 February 1854 and, after initial conversations with the Jesuit provincial, the president of Maynooth and sundry bishops, quickly concluded that he had been asked, in his own words, 'to attempt an impossibility.' Impossibility or not, Newman threw himself into preparations for the opening of the university. He started the *University Gazette*. He began a scholarly magazine, *The Atlantis*. He engaged professors and secured premises for the first Catholic medical school in Dublin.

The Catholic University of Ireland, Newman's university, opened its doors on 3 November 1854 in what is today Newman House, St Stephen's Green. Soon thereafter, on 1 May 1856, the adjoining University Church was opened, funded in various ways by Newman himself after he was refused a loan by the bishops. He also donated a large part of his salary to student support and is reported as having had 'the support of his entire professorial staff'. I don't think it's unfair to say that neither trait has been omnipresent in the subsequent history of Irish university leadership.

After four disappointing years, during which he failed to secure a charter for his university and student numbers remained low, Newman resigned his post as Rector of The Catholic University of Ireland on 12 November 1858. Whatever Newman's difficulties in Dublin, it was 'the occasion and stimulus for the composition of works of outstanding value', as one of his postulators has put it. His discourses of 1852 were published as Part I of *The Idea of a University* on 2 February 1873 – nine years to the day before the birth of one James Augustine Joyce, the most celebrated graduate of the Catholic University's successor institution, University College Dublin, and a man who regarded Newman as among the greatest of prose stylists.

On another topical matter, Newman wrote to the parish priest of Scarborough in 1868, concerning Darwin's *Origin of Species,* that the theory of natural selection 'may simply be suggesting a larger idea of Divine

Prescience and Skill'. This refusal to plant theology's flag in other spheres echoed similar points made in his Dublin writings about the autonomy of academic disciplines, including the natural sciences. Newman was a classic 'both-and' thinker whose first sermon in University Church refuted explicitly the assumption 'that, to be religious, you must be ignorant and to be intellectual, you must be unbelieving'. In this, as in so much else, he is a saint and scholar for our time.

CROKER

Noel Ellis

For five years it was like an annual pilgrimage. November in Scoil Mhuire meant only one thing: a trip to Croker to support our school football team in the Cumann na mBunscol final. From 1994 to 1998 we made six visits (yes, two in one year) to the home of Gaelic football.

And we thought it would last forever.

Of course it didn't.

And maybe that's what makes those years so special.

Especially for the boys and girls who were lucky enough to pull on the Scoil Mhuire jersey and run out onto the sun-splashed carpet in front of 82,000 screaming fans and a TV audience of mill—

OK, OK, our memories are playing a few tricks on us here.

It was more like a few hundred.

And the weather was pretty miserable.

And somebody somewhere probably has a video recording of the match stashed away in a dusty attic (probably focusing on his own darling child doing his best to keep warm while a goal is being scored off camera at the opposite end of the pitch!).

But did we care?

We were in Dreamland.

We were in Croker.

And we had a ball.

And for every one of our six adventures, the teachers' prayers were answered, as we always got an early slot for our final instead of the dreaded 2.15 p.m. graveyard shift.

The excitement would begin with the children getting their wristbands and banners and hats and colours ready in art class in the days leading up to the match. Articles would be submitted for the match programme and teachers would be pulling their hair out as money arrived in for the bus.

'Me da wants to go on the bus. Can me sister and her friend come?'

'Me brother is in fourth and me sister is in first and I'm payin' for the three of us. Do we have to pay the whole lot?'

'Me ma says I can't go cos last year I got sick on the bus on the way back cos I drank me full 2-litre bottle of coke.'

But between the jigs and the reels it'd be all sorted. Then on the morning of the match the shout would go up. 'They're here!' And a fleet of double-decker buses would pull up outside the team hotel (sorry; getting carried away again). Children from first to sixth class were allowed to go and it became customary for the infants to wave the supporters off as the buses pulled out. On one of these auspicious occasions a senior infant was overheard commenting to his pal:

'Can't wait till next year.'

Scoil Mhuire expected!

Rumour has it that some of the poor Dublin Bus drivers who brought our supporters to Croker are still receiving counselling for the torture they endured while being subjected to:

'You'll Never Beat Scoil Mhuire'

and

'Ninety-nine Bottles of Beer on the Wall'

Over and over again.

THE SWEETEST THING

Josephine McArdle

It was ten past nine and I was sorting the newspapers on the counter when he marched in and stood in the middle of the floor.

'You work here?'

I assumed my serving position behind the till and waited.

'I'm to ask for Mr Heavey,' he said.

And at that moment the shop-owner pulled up in his F Escort Estate onto the footpath directly outside the front door.

He came in and looked at the skinny young teenager.

'You must be Michael.'

They shook hands.

'Come and help me unload the order from the cash-and-carry.'

He threw an eye in my direction before walking obediently after his new boss.

I watched him carry the boxes and crates inside and stack them neatly at the back of the shop.

He brushed the dust off his clothes and waited for his instructions.

'Josie will give you the prices, and tell you where to pack them,' said Mr Heavey.

'I'm going to the bank. Keep busy. There's plenty to do.'

That was our introduction.

Michael didn't say a whole lot. He whistled and drummed his fingers along the counter when he walked by.

He made me nervous.

He had a short back-and-sides haircut, and his face was pale, almost white, so that his green eyes seemed all the more vivid and alert.

'What age are you?' he demanded, pulling a packet of cigarettes out of his jeans pocket.

We were on our break in the little kitchenette in the storeroom.

'You still go to school?'

I didn't ask any questions.

I knew all I wanted to know about him. I'd heard Mrs Heavey tell one of the customers earlier that he was from Artane, and that the McGraths had taken him out for the summer. Michael McGrath was his name. No relation to his benefactors, she said.

I'd heard all about Artane. It was an industrial school, a reformatory, like Daingean and Letterfrack. I knew about reform schools because my two younger brothers were forever being threatened incarceration in one or other of them when their behaviour crossed the line of sufferance and my mother's patience had expired.

'Letterfrack is too good for you,' she'd wail. 'It's Artane you'll be heading for. And don't expect me to visit you either.'

Not good. There was nothing nice about Artane, and Michael became more and more a curiosity for me as I got used to his presence about the place and gradually came to enjoy his tales of bravado and high drama about his Alma Mater.

He vowed he'd go back and burn the place down when he made his fortune.

He was good at blowing his own trumpet.

He was fourteen and I was thirteen.

I told my mother about the Artane Boy in the shop.

'Watch out and don't let him cod you,' she warned. 'He's not in there for nothing.'

My fear was turning to fascination.

At lunchtime he'd wait until I was ten paces ahead of him and then leave the shop. He'd trail me up Garden Vale Terrace. I could sense him there behind me, but I wouldn't turn around because then I'd have to wait up and walk with him.

Then he began to wait for me at the junction where our paths converged, pretending to be having a casual smoke.

There was no avoiding him.

We walked past the Brothers' house and he spat his chewing gum at their front door.

I winced.

The Adelphi Cinema was next.

'I love the pictures,' he said. 'Do you?'

The Adelphi was rough, I told him, and it was smelly. The Ritz is nice.

'Oh!'

The summer was coming to a close when he made his move.

I'd soon be finishing work in the shop and taking a week off before going back to school.

I said nothing to Michael about my intentions.

I'd left the shop and it was my half day. A glorious August afternoon.

'Get out in that sun and make the most of it,' Mrs Heavey called after me.

I was halfway up the street and just past McGrath's, safely as I thought, when he appeared, keeping in perfect step alongside me.

I smiled nervously and quickened my pace. He ran ahead and stood in my path.

I could smell the Lifebuoy soap.

Oh no! I thought wildly. He's going to kiss me!

My cheeks burned.

'I was just wondering,' he said, and I caught the tiniest hint of hesitation in his voice.

'I was thinking that you might come to the pictures with me.'

'I can't,' I heard myself tell him.

'You see I already have a boyfriend,' I lied.

He shoved his hands into his pockets and spun around.

Never said a word.

Never said another word to me.

'Where's Michael?' I casually asked Mrs Heavey when he failed to appear for the rest of the week.

'Gone back,' she said matter-of-factly.

'Oh!'

'He has to rehearse. He's the drum major you know.'

I didn't know.

I felt the queerest, tightening sensation in my chest and I took a deep breath. But my eyes were stinging, and then, without warning, I began to cry thinking of my lie.

That big black lie.

On All-Ireland Sunday I watched the final, for the first time, in our front sitting room.

Kerry were playing Offaly, but that was of little interest to me.

My attention was focused on the Artane Boys' Band, and when they took to the pitch on that Sunday in September there he was.

The drum major, in his majestic scarlet and blue uniform, commanding the band with an air of authority that I recognised immediately.

Michael Mc Grath, the first boyfriend that I never had.

Ain't love the sweetest thing!

UISCE FAOI THALAMH/ UNDERCURRENTS

Leo Cullen

Help me, this Sunday morning, the sink hole rancid with crusts,
Why must I always throw spent matches in there; why must
My brother be standing beneath a whitethorn bush
in the rain, My brother, scribbling out a poem
a few days, a few green years, before he dies?
Help me to stay calm, to slop out the glug of stuck
sink. I'm a wiry little man, aren't I, is that not enough?
I have hard little muscles like the chain of a bike
That got me this far and will keep me going on.
So why am I crying, 'help me, help me'?
For today I'll be crying in Croke Park's auditorium:
'Up Tipp,' and be carried far away from my needs
or is it carried with longing for all that I am
drowned in a crowd, a wiry little man?
Is it me is the man that now calls for help?
Or am I my brother as he called those few years
before he died writing poems beneath
a whitethorn bush in the pouring rain?
That's what I remember about him the most
And trembling lips on a day that Tipp lost
Against Kilkenny in 1967.
We were on the old Cusack, the wind clattering the roof stays,
lightening across his forehead, he was fifteen,

phalanx after phalanx of black and amber men,
while he sucked his thumb with each surrender
And blue were his lovely lips, yellow his blood-dry thumb.
As a child he had sucked it and even once
When he won a rosette at a juniors' gymkhana
in Boherlahan in went the thumb
despite mustard the elders coated up to his elbow
to stop the sucking, in went the thumb
Oh my muscles are tensed as a hurling *sliotar*
here I am today, lost in my brother,
in his disappointment at his first and last
All-Ireland in the Capital, and I wanted to offer
solace – for how can it be when you are a child
without insight that you won't grow to wisdom of manhood –
but my own grief was enough that day for me
not to smother him with love and say it's ok.
Years passed, walls gathered moss and my brother
fell sideways one night at the side of the mountain
of Slievenamon and was laid out in the hospital
like his man Fionn Mac Cumhail or lithe Cúchulainn,
Oh he told me once about the time
Fionn arranged the race for the fast women
to the top of Slievenamon to decide
who would be his wife and a goddess slid open
the cave to the Underworld and Fionn, trying to enter
before it slapped shut, prised in only his thumb,
so Fionn's thumb, said my brother, glimpsed the Underworld
and what would any warrior do, but stick it in his gob –
knowledge of the Underworld to course, thumb to heart!

Oh brother dear, we are lost in our fathers
Help me, help me, let us know our loves.
Brother dear, we are lost in our mothers
With rapparee Patrick Sheehan on Aherlow roaming
Brother dear, beneath a whitethorn cloud
You wrote that night, and not rain but sunshine
peeped through some corner and when the cloud dispersed

Nature's light shone brightly
With the gift of birth.

Brother dear, today for Boherlahan
I will swell up my chest muscles into a bundle,
For you and your living, and please suck your thumb
today please, for us, and ask your man, Fionn,
to suck his, let the Underworld undercurrents come,
uisce faoi thalamh, and wash over us all.

WE SHUDDA WON

Larry McCluskey

'You're comin' home this afternoon captain of the All-Scholastic Championship Team of the City of New York, y'hear?'

That's what Willie Loman promised his son, Biff in the play, *Death of a Salesman*, written in 1949 – ten years before we played in the minor final in Croke Park.

But Biff did *not* bring home the Cup. And, equally sadly, neither did we.

Five of us, all members of that minor team of 1959, met in Kells recently to arrange the golden anniversary of that event.

There was a silence after we looked – for the fiftieth time – at the team picture of fifty years ago. One of the men, now approaching seventy, said – simply, despondently – 'Frig it, lads, we shudda won.'

There were murmurs of agreement. 'They hadn't a buckin' clue,' says Frankie. 'Sure, we weren't prepared for Croke Park at all.'

'Jaysus,' says another, 'when I came out on the pitch, after runnin' down from Barry's Hotel with my togs and boots in hand, I thought the stands were goin' to fall in on top of us!'

'It was worse for me,' said Des. 'Hugo and myself went to the wrong gate. The stewards wouldn't let us in till we showed them the boots. We were late getting to the dressing-room, then the top priority seemed to be that we get out on the pitch at exactly the right time!' In that confined and frenzied space, advice about the game or tactics or anything like that went well over our bedazzled heads.

Sunday, 20 September 1959 – All-Ireland final day, fifty years ago. Galway v Kerry in the senior final; Cavan v Dublin in the minor final. We were playing for Cavan.

Now, there may be fifty reasons why footballers remember the day they played in an All-Ireland final in Croke Park, but for the losers there's only one – that they didn't win.

Standing on the front steps of the college in Cavan that bright September morning, light-headed with excitement and fitness, defeat was unthinkable. Paul Fitzsimon's Volkswagen Beetle came up the avenue, two players already in the back seat. Three more of us piled in, and off we headed for Dublin. Outside Navan, we stopped along the road for one of the lads to get sick.

Into the city, to Barry's Hotel for tea and sandwiches, apple tart and custard. Then, suddenly, everything was frantic. Half-walking, half-running through the crowd across Mountjoy Square, down Fitzgibbon Street into Jones' Road, to the Mecca itself: Croke Park, famed in song and story, then as now – my first time there.

Dressing-room a-bustle, the sacred Cavan jerseys being handed out – mine, No. 13. Everyone shouting instructions and advice, all of it confused, much of it contradictory. Paddy Flood, our becalmed captain, with his bottle of 'stuff' (what was in it? I often wondered since – probably egg-flip in those innocent, pre-wintergreen days).

Out to the pitch – a thunder of sound, a blaze of colour. 'The ball is in and the game is on!' Early in, I score a flukey goal, get a wallop that splits my eyebrow and have to go off. 'One of our best players,' I hear Mick Higgins, our trainer, say – and the pain eases a bit. At half-time, Dr Carroll stitches the cut – no anaesthetic, of course. I feel sick in my stomach as I'm ushered back into battle for the second half, of which I remember little, except my brother Declan scoring a point and the sinking realisation that we are going to lose.

Then it's all over: 1–4 to 11 points. Coming back out on the side-line to watch the senior match, Patsy Marron from Magheracloone shouts hello through the wire, the only familiar face I see that day, though our parents – their first time, too – are also in Croke Park. Afterwards, to Clontarf Castle, where we aren't part of whatever celebration is going on.

Then, tired, dejected, silent, the long road back to Cavan. No cup, no crowds, no bonfires. Cavan's heady days of All-Ireland victories were over. But we didn't know that; we (at seventeen) were sure we'd be back in Croke Park the following year. How wrong we were! – no Cavan team has been in Croke Park on All-Ireland final day since.

And, now, fifty years later, we gather to celebrate – 'renewing our deeds of past glory', as the song says. But to celebrate what? What might have been? What could have been? What nearly was – but wasn't? We shudda won!

In Kells, the talk turns to the set of jerseys we are ordering for the event. (One supplier has joked that for an extra tenner he'll throw in a shroud as well.) The sample jersey reads: 'All-Ireland Finalists, 1959'. 'I don't like "finalists",' says Hugo; 'it begs the question: did yiz win? – just say "Final".' Then Tony says, 'Ah, to hell with "Final", put "Winners" on them – sure, at this stage, who will know but ourselves? And, anyway, we shudda won.'

And so it is that, on this All-Ireland final day, a full Cavan team and subs – less only the three who have gone to their eternal reward, where finals are *never* lost – will each don a Cavan football jersey bearing the legend, 'All-Ireland Winners, 1959'.

And, sure, in the twilight, isn't it often difficult to see things clearly, to tell the difference between what is and what ought? And isn't everyone – especially old footballers at this time of year – entitled to dream? And aren't All-Ireland finals the very stuff that dreams are made of – sure, didn't Shakespeare tell us that?

Ah, dammit, lads – we shudda won!

THE OATH

Bairbre O'Hogan

Sometimes the answer is so obvious when you hear it, that you wonder why you never asked the question. I always knew my grandparents' marriage had GAA roots. He was John J. Hogan of Tipperary, a hurler, a referee, an office holder. She was May O'Kennedy from New Ross, of the famous footballing family.

My grandfather was educated with the Christian Brothers in Nenagh. Following exams for the British civil service, he was employed as a postal sorter in London. There were plenty of Irish working in the London postal service around that time, including Sam Maguire, Liam Mac-Carthy's mother, and, a couple of years later, Michael Collins. In 1902, John J. Hogan transferred to the Central Sorting Office in Dublin. Within a year, he was on the winning team in the Dublin Junior Hurling League. Was it in his role as player or referee or Chairman of the Leinster Council that he met up with the O'Kennedy brothers – Tom, Seán and Gus – who were to be instrumental in bringing Wexford to six successive Leinster Football Championship wins and four successive All-Ireland wins? The friendship between the men somehow led to an 'introduction' and John J. Hogan met, courted and married their sister, May. His friend, fellow referee and Chairman of the County Dublin Committee of the GAA, Harry Boland, was best man. May's bridesmaid was her cousin, Nellie Cooney from Waterford; in the newspaper reports of the wedding, the bride and bridesmaid were described as being 'members of popular and rightly respected families'.

Life was busy with GAA business in the newlyweds' home – my grandfather was one of nine trustees who signed for the purchase of the

Jones' Road grounds in 1913. Hospitality was regularly extended to family and friends who travelled to watch my grandmother's brothers embark on the historic run of football successes. Seán already had a 1910 All-Ireland hurling medal. He captained Wexford in '15, '16 and '17, but was in hospital for the 1918 final. Gus, his younger brother, was one of nine who played in all four football finals.

So, the GAA was central to the comings and goings of the growing Hogan household. And yet, my father, the eldest boy in a family of eight girls and six boys, played cricket and hockey as a young man, two of the games banned by the GAA as 'foreign games'. Although he passed on his love of Irish, and of Irish history and archaeology to me, there was no transfusion of the GAA blood in him, blood which he inherited from both sides.

It often seemed strange to me that there was no follow-on in his life from his parents' involvement, and no burning desire in him to rekindle the GAA spirit in his children. But on a recent visit to the museum at Croke Park, I found an answer – maybe not the definitive one, but certainly a possible one.

As a civil servant working in the postal service, my grandfather had to take the Oath of Allegiance to the crown: that or lose his job. The Central Council of the GAA had adopted a Resolution in December 1918 relieving any member who had taken the Oath of membership, pending the next Convention. Sadly, his erstwhile great friend, Harry Boland, was one of those who championed the expulsion of the civil servants, which, incidentally, also included national school teachers, to the detriment of the association at the time.

My grandfather, having taken the Oath for his job, had to step down from his role as chairman of the Leinster Council. Though nominated as chairman again at the April 1919 Congress, he had already made his mind up not to stand. He thanked those who had nominated and supported him during his terms of office. The GAA in turn thanked him for 'improving the discipline, punctuality and good order generally', and for his thorough knowledge of the rules and the impartiality of his decisions.

My grandfather's traits of discipline and punctuality, of knowledge and impartiality, and of integrity, are exactly what I would also associate with my father. So even if my father wasn't imbued with a love of the GAA, the GAA and I have shared the benefits of those Hogan qualities.

A TRIBUTE TO MICK LALLY

Orla Shanaghy

The façade of the Forum Theatre in Waterford looks down on a sloping plaza that is surrounded by the small terraced houses that mark this historic part of the city. Here and there between the houses run narrow streets with centuries-old names, some leading down towards the Quay, others up the town to Ballybricken and beyond. It was down one of these streets, as I stood outside the theatre after a performance of *The Castlecomer Jukebox* in 2004, that I watched a solitary, tall, hunched figure lope away, hands in pockets, probably off for a quiet post-performance pint in one of O'Connell Street's pubs. That figure was Mick Lally.

I never had the good fortune to meet Mick Lally in person, but I cannot shake the feeling that I have known him all my life. To me and my brothers, like many Irish children in the 1980s, the *Glenroe* theme tune signalled the dreaded Sunday-night bedtime (as much as it probably signalled to our parents the time when they could finally sit down and watch some TV in peace). Even when we were too young to actually watch *Glenroe*, we and our school friends knew all the characters and especially Miley, the beleaguered everyman with the bewitching voice and a brilliant catchphrase that we repeated with delight at every opportunity.

Being finally allowed to stay up beyond 8 p.m. on Sundays to watch *Glenroe* was a real rite of passage. As well as being a staple in that show, to those of us growing up in Ireland in the 1980s Mick Lally always seemed to be around, be it on TV or radio. He even managed to turn a TV ad for cheese into a memorable experience, his mellifluous tones combining deliciously with the thrumming of a bodhrán's beat.

The years passed, I moved to Dublin, and even though as a student I no longer had access to a TV, Mick remained a constant. My Austrian friend Sabine visited Dublin and, to give her a taste of Irish theatre, my boyfriend and I took her to see *A Skull in Connemara*, with Mick in the lead role. We had great seats looking down on the stage. I remember being overawed by Mick's looming, menacing presence in that role. I was also delighted that we had an actor of such calibre in this country that enabled me to show off our culture to a visitor so successfully. In the pub afterwards, Sabine's English was tested to the limits as she tried to put into words the impression his performance had made on her.

These days, my husband and I, now with three children, rarely get to listen to an entire radio show, so we considered it a special treat on a recent drive to Dublin to turn on the radio and hear Mick's voice. He and another wonderfully familiar actor, his *Glenroe* co-star Mary McEvoy, were being interviewed by Miriam O'Callaghan. As the children, miraculously, slept in the back, it was a delight to hear him describe his life and career with endearingly self-deprecating good humour, and just as much a delight to simply sit and listen to his voice. To hear his gorgeous spoken Irish was another pleasure.

Perhaps it was because that interview was so recent that the news this morning comes as such a sad shock. It strikes me that as we advance into our mid-thirties, us *Glenroe* children have now reached the age where the death of a well-known person can feel like the death of something in us. Mick Lally was part of the background of our lives, whether we paid his presence there much heed or not. Now that he is gone, I personally, for the first time, feel the loss of a person I never actually knew.

Although thanks to that radio interview, it is not long since I heard him speak, my last, and lasting, visual impression of Mick Lally is that evening in Waterford in 2004, when I watched him walk away down a dark street after another brilliant performance, alone, seeking no accolades, a quiet master.

LEAVING HOME

Alex Miller

More than fifty years after I left England to go alone to Australia, my younger brother Ross came out to Australia to visit me for the first time. On the last evening of my brother's visit, he and I were sitting in my back garden under the apple tree enjoying the last of the very large bottle of duty-free Glenfiddich he'd brought in with him. Ross is nine years younger than I am and was not yet eight years of age when I left home as a boy of sixteen. Since my departure from England I had retained an image of them all standing there on the platform at St Pancras station in the steam and smoke of that dark November day in 1953 – the tight little group of my family watching my train pull out for Southampton and the other side of the world.

In this last-remembered image of my family, Ross is standing between my father and mother holding my father's hand. My older sister Kathy and my younger sister Ruth are holding each other's hands, standing close up against the skirts of my mother's coat. Sitting under the apple tree that autumn evening with my brother, now a man nearing sixty, I turned to him and said, 'Do you remember seeing me off for the boat?' His wicker chair creaked. 'Of course I do,' he said and laughed. 'We were all crying.' 'Was our Dad crying?' I asked him. I was surprised. My memory of my father was of a tough, kind-hearted Glaswegian who never cried. 'No,' my brother said. 'No, Dad wasn't crying.' How could I have thought our father might have been in tears? It surely showed how little I'd known him. We sipped our whiskey in silence. After a minute or two I said, 'And you? Were you crying?' I wanted to know. I loved my brother. I had been the one who had made up stories for him when he was little, to get him to go off to sleep at night. And I remembered his birth; my father coming out of our parents' bedroom, his collar off and his sleeves rolled up, his face shining in the light of the coal fire, the three of us children sitting close together on the hearth rug in silence after all the wailing and screaming from the bedroom. 'Come in and meet your little brother,' my father said. He had a lovely happy smile on his face such as none of us had ever seen since he'd come home from the war. Our little brother's arrival healed my father's wounded soul and we loved Ross in a special way for it. His presence restored harmony to our family, and there was always a deep gratitude in the way we loved him.

Fifty years after leaving my family, sitting under the apple tree with my brother here in this little country town in Australia where I am writing this, I wanted to know that Ross had shed a few tears at the moment of my departure. When he didn't respond to my question I let the silence go on for a bit, then said again, 'So, tell me – were you crying or not?' My brother's laugh was light and untroubled, as it always was. 'Of course I wasn't crying. Whenever we had a bit of a crisis in the family, Dad's way of dealing with it was to promise we'd all go to the pictures when it was over and done with.' He twisted around in his chair and looked at me. 'I couldn't wait to see the back of you.' He picked up the whiskey bottle, eyed it, then carefully poured equal shares of the last of it into our glasses. 'Whenever anyone in the family has ever mentioned the day you left home, I've always thought of Deborah Kerr and Burt Lancaster kissing in the surf.'

By now the sun had gone down and the air in the garden was getting a bit of a chill in it. I suggested we go in and see how dinner was coming on. 'At the end, when our Mum was dying,' Ross said, 'I was sitting with her holding her hand. The last thing she said to me was, "It will be all right when Alex comes home."' He turned on his creaky chair and looked up at me. 'Mum spent her life believing you'd be coming home one day.'

My mother's people were from Kilkenny and I've always promised myself that one day I'd visit the country of her beginnings. This is my first visit to Ireland, and this little piece I've been reading to you is a homage to my mother. She never returned to Ireland herself. But I'm glad to be here in her place.

NESSA DEPARTS, FINN ARRIVES

Nuala Ní Chonchúir

In May your phone call came; knowing it was you, I grumpily didn't answer. I was still battling with jealousy for your good fortune as well as with my own losses. I saw your number come up and turned my back on the telephone. Our older sister rang me the next day with your news; it wasn't good.

In August, almost a year after your daughter arrived, I got the coveted two pink lines for myself. While I grew, Russian doll-like around my baby, you were being slowly taken apart by your own body. With each new test another area of you was declared invaded, unsafe.

As autumn arrived, my shape changed; I bloomed forward, the egg of my belly announcing me as public property. Your shape changed too – under blue men's pyjamas you ballooned and your legs weakened. With the arrival of chemotherapy, new changes occurred. Your jackdaw-black hair fell out and your skin took on the blue hue of your pyjamas. The pills you took were as varied as a sweet shop's; you marvelled at it all and said when you were better you would take your daughter to Africa to learn drumming.

September arrived and, with it, radio-talk of the Euro we would all soon be using; then the shock and sadness of the 9/11 attacks. You started to plan what would be your final plane trip.

October arrived and my first hospital visit for an antenatal scan – on the screen the baby pulsed and waved like the most beautiful jumping bean in the world. Your hospital stays got longer; each one brought more tests; none of the results brought good news.

Late November arrived and you took a plane to Lourdes. I worried about terrorist attacks the way we all worried then.

On the postcard you sent me, you said Lourdes was 'a tackfest'; 'Blackpool meets the Vatican' you wrote. You brought me home a red-robed statue of Saint Michael – you said you thought he looked sexy.

In early December I arrived in Dublin from my Galway home to see you in hospital. You had high praise for the nurses and doctors; you chatted and laughed, talked about writing a novel. In your scarlet bandanna and shapeless gown, to me you looked shockingly sick and were shockingly cheerful. I didn't know then it would be my last time to talk to you in person.

In late December our ma's phone call arrived; she told me to come home, it was time. Two days before Christmas we set off before dawn, hoping you would hang on so I could say a proper goodbye. We stopped to watch the sun rise over Galway Bay – the sea was salmon and orange coloured; your artist's eye would have loved it. Back in the car, I cried and cried, willed us forward to Dublin. In the rear seat, my 7-year-old son sang 'Jingle Bells' over and over again.

You had departed only minutes before I arrived at your hospice bed. Your beautiful slim fingers were still warm when I held them. I couldn't believe you were gone. The nurse said you sat up the night before and ate Cornflakes; in typical fashion, your last meal was cereal. You were always mad for your breakfast.

Your second departure took place after Christmas – you sailed through the red curtains in the crematorium and we all agreed you would have approved of the theatre of it, the drama.

You always liked to give presents; you put a lot of thought and time into them, often making them yourself. Even in death you were still giving. Months after you died, a letter arrived to our parents, thanking you for the gift of sight you gave to one old person, one young.

In May, my baby son arrived, a cousin for your little daughter. My hope was that as they grew, they would be friends as we were friends. More than cousins, the way we were more than sisters. I'm happy to tell you that they are.

PATTI SMITH

Joseph O'Connor

I can remember the moment she came into my life. It was on the afternoon of my fourteenth birthday, 20 September 1977. I was in a record store called Freebird on the north quays of the Liffey, a murky little basement that reeked of mould and patchouli oil. An aunt had sent me ten pounds as a gift, and I didn't know what to buy.

I was flicking through a rack of second-hand punk-rock records, with their splatters of graffiti and blackmail-style lettering, when my fingers stopped at an unusual sleeve. It showed an extraordinary looking woman of skeletal build. It was like a still from one of those cool French movies. The record was *Horses* by Patti Smith.

I had never heard of this Patti Smith. I'd never seen anyone who looked like her either. You couldn't have called her pretty; she was something much more troubling. Yeats wrote of Maude Gonne that she had 'beauty like a tightened bow', and the old priest who taught us English (and who had himself once seen Maude Gonne on a Dublin street) used to try and explain the phrase. But when I saw that photograph, I knew what it meant. Androgynous, sullen, unconventionally gorgeous, she had the air of a young Keith Richards about to embark on a night of debauching debutantes. Her confidence and raffish self-possession were enthralling. It sounds mad to say it now, but back in the 1970s you just didn't see women presenting themselves in this way.

This was an era when the monthly *Top of the Pops* anthologies of chart cover versions still featured models in crochet bikinis simpering on the covers. Patti didn't strike you as a bikini kind of gal. On a beach, you felt she'd be wearing Doc Martens, sipping absinthe, and kicking sand into the faces of passing skinheads. Camille Paglia would later write, of the cover photograph of *Horses* (taken by Smith's then lover, Robert Map-plethorpe): 'It was the most electrifying image I had ever seen of a woman of my generation. It ranks in art history among a half-dozen supreme images of modern woman since the French Revolution.' I confess I wasn't pondering the art historical implications, but in thirty years of buying records, it's still the only one I've ever bought purely for its cover.

In every life there are moments remembered in a kind of emotional slow motion. The first kiss, the first heartbreak; the first time you lost out; that instant when your eyes met across a crowded party. The first time I heard Patti Smith singing is one of my moments. As long as I live, I won't forget it. I grew up in a home where there was music of all kinds, but I had never encountered anything quite like this. So stark and raw; so beautiful and yet so violent. It was like listening to someone holding their heart in their hand.

The band was on fire. They played with a fierce passion. They speeded up songs to a punkish thrash, then slowed them down to a gin-soaked blues. Over this extraordinary sound came Patti's voice like a whipcrack: mischievous, scheming, prowling, transgressive.

In the mid-1970s, women didn't sing like this. It was the era of Karen Carpenter, Agnetha and Frida, all swaddled in cheesecloth and lurid batik. But this voice reminded me of Janis Joplin, of Howling Wolf, or Screaming Jay Hawkins. It also brought to mind the traditional *sean-nós* singing I had heard with my father on trips to rural Connemara.

It would swoop from a growl to a scream in a single phrasing. It soared and hollered, it crooned and barked. It could squeal like a saxophone or rumble like an ancient cello; you'd get goosebumps listening to it, and I played it at full-blast: loud enough to hurt my teeth. She'd snarl and spit and shriek the lyrics, but at other times there was a heartbreaking tenderness in the tone. In between singing she'd mutter streams of incantation that were more like crazy prayers than rock 'n' roll lyrics.

Listening to her was a crash course in popular culture's rebels. Rimbaud, Bessie Smith, Chuck Berry and The Who, Lou Reed, Allen Ginsberg: all of them were included in Patti's worldview. Maddening, beautiful, pretentious, disgraceful, there had never been anyone like her and there never will be again. No Blondie or U2 would have been possible without her, no Polly J. Harvey, no Nick Cave, no White Stripes. As

Bob Dylan once remarked of Johnny Cash, 'Some people drive the train, but others built the tracks.' That's how Patti Smith should always be remembered. As one of the truly great track-builders of pop music.

MUSEUM OF BROKEN RELATIONSHIPS

Cathy Power

The Museum of Broken Relationships was in Ireland last month. Two Croatian artists, who had comforted many broken-hearted friends, created the museum to preserve the heritage of relationships that end, happily or unhappily.

Every item in the collection has been contributed anonymously and each one has a short explanatory text with it. It came to Kilkenny from Croatia and went on to Slovakia. Wherever it goes, the locals have the chance to contribute relics of their individual broken hearts.

There is a fine collection including seven bras, a wedding dress, assorted photographs, cuddly toys, a mobile phone and, of course, love letters and poetry.

Someone living in Kilkenny had contributed a neatly pressed and folded blue blouse, accompanied by a short, sad description of how the woman who wore it was taken out to lunch by her husband so that he could tell her he was leaving her. Six weeks later he was gone, she said.

A prosthetic leg was contributed by a Balkans war veteran who fell in love with his physiotherapist. He explains in his little note that the leg lasted longer than the relationship.

How could anyone look at the collection and not think of something they could or should contribute and relive the broken relationships in their lives and the bits and pieces around the place that remain from them.

I was in love with a man from New Zealand once. When I met him he was already decided on going home. He had come to Europe to do the year out which was almost obligatory for Antipodeans back in the 1980s. He had already stayed longer than he had planned and the call of cold beer and warm weather, the cricket, his family and the food was proving too hard to resist.

However, one thing led to another between us and soon we had set up house. He was an engineer, working illegally here in a potato-crisp factory and, like most people I knew at the time, I was mainly unemployed.

It is hard to believe that we didn't have email, text, video phones or cheap phone calls then, and that people used to write to each other regularly. He was a great man for the letters and parcels home. He used to type a standard newsletter, photocopy it and then add personal notes and send it to a dozen or so friends and family each month.

It was because of the monthly parcels and because of the universal phenomenon of not-being-able-to-find-the-Sellotape, that he went down to a stationery shop called Evans' of Mary's Abbey and bought an industrial-sized roll of adhesive tape. It was about the size of a big round of cheese.

He used it to make up the parcels of Irish calendars, corny tourist T-shirts, photographs and other bits and pieces to send home. We never couldn't find the Sellotape, as this roll was so enormous and sat on top of the fridge in the house we shared in Dublin. However, he left Ireland and me after two years and went back down under. He left the Sellotape in its place. Six months later he sent me a ticket to Auckland. I went, had the best and one of the longest holidays of my life touring the North Island of New Zealand in a camper van. At the end of that six weeks, we sadly decided that he could not live anywhere else. I, on the other hand, decided that if I was going to live 13,000 miles away from Ireland, I wanted to go somewhere much more exotic than 1980s New Zealand. At the end of February 1986 I left him at Auckland airport and never saw him again. Soon the expensive phone calls became further and further apart and eventually we admitted that this was going nowhere and we stopped.

However, his relationship with my mother survived and they exchanged letters and cards regularly, so although we had no direct contact we knew what was happening in each other's lives. When she died suddenly in 2003, I wrote him a little note to let him know and, instead of writing back, he lifted the phone and rang.

I told him I still had the roll of Sellotape. It sits in the bottom of a press in the kitchen and it is still big enough not to get lost, although it is now about the size of a saucer and not the huge circle that it once was.

I should donate it to the Museum of Broken Relationships before it shrinks to nothing but a small ring of cardboard. The Sellotape has lasted twenty-four years longer than the relationship, but every time we wrap a present in our house I think of him.

FLOYD ON HAT

Donal Hayes

In the spring of 1986 I shared a house in Dorset on the south coast of England with a number of friends from Cork. We had all recently graduated, all had jobs and were living in our shared domestic bliss. Well bliss maybe, but looking back, the domesticity played second fiddle. We were all away from home for the first time and all coping with our new freedoms and responsibilities with different levels of enthusiasm. Everything was new and everything was possible. My housemates discovered love, money, soccer, travel and work – all to greater or lesser degrees of success. I discovered Keith Floyd.

In our house the idea of being interested in cooking would have been looked upon as being decidedly uncool. Until Floyd. From the opening strains of 'Waltzin' Black' by The Stranglers to the closing 'Walking on the Beaches Looking at the Peaches' he gave a healthy and passionate two fingers to the conventional food programme. He was not putting on an act; he was allowing the camera to follow him. He drank, he smoked, he was funny, he was rude, and he was consciously unprofessional. He left the security of the kitchen to cook mackerel on trawlers and boil shrimp in huge pots on the beach. If food was the new rock 'n' roll, then Floyd was Johnny Rotten.

So that summer I followed Floyd around the coast of England as he cooked and drank his way from obscurity through cult status and on to be the definition of the now much overused expression, celebrity chef.

I followed him, slurp for slurp, through the following summer, as he cooked bouillabaisse in Marseilles to the smell of Gitanes and the snarl of the *deux chevaux*, and rustled up truffle omelettes in the Périgord, on a pan, over an open fire. A white suit, dark glasses, a red handkerchief and an outsize glass of Bordeaux. And that, my little gastronauts, was that.

In 1988 we drank our way through Britain and Ireland, boiling bacon and cabbage in West Cork and trading tetchy comment for tetchy comment with a fresh-faced Darina Allen. We shared rabbit in gooseberry and champagne in a little pub in Somerset. It was summer, and we were set.

The world was his freshly opened oyster. Onto America, Australia, India, Asia, Spain, Italy and, rather optimistically, I felt, to Africa. The Scandinavian series was surely done for the sole purpose of being able to use the wonderful title of *Floyd's Fjord Fiesta*. He had finally cooked his way around the world. And his star was now on the wane.

In late 1995 he moved to live in Kinsale and, coincidentally, so did I. Kinsale was small and Floyd was big and the marriage was doomed to fail. But for a couple of years he loved Kinsale and Kinsale loved him. I would see him around town on a daily basis – the white Rolls Royce with the personalised number plate was difficult to miss – but, despite my hero worship, I respected his privacy too much to speak to him. I needed a casual encounter.

Then one night, in the winter of 1996, my wife and I went for a late-evening pint to one of our local pubs. It was a Tuesday night in November so the place was virtually empty. Empty except for Floyd and the landlord, Alex Hogan, sitting at the far end of the bar eating prawns. We sat at the bar with our drinks and Alex chatted idly to us, as both he and Floyd worked their way through a mountain of prawns. Still no acknowledgement or word from Floyd, concentrating all the time on his shellfish and wine. And then, without as much as a bye or leave, he got up and was gone. Out through the bar and into the kitchen. I was gutted like a fresh cod to have missed my opportunity.

But I could not have been more wrong. Five minutes later Floyd reappeared from the kitchen with a large plate of prawns, pungent with ginger, garlic, chilli and coriander. He put the plate between my wife and I, saying he would hate to see us left out. And that was it. I muttered something unintelligible and unintelligent but he was gone.

The following year he left Kinsale for good. He sold his house and auctioned off all the contents. The auction attracted people from far and wide, all eager to buy their little bit of Floyd. I was torn between going to bid on my own piece of Floyd memorabilia and the fact that it was all a little unseemly. I decided not to go.

Some weeks later, at a dinner party, I was given a present of a hat that a friend had bought at the auction. It was a felt, western-style hat with a leather band around the brim, custom-made by Texas Hatters of Austin Texas and embossed in gold lettering on the inside was 'handmade especially for Keith Floyd'.

I was embarrassed by my friend's generosity and thrilled to become the owner of part of my own coming of age.

The hat doesn't fit, incidentally, but then again, I wouldn't have expected it to.

TRANSLATIONS IN DERRY

Nuala Hayes

Recently, I watched a scene on television which brought tears to my eyes. It had drama, it had tension, it had crowds, it was stage-managed and it had a resolution.

It was from the Guildhall Square in Derry, where thousands of people waited for the results of the Saville Inquiry. After eight years of deliberation, the inquiry would deliver its findings on the truth behind the killing of thirteen people on the streets of Derry on Bloody Sunday in January 1972. The findings were clear and unequivical. But the moment when the British Prime Minister David Cameron projected on a huge screen, live from London, apologised to the people of Derry, on behalf of his government, for the behaviour of the forces of the Crown, stopped me in my tracks. The crowd erupted with approval and relief. That was a first, I thought.

It also brought me back then to another, more personal experience. Another piece of history, but of a different kind. It had drama, tension, an audience, and was also stage-managed. It was the last few moments of the opening night of Brian Friel's play *Translations*, which opened inside that same Guildhall in September 1980. An occasion that those of us who were part of it will not easily forget.

The rich Donegal tones of actor Ray McAnally's voice spoke the last lines, as the lights faded to black. There was silence. Applause erupted, the lights came up and the cast appeared for a well-rehearsed bow. The applause continued, so we returned again and again. The playwright joined us on stage to cheers of approval. He said something about a prophecy of St Colmcille coming true. My memory is blurred at this stage, but can it be true that he said that St Colmcille prophesied that a theatre company called Field Day would take Derry by storm on 23 September 1980?

In the days that followed word spread that the play, *Translations*, which against all the odds had its world premiere in Derry, seemed to have hit a chord with both audience and critics. By any standards, the 'enterprise', as the playwright liked to call it, was, to say the least, hazardous. The Guildhall, though a great building, was no theatre. Voices bounced around the walls like echoes down the centuries. A plaque on the stairwell marked the dates of its restoration after numerous bomb attacks. Few buildings had escaped the explosions that had shaken the city throughout the 1970s. The streets were patrolled day and night by the British Army and the police. Helicopters circled constantly. A trip to a city centre store meant a body search at the door. Tension was a normal part of everyday life.

It was a risk for the founders of Field Day, Brian Friel and Stephen Rea, to launch a new theatre company in such circumstances. It was a risk for the cast and crew, from both sides of the border in Ireland and from England and Scotland, to come to Derry at that time. Our entire family moved there. Our two lively little boys, aged seven and four, went to school in St Eugene's, within the walls. We lived on the opposite side of the river, on the Waterside. The marching season was in full swing. Graffiti on the side entrance to the house we were staying in said 'Fenians Out'. We didn't take it personally. It was a marking of territory, we decided. The people of Derry were warm and welcoming. The City Council had pulled out all the stops to make the project possible and the context was perfect for the play. Deep down we knew that if it wasn't a disaster, then a piece of theatre history was in the making.

Translations is set in a hedge school in the fictitious townland of Ballybeg in County Donegal in 1833, long before partition. The Royal Engineers of the British Army are engaged in an ordnance survey of the entire Island. The Irish place names are being translated into English for the purpose of the new map. At the same time, a new national education system is being put in place to ensure that the children learn English at school instead of their own native Gaelic. On face value, it seems simple enough, and practical and logical to the British rulers. But it had far-reaching consequences for the entire Island that have lasted right up to the present and the unfinished business was still being played out on the streets of Derry as we rehearsed the play.

At the first reading of the script in the rehearsal room in the Guildhall, there was spontaneous applause from the cast and crew. Sitting around that table were Ray Mc Anally, Stephen Rea, Liam Neeson, Mick Lally, Ann Hasson, David Heap, Brenda Scallon, Shaun Scott, Roy O'Hanlon, along with the author, and the director Art O'Briain. Some of those names are still well known; some of them, like the recently much-lamented Mick Lally, are sadly no longer with us. The sense of anticipation and excitement and apprehension of that morning lasted right throughout rehearsals. Those rehearsals were not without their tensions. We realised that a perfect score had been created by Brian, and our responsibility was to play it as well as we could.

Following on from that opening night, we travelled with the play to towns and villages throughout Northern Ireland. After Derry and Belfast came Magherafelt, Dungannon, Newry, Carrickmore, Armagh, Enniskillen. We played in school halls and community centres. We changed in classrooms and in sweaty school gyms. The crew packed up each night and moved straight to the next venue to prepare for the following night's performance. These were troubled times, and at night the streets were deserted and dangerous. In Carrickmore in County Tyrone, it seemed that the entire village was under Army surveillance from the huge barracks which overlooked us. Still, people came out in their hundreds to pack the halls. Tea and sandwiches and stronger stuff were always proffered at the end of the night before we set off in the darkness again, high as kites in our transit van. As the weeks passed, the players and the characters we played bonded as a family.

I played the part of Máire Chatach, the local girl who falls in love with a British soldier, one of the map-makers. It is his job to translate the local Irish place names into the Queen's English. They are divided by history and language. She speaks only Irish and he, English. In their attempt to communicate, the lovers resort to the only words they share, the words of the place names which are being translated: *Bun na hAbhainn, Druim Dubh, Poll na gCaorach, Lis Maol, Lis na nGrádh, Mullach, Port, Tor, Lag.* The sound of those words still gives me the shivers and brings me back to the famous love scene, the tragic consequences, and the strange brave ending to the play.

Máire asks Hugh Mór, the master of the school and a man who prides himself on his knowledge of the Classics, what the English word 'always' means. He is drunk and defeated but he has eventually agreed to teach her English.

'*Semper, per omnia saecula.* The Greeks call it *aei*. It's not a word I'd start with. It's a silly word, girl.'

The play ends with a downbeat: only change is constant. And all has changed.

It is now thirty years since that first production of *Translations*. The play has become a classic. It is studied by students for the Leaving Certificate, and in theatre schools, and has been translated and produced all over the world.

It is true, that nothing lasts forever, that 'always' is not the word to start with.

There is peace now, however uneasy at times. And Derry/Londonderry has recently been named the first UK City of Culture.

One thing is sure; the play itself, *Translations*, will last longer than any of us.

That ritual of the first day of rehearsals, when a group of people begin the process of reading together for the first time, will be repeated over and over again. *Translations* explains something that is difficult to put into words and it is only by playing it out and witnessing it in real time that it works.

But the memory of that first time, in September 1980 at the Guildhall in Derry, is only for those who were lucky enough to be present.

OCTOBER

AT HOME AMONG TREES

Denis Sampson

Our first autumn in this house, I planted a Norway maple in the front garden, and now it is taller than the house. Some lighter branches gently touch my bedroom window and often the sun shimmering on the leaves is the first thing I see in the morning. I chose a Norway maple because my neighbour had just planted one, and together they have grown, their countless yellow leaves the last to fall after the reds and oranges have come down.

Our single trees here on the street are like scattered reminders of what envelops Mount Royal, which begins its steep rise just a block away. Within minutes I can be on the mountain among the trees, high above the city. It is October now and the mountain is ablaze with all the shades of maple, and so this is where I go for an hour each morning, walking.

In my first winter in the city, I was persuaded to try cross-country ski-ing, and so, equipped with two narrow wooden skis, I tried my luck on the trails that encircle the summit. I persevered for some winters and in-troduced my young sons to the magic of zipping through snow-laden trees, although, of course, they soon wanted to go for the downhill action on the real mountains.

But it is as a place for walking on the gravelled avenues that I have al-ways loved the wooded mountain, in all seasons until the snow and the skiers take over during the freeze-up. I walk on the mountain alone, with my wife, my daughter, with friends. Unlike many who go to the mountain to picnic in family groups, or take the sun, or exercise vigorously, or have a romantic interlude, or just relax away from the traffic and the com-merce, I go there for the trees themselves.

On the mountain in the heart of Montreal, I am back in the country, walking among old trees as I did in my first years in County Clare beside Lough Derg.

One of my earliest memories is of the low-hanging branch of a huge and very old chestnut tree that occupied a central spot in the large field that encircled our house. My father sat me up on it and gently bounced it up and down. The excitement of that swing must have been intense, for it is an indelible part of my childhood, and I often returned to it later under my own steam. I think it may well have been a swing in the days of my father's childhood too, but now there is an empty space, for the chestnut came down in a storm some years ago.

Storms. The wind in the trees. That's the other memory, possibly an even earlier one. My mother feared the wind. She expected a falling branch to hit the old house. But I remember all the stormy nights I lay in bed listening to the gusty creaking of the old trees or, more often, to the soothing constant hush through the leaves that sent me off to sleep. Listening to the storm outside was high drama for my parents, but the trees that enveloped the house were all comforting to me; I could not really grasp the idea of another kind of paradise in which there was a tree of knowledge, of good and evil.

I graduated from having my own house in the trunk of the old chestnut tree, and from other structures built with my brother in other trees, to the woods by the lakeside, to the true adventure in unknown lands. Down here, I knew the eel-fishers camped in secret, for my father sometimes helped them out, and when my mother read us *Robinson Crusoe*, it was an entirely real scenario to me. I imagined myself living in the woods, even running away from family troubles to my own lost place. In my father's childhood, a soldier had deserted from the British Army during World War I and had lived there for some time.

The magic of trees and woodland was compounded for me by some of the earliest poems we learned off in school. 'The Daffodils': 'beside the lake, beneath the trees, fluttering and dancing in the breeze,' although at my house the hundreds of daffodils did not actually spread down to the lakeshore and the woods. And before I came to North America, it was not television or Hollywood movies, the glitter of New York City, or the music of Elvis or the Beach Boys that prepared me. It was the poems of Robert Frost. The memorable ones that everyone knows took on an extraordinary charge for me as I travelled down into Vermont and New Hampshire, hundreds of miles of trees blanketing the Adirondacks. The man who stopped by woods on a snowy evening somehow knew my feelings: 'These woods are lovely, dark and deep/But I have promises to keep.'

Even more than that, Frost was there ahead of me: 'Two paths diverged in a yellow wood,/And sorry I could not travel both.' At this stage, I was already 'deep in Canadian woods'. But when I turn back to try to keep the other path into the woods open, I am moved by Seamus Heaney's elegy for his mother:

> Deep planted and long gone, my coeval
> Chestnut from a jam jar in a hole,
> Its heft and hush become a bright nowhere.

My mother is still alive and well in County Clare among the trees and beside the lake, the chestnut tree she feared 'long gone', but it is my 'bright nowhere'.

Even in absence, I am rooted in my world by trees.

MEETING MICHAEL HARTNETT

Bill Tinley

Details of the first time I met Michael Hartnett are a little hazy now, but what's certain is the encounter was rather brief and somewhat awkward. Earlier in the day, as a guest of the Irish Department at Maynooth College, Hartnett had recited his poems *as Gaeilge* and in English to a large audience of students. I don't recall the date, but reckon it must have been shortly after the publication of *O Bruadair* in December 1985. I was still an undergraduate at the time and president of the English Literary Society, alert to the world of Irish letters and on the lookout for authors to invite to our Friday morning readings.

Some hours later, catching the mid-afternoon 66 bus to Dublin on the first part of a two-leg journey home for the weekend, I made my way to the upper deck. It was virtually deserted. Towards the back sat an acquaintance of mine, on his way to a basketball match; towards the front sat the slight figure of Michael Hartnett. My nerve failed me and I opted to sit with my college mate. I half-listened to what he said, uncomfortably conscious of the poet further up the bus, an esteemed guest of the university abandoned to the grimness of 1980s public transport in the depths of winter. My friend alighted near the West County Hotel and, as the bus descended into Chapelizod, I summoned up sufficient courage to take a seat beside Hartnett.

A brief conversation ensued in which I complimented him on his reading. In the short journey between the Mullingar House and Islandbridge, where he got off to make his way to Inchicore, I recall only that he told me that the raincoat he was wearing in the Edward Maguire painting adorning the cover of his Raven Arts *Collected Poems: Volume 1* had been given to him by Derek Mahon and that he had subsequently left it behind him in O'Neill's of Suffolk Street. Then he was gone into the already fading light of the afternoon.

By the time of my second encounter with Michael Hartnett, some two years later, our paths had crossed again, albeit at quite a remove. The *Dundalk Democrat* newspaper had run a poetry competition in the summer of 1987, of which Hartnett was the judge. I had entered a poem entitled 'The Dead Sea Scrolls', composed in a down-at-heel apartment overlooking Main Street that a friend and I were renting in advance of autumn exams. The poem didn't win or make the medals, but to my surprise was included in an anthology of poems selected by Michael Hartnett. The thrill of his endorsement was only slightly diminished many years later when a more attentive reading of his introduction suggested that the poet had not been alone in choosing the thirty-nine poems that made the cut.

Another academic year was already more than halfway through. The English Literary Society at Maynooth, of which I was no longer president, had invited Hartnett to the campus to read in the usual Friday slot and he was to follow this with an informal workshop with interested students. It was 5 February 1988, a surprisingly sunny day for the time of year. Hartnett performed splendidly, charming the assembled students and feeding off their enthusiasm and interest. During the reading he told a story of having read in similar circumstances in a university in Spain some years previously. He recalled how, in a moment of extravagance brought on by the setting and the attentiveness of his audience, he had tossed his cap, like a cocky matador, into the tiered ranks of students. Back home in Ireland several weeks later, the cap was returned to him through the good offices of the Department of Foreign Affairs.

It wasn't until a small group of students – aspiring poets and some Literary Society officers – decamped to the staff area of the Arts Building where the workshop was to be conducted that we learned of Hartnett's rather extraordinary trip to Maynooth earlier that morning. He had made his way in good time to Middle Abbey Street, there to catch the 66 so as to be in Maynooth for the 11 o'clock reading. His partner, Angela, had accompanied him to the bus stop and had seen him off safely. Only then, as the bus pulled away, did he realise that he had left his glasses in her handbag. Far-sighted, there was no way he could read from his numerous collections of poems without the aid of his glasses. From the upper deck he saw Angela make her way towards the Ha'penny Bridge: there was nothing for it but to get off the bus and catch up with her. Not without some effort he did so, successfully retrieving the necessary spectacles. But the next 66 would not get him to Maynooth until well after his appointment. He had no option but to hail a taxi which he did along the quays. Once more Angela saw him off.

He had just settled into the back seat of the taxi, composed himself again after his panic, though probably sore now at the prospect of losing a good part of his fee to a taxi fare, when the driver, eyeing him in the rear-view mirror, asked him, 'Are you Michael Hartnett?' It's doubtful, even in the heyday of notorious writers like Behan and Kavanagh, if their celebrity would have extended to instant recognition by taxi-drivers. Startled, Hartnett replied that it was indeed he. 'I knew I recognised you,' the driver said. 'I bought your first book back in 1968.' The poet was almost dumbstruck. What were the odds on such a coincidence?

When he explained his situation to the taxi-driver – if memory serves his name was Oliver – and told him his destination was Maynooth, the meter was turned off. Not only was Oliver not going to charge him for the ride but he had decided there and then to take off whatever part of the day was required to bring Hartnett to Maynooth and back again to Dublin. Like brothers in arms out of touch since being demobbed and now unexpectedly reunited, the two set off through Chapelizod, Palmerstown and Lucan on their way to St Patrick's College. With time to spare on reaching Leixlip, they reckoned a break was in order, repairing for a quick one to the Salmon Leap beside the Liffey Bridge.

After the reading – which, of course, Oliver attended – and surrounded by a coterie of admiring students, Hartnett was effervescent. The perfect serendipity of the whole morning had completely animated him. He had probably been tempted to toss his cap to the audience again. As he settled into the informal dialogue of the discussion, Oliver was dispatched to the dilapidated Students' Union bar – fondly known as 'The Barn' – to bring 'refreshments' to him, fortifying him for the rigours of an audience with us. We camped around him, the oatmeal-coloured easy chairs drawn into a semi-circle, cold, clear sunlight brimming in the enclosed garden outside the plate-glass windows, a counterpoint to the deep amber of the brandy in the poet's glass. Oliver sat in attendance, on the fringe of the workshop but clearly absorbed by the proceedings, a smiling face behind large, reactalight spectacles. To finish off the day, Hartnett told us, on their return to Dublin they would stop off at Oliver's house so that, after all these years, he would have his copy of *Anatomy of a Cliché* signed.

I encountered Michael Hartnett just one more time. It was early summer 1996. My brother and I had met in The Duke one evening for a few pints over photographs and stories of his recent visit to Nepal with his girlfriend. Strolling from Duke Street onto Grafton Street, shortly after ten, I saw, not far away, the thin figure of Michael Hartnett, arm-in-arm with Angela, making his way somewhat unsteadily up that famous thoroughfare. When he had drawn level with us he stopped and made some good-spirited but incoherent banter with us before moving on. I tried to do him the courtesy of letting him know I knew who he was, but doubt if it registered with him or that it mattered.

'Who was that?' my brother asked when he was out of earshot.

'That,' I said, 'was the poet, Michael Hartnett.'

THE GREEKS AT VENTRY

John O'Donnell

The crew of the Greek cargo-ship *Diamantis* may have expected high winds, rough seas and perhaps even the odd whale on their voyage from Freetown in West Africa to Barrow-In-Furness in England. But on 3 October 1939 they were spotted off Land's End by a German submarine. Already queasy in the foul weather that afternoon, the sight of the submarine coming to the surface nearby must have set Greek stomachs churning. They were carrying 4,000 tons of iron ore to enemy territory. The U-boat was perfectly entitled under the Geneva Convention to sink the loaded ship.

Having stopped the freighter, the submarine commander Werner Lott wanted to examine the ship's papers, but could not board in the boiling seas. To persuade the ship to follow the sub towards the Irish coast – where seas were calmer – he fired a shot across the bow of the ship. The Greeks panicked, jumping lemming-like into tiny lifeboats carried on deck. Lott could see how rough the seas were; it was clear that they could not possibly survive. Already crewmen had been flipped out of capsizing lifeboats into the foam. What was he to do?

In a remarkable act of humanity and chivalry, Lott decided he would rescue the terrified Greeks. Somehow he managed to pluck the entire crew from the waves, taking them aboard his submarine. Having sunk the freighter, the U-boat dived. Now Lott had a problem. He already had a crew of forty-three; now he had twenty-eight frightened, soaking sailors who spoke no German. He had barely enough provisions for his own men. Obviously he could not offload the Greeks in England; British warplanes were already on the lookout for U-boat 35. And so he headed west to where German warships had in the past been welcomed; the neutral waters of Ireland.

A little over a day later, the submarine surfaced in Dingle Bay and cruised into Ventry Harbour. Astonished locals gathered, watching as the U-boat steamed in. Fifty yards off the beach, a little rubber dinghy was lowered; and, as if emerging from the Ark after the deluge, a single German seaman rowed the exhausted Greeks, two by two, ashore.

The Greeks had been well treated aboard the submarine, though some were still in shock. Five were brought to the local hospital in Dingle. They craved cigarettes, and no doubt would not have refused anything stronger offered by their hospitable west Kerry hosts. Then a schoolboy, the late Jimmy Fenton, remembered that while their English was extremely poor they kept repeating one phrase in praise of Commander Lott: 'German, gut man.'

But Commander Lott had little time to lose. In entering Irish waters he had technically breached Irish neutrality. Having landed his special cargo, Lott and his crew turned the bow around and headed slowly out of Ventry. Crew on deck waved goodbye to the bemused Greeks and excited locals. Soon the U-boat disappeared beneath the waves. A little while after, the Gardaí arrived. Later an RAF plane searched unsuccessfully for submarine U-35.

Eventually the Greeks travelled to Dublin and from there to Greece. But they never forgot the kindness of the German commander and his crew or the hospitality of their new friends in west Kerry. The Greek government erected a plaque at Dingle Hospital as a tribute to the kind deeds of the locals. They wanted to award a medal to Lott for his act of humanity, but the German government wouldn't hear of it. The British government, already suspicious that Irish ports were being used as refuelling stops by German warships, protested bitterly. At a cabinet meeting three weeks later, Churchill condemned the Irish attitude to the use of Irish ports as intolerable, demanding that the ports be invaded and seized immediately. Wiser counsel prevailed.

And Commander Lott? He returned to Ireland on numerous occasions, visiting Kerry and meeting forty-five years later in Ventry the now-grown schoolboy Jimmy Fenton who had been one of the first to see the U-boat entering the harbour. Reprimanded by the German high command for the reckless endangerment of his crew in carrying out his humanitarian acts, two months after the event Lott's U-boat was sunk off Norway by a flotilla of Royal Navy destroyers. He and his crew made it to the surface where they were hauled aboard by the British. Lott made a point of thanking the commander in charge of the flotilla for their rescue efforts. 'That is how life is,' the British officer replied. 'You were extraordinary picking up the Greeks.' After the war Lott and his opposite number became friends, corresponding regularly until the British naval commander who had rescued the German rescuer died suddenly at sea on a sunny day in 1979. His name was Lord Louis Mountbatten.

THE COMMENTATOR

Joe Ó Muircheartaigh

Sheehy's house in a place called Ballintaggart near Dingle was always surrounded by sport. A few fields away and you had Casey's land that was home to the greatest flapper meeting of them all. Still is. Half a mile in the other direction nestled Dingle's nine-hole links in the townland of Dúnsíon, while the greyhounds and football were everywhere.

The greyhounds were brought into the Moriarty household by the original Joe Ó Muircheartaigh – the clan's *cigire* who coursed greyhounds and who had a litter brother of the great Dainty Man, the dog belonging to All-Ireland footballer Con Brosnan who won the Derby in Clonmel in '32.

The hounds coursed around Ballintaggart, for fun I suppose, but with Joe dreaming and talking of a Derby. Joe talked football too, having won a Munster junior medal with Kerry in '26, while he also gave golf clubs to his young nephews.

It meant they were spoiled for sport on their doorstep, but what lay beyond the front door of Sheehy's house was different – something almost mythical in attraction. A radio. The only one for miles around.

Sunday afternoons became great social occasions, as people of all ages came to listen. Micheál Ó Muircheartaigh was one of them.

The Sheehys had fourteen children, so it was a busy place – and it was there Micheál got to listen to the 1938 All-Ireland football final between Kerry and Galway.

Nobody would dare go near the radio. Back then radios were regarded as temperamental and delicate and if you had too many people messing with it, it could let you down. The only person allowed to touch it, turn it up, down or sideways, was Mickey Sheehy.

And he took his job very seriously. During the week leading up to an All-Ireland he'd carry the battery into Houlihan's in Dingle to get it charged up. Then the radio would be used very sparingly in the days leading up to the match.

You had to be in Sheehy's early or else you wouldn't be able to get in. It was a great occasion for the Sheehys because they were facilitating people and showing off their product.

That All-Ireland day in Sheehy's, Micheál's introduction to Croke Park couldn't have been more dramatic. It was Micheál O'Hehir's first All-Ireland football final broadcast. For Micheál and his brothers, Paddy, Náis, my own father Dónal, my grandfather Thady, and everyone else listening, the game had a special dimension.

It was the Dingle connection to the team. The Brosnans, Seán and Paddy 'Bawn', 'Gega' O'Connor, Billy Casey and Bill Dillon were all Dingle players – Paddy Kennedy was from over the road in Annascaul.

These were the players everyone visualised in the hushed kitchen of Sheehy's. The 'Bawn' being uncompromising in defence, Billy Casey and Bill Dillon the same outside him in the half-line; Kennedy and Brosnan ruling the skies at midfield and 'Gega' leading the attack.

That afternoon Kerry thought they'd won their thirteenth All-Ireland in a dramatic few last seconds. Tony McAuliffe, who became my neighbour in Ennis over sixty years later, passed to John Joe 'Purty' Landers and the Rock Street man kicked the lead point, but as the ball was sailing over, referee Tommy Culhane from Glin blew his final whistle.

For Micheál it was back to Sheehy's for the replay and more drama – this time, with Galway leading by four points with three minutes to go, a whistle from referee Peter Waters was mistaken for the final one and Galway supporters rushed the field. Kerry left, with some of the players gone from the ground and on their way home before order was restored to finish the game.

Micheál listened intently, not to know that eleven years later the same Micheál O'Hehir would hand him the microphone for his maiden voyage in Croke Park – the Railway Cup football final between Munster and Leinster.

His own voice coming out of Sheehy's radio, or from the one his Auntie Mai brought back from America and sat proudly in the middle of the Moriarty kitchen in Dúnsíon.

And so it began. Our family's radio man, who's touched our hearts and others with his words – the way he says 'em, the bilingual journey through the GAA ages, but always rooted in the present day.

Everyone has their favourite Micheál moments.

The Donegal man will speak of '92 when he talked the Annals of the Four Masters from 1616 – An Bráthair Bocht Micheál Ó Cléirigh, his brother Conaire Ó Cléirigh, Cuchoccríche Ó Cléirigh and Flaithaire Ó Maolchonaire. Wish they were here, said Micheál.

The Meathman will pick the blitzkrieg move for that goal in Game Four in '91 that broke Dublin hearts; the Downman will think of D.J. Kane – or Lawrence of Arabia as Micheál called him – returning to battle with head gear like Peter O'Toole's famous character; the Kerryman doesn't know what to pick because he has so many big days.

The list goes on and on, but I'll always go for Clare. My adopted place, my home, my family's home. The Clare shouts around Micheál in '95 when they came in from a desert of eighty-one years and won an All-Ireland. The way he rattled off the names of the 1914 Clare team when when Jamesie O'Connor scored the final point.

Fowler McInerney, John Shaloo, The 'Dodger' Considine, John Fox who went straight from Croke Park to the Western Front but who lived to tell the tale, James Guerin who got three goals in the final but was a victim of the Great Flu epidemic a few years later, captain Amby Power and Sham Spellissy and more.

And there's more, because other Clare folk go back to the famous Oireachtas final of '54, when Clare beat Wexford.

The commentary was *as Gaeilge* and Big Dan McInerney became *Dónal Mór Mac Airchinnaigh*; Nickey Rackard became *Nioclás Mór*; Jimmy Smyth was *Séamus MacGabhann,* and so on … and Wexford was *Loch Garman*.

And therein lay a tale.

Clare won and believed there'd never be another bad day, with local Ennis wag Peter 'Slavery' Guilfoyle going down in history when he said: 'My God, that fella Gorman must be a great player, he's all over the field, he's brilliant.'

That was Micheál. You didn't have to be able to understand him to love him. We'll miss him on big match days.

But, I'll tell you what. The radio was on in Sheehy's of Ballintaggart on Saturday evening for his final commentary after sixty-two years and in Auntie Mai's old kitchen too.

And all around Ireland, and beyond.

And it was emotional.

TWO GAMBLERS

Christine Dwyer Hickey

My father was a gambler. In the late 1940s he owned a garage in Baggot Lane. He was a single man and a long-term resident of the Ormonde Hotel, where he lived for eight years prior to his marriage in 1956. He was young – still in his twenties – and in those stricken times, relatively well off.

One day, he goes into his then local bookies, Kilmartin's on Baggot Street, to collect on a bet. He is told there are insufficient funds on the premises to cover a pay-out of that size and asked if he will accept a cheque. No, he will not – he's put a cash bet on and expects a cash pay-out in return. In that case, the counter hand explains, he will have to go to head office. He most certainly will not! He has a business to run and has no intention of chasing after money that is rightfully his. A man who has been standing at the back of the shop takes a step forward. There may be other bystanders there, but I can't see them. I only see the young man, who is my father, and this other man, older by more than twenty years, coming up the rear; long coat and hat, collar on his shirt, slightly dog-eared – clearly a countryman. I see him, hand on hip (always with the hand on hip), head cocked to one side, peering through heavy-rimmed glasses. He throws in a remark in support of the young man: 'The bet had been placed in good faith, the bet must be honoured.' The counter hand now has two cranks to deal with. She goes out to the back to telephone head office for advice. The older man by now, with both hands on both hips, is rocking on his heels, his coat pushed back like a tail. While they wait, the ins and outs of the winning bet are discussed – the whys and whynots – the sort of talk so beloved of gamblers as if it's all about knowledge and divine inspiration; nothing so vague or frivolous as mere luck. The girl returns and announces that a taxi, to be paid for by Kilmartin's, will take the young man to head office. The two men continue the conversation out onto the road, and when the taxi arrives, it seems completely natural that the older man should also climb into it. At head office, they stir up another scene before, business concluded, they finally come back out onto the street. There my father, pocket stuffed with money, turns to the country man and asks that immortal and peculiarly Irish question: 'Tell me, do you take a drink yourself?'

And so the friendship begins between Dinny Dwyer and Patrick Kavanagh. A friendship that would last until Kavanagh's death over twenty years later.

If Kavanagh did not know Dinny Dwyer that day, I am certain Dinny knew him. Anyone who lived or worked in the area would surely have noticed him, ambling along, muttering to himself, stopping to look at this or that thing, to chat to this or that person. One thing is certain, Kavanagh would not have to wait 100 years to be inquired about in Baggot Street. Dinny would have known him by sight but also by reputation. He knew his poems, certainly. He was an avid reader and reciter of poetry (I heard Auden's poems from him long before I was able to read them). My father may have been a gambler, and a man that sold cars to make a living, but what he really wanted to be at that time of his life was a poet. Perhaps this was what attracted him to Kavanagh in the first place.

And what of Kavanagh – what drew him into the friendship? It is said that he only started to gamble in his middle years, which would have been around the time he met my father. But it is most unusual for a man of that age to suddenly become hooked. Usually, and my father's case would be a typical example, it starts in early adolescence. Not that it really matters; both men would become addicted to gambling, as both would, in time, become addicted to alcohol. Gambling, as the more insidious, can often be the more destructive. A gambler will sacrifice everything to his addiction: time, money, above all hope. It will always come first; before family, before duty – yes, even before poetry.

Still, in the early days of the friendship, while the gambling was still at its seductive best, it was the principal bond between the two men. There was much to discuss and calculate, post-mortems to be carried out, triumphs to be celebrated. There were several trips to the races both at home and in England. Dinny was one of those expansive gamblers who care nothing for money; a carelessness – a lack of desperation if you like, that paradoxically can keep the winnings rolling in. Having spent the war in Belfast working in Harland and Wolff – one of the very few Catholics to have done so, and having survived *that* particular experience intact, and moreover gone on to survive the Belfast blitz – he had had his fill of death and destruction. From now on, life was for living. These sort of gamblers tend to look out rather than in. They are reckless and entertaining and above all optimistic. Their company is often invigorating. And perhaps this was just the tonic for a middle-aged poet of little or no means, tired of whiling away the lonely hours, nursing a drink in the hope that someone would buy him another, in the darkening light of an afternoon pub.

ELEVEN

Declan Hughes

The bike was big and black and heavy, with a frame at the front for the brown cardboard box. You had to fold the four flaps of the box shut, or the parcels might shoot out when you were coming down a steep hill, and since they contained glass bottles and jars, you couldn't let that happen. Mostly though, it felt like you were going *up* steep hills: Dalkey Avenue, and Killiney Hill Road, and the steepest of the lot (if the shortest), that stretch of Cunningham Road, that runs up from the railway. You needed to swing onto Cunningham Road with as much speed as you could muster, and trust in momentum and will to see you to the top. It was a matter of pride – professional pride, you might say – never to get off the bike and push, and through the combination of momentum and will, I'm proud to say I never did. I was the chemist's delivery boy for Hayes, Conyngham and Robinson on Railway Road, earning two pounds a week. It was my first job. I was eleven.

Up on the bike and out across Dalkey, delivering to nursing homes and to big, damp old Victorian and Georgian houses on darkening afternoons. My grandmother had died the year before, and sometimes the old ladies (it was almost all old ladies, and they would not have thanked you for calling them 'women') reminded me of her: their dignified hauteur, their bony parchment hands, their musty cake-mix aroma of boiled sweets and dried fruit and face powder.

I came in after school, and if there was nothing there at three, I'd have to come back around five. I could have been home in ten minutes, but I didn't want to go home. I would haunt the supermarkets, Power's and Five Star, wandering up and down the brightly lit aisles buying Maltesers and Lilt. I would study the second-hand books in the window of a women's clothes shop called Mother and Baby. Why did a shop called Mother and Baby have second-hand books for sale? I tried to buy three James Bond paperbacks, the Pan ones with the cool Raymond Hawkey covers – two pounds a week, I could pay my way – but the smirking assistant wouldn't sell them to me, on what grounds she declined to say.

Something was wrong at school. I had mislaid my friends, and I was being bullied. Something was wrong at home as well; I never really figured out what, but I was not much use to them, nor they to me. In dreams, my grandmother appeared to me in her coffin, her eyes gleaming.

On the delivery bike though, all of this fell away. On the delivery bike, I was looking to the future. There was a house I delivered to on Glenalua Road called 'Hendre', which I decided would be the name of the science-fiction novel, no, science-fiction *trilogy* I would write. That was after I had finished *Murder on Markham Island*, a detective novel I had high hopes for, going so far as to write down the names of the characters in a special notebook I bought with my first week's wages, although not quite as far as to write any of the actual book; all my momentum and will back then were channelled into climbing one steep hill after another.

Coming up to Christmas, outside a house on Ulverton Road, after ringing the bell half a dozen times, I was about to leave when the door finally creaked open and a female figure appeared, hunched with age. It was dark outside, streetlamps not on, and dark inside, the hall pitch-black. The only available light was in the old lady's eyes, unsteady, precarious light, like a candle guttering in a draft. She took the package, and caught me in the gaze of her gleaming eyes, and snapped the door shut.

I was on foot that day, the last delivery on my way home, but I went back in the other direction through Castle Street and into Five Star, and I walked up and down the brightly lit aisles until the chill had left me.

I bought some Maltesers.

I bought some Lilt.

Things would change soon. Of course they would. They always did.

I would get those James Bond books, and not from any shop with a name like Mother and Baby.

I was earning two pounds a week.

I could cycle up any hill in Dalkey.

I was eleven.

MARY WARD

Dolores MacKenna

On 21 October 1621, a group of eight women set out to make a 2,000-mile journey, on foot, from Brussels to Rome. The women, all English, were led by a Yorkshire woman named Mary Ward. Dressed as a pilgrim, Mary wore a dark brown dress trimmed with lace and a short cape. On her head was a tall, slightly conical, beaver pilgrim hat with a narrow brim. In her hand she carried a staff. It was her intention to reach Rome in time to celebrate Christmas.

Such a journey, undertaken at the onset of winter, was extremely hazardous. The pilgrims must cover an average of thirty miles a day. Roads were rough and uneven – sometimes overgrown. The countryside was a wilderness and people were frequently robbed. What was to be known as the Thirty Years War was raging all over Europe and disaffected soldiers from the many engaged armies roamed about, threatening civilians. Cities promised some shelter, if travellers were inside by nightfall when the gates closed. Mary and her group made all possible haste, stopping only for one meal a day – usually in the evening – since to qualify for a bed at an inn, guests had to pay for dinner.

The little party crossed the Rhine by a narrow bridge at Basle and took a winding road south, overlooked by lofty, snow-capped mountains. Below were slate-grey lake waters and in the distance could be heard the sounds of Alpine horns.

Soon the paths rose into the high Alps, where freezing winds added to the pilgrims' hardship, as they negotiated their way over thread-like tracks, running alongside ravines which dropped hundreds of feet below.

But these women were not easily intimidated. They had already known difficult times and had become used to dangerous living. Devout English Catholics, they had first-hand experience of the penal laws in their own country. Mary's grandmother had spent fourteen years in prison for her beliefs, while two of her uncles had been executed for taking part in the Gunpowder Plot in 1605, when Mary was a young woman of twenty. In fact, of the seven men who spearheaded that plot to blow up the English parliament while the king was present, all but two – one of them Guy Fawkes – were in some way related to her.

Mary had left England the year following the abortive Gunpowder Plot, with the intention of joining a religious order in Flanders. Having spent some time as a postulant in the Poor Clare convent in Saint Omer, she decided to set up a Poor Clare monastery nearby, specifically for English women. She then entered its novitiate herself. Soon, however, she came to realise that this was not the life she was meant to lead. She decided therefore to found a religious order for women who would not be restricted to the contemplative life. Instead they would remain active in the world, involving themselves particularly in the education of girls. Their institute would take as its model the Jesuit order of priests and would be self-governing. Mary Ward's journey to Rome was to seek papal approval for her venture.

As the travellers descended into the soft pasture lands at the foot of the Italian Alps, they made a diversion to visit the little town of Loreto – at the time a major place of pilgrimage – where it was believed the Virgin Mary's house at Nazareth had been miraculously transported. Even with this detour the women reached Rome, as planned, just as the bells were ringing in Christmas.

In spite of letters of introduction from prelates and princes, however, Vatican approval was not forthcoming. Pope Gregory was amazed by his English visitors. Even their appearance astonished him and he remarked that if they wore hats like that all day, they would surely have headaches. But much more serious was their notion of women religious working outside the cloister and expecting to run their own affairs. Mary Ward and her companions soon found themselves condemned as 'a disgrace to the Catholic religion', no better than 'chattering hussies' and 'galloping girls', gadding about unveiled and unchaperoned, with neither the walls of a convent nor husbands to keep them in order.

Mary was to survive suspicion, humiliation, and even imprisonment at the hands of the Inquisition. Papal approval was not obtained in her lifetime for the religious order which became known as the Institute of the Blessed Virgin Mary, or, in Ireland, the Loreto Sisters. Centuries would pass before the Institute, as she envisioned it, was fully recognised. Today, four hundred years after its foundation, the followers of Mary Ward are to be found working, particularly in education, throughout all five continents, their work bearing out her prophesy that 'women in time to come will do much'.

ATTENTION ALL SHIPPING

Marie Hannigan

In our household, the radio was permanently tuned to 2211, the frequency used by fishermen to communicate at sea. Skirled with static, it was far from pleasing to the ear. No amount of pleading would persuade my mother to move the dial, until *Mrs Dale's Diary* released us from the ear-grinding racket of the Trawler Band. My father's signature, a few whistled bars of 'Rose Marie', informed his fellow skippers that Johnny was on air, and my mother would lower her head to the set; straining to hear the brief transmission.

Those were the days, she confided, later, when the sound of his voice still brought a thrill.

'We were in love,' my father agreed. 'Too much love is not a good thing.' Alluding to their tempestuous relationship, he might well have been speaking of his other great passion.

Marie Angelique was – he claimed – a more demanding mistress than any wife. He had christened her in tribute to her origins in a Lorient shipyard. That she shared a name with the eponymous heroine of a naughty French novel was a source of great amusement. Without question he lavished more devotion on her than he ever showed my mother.

The tradition of listening to the Trawler Band was not unique to our family. Many skippers' wives tuned in to find out how the fishing was going.

There were other reasons.

In the decades before affluence, the silver darlings were the lifeblood of coastal communities. Autumn heralded the frenzy of boats gearing up in the hope that this year would be the big one, when the herrings wagged their tails.

They were rare, those wonderful bumper years. The storms were perennial. We dreaded the words 'attention all shipping', the prelude to a severe weather warning. Coming at the turn of the season, a change in the weather brought a cycle of gales that hampered fishing in the months leading up to Christmas.

Those were the most hazardous times.

'He is like *your* people,' an elderly woman said, on meeting my son. Tearfully, she explained that the family resemblance had stirred the memory of a dance in the Foresters Ballroom. She had waited in vain for her gorgeous young man, unaware that 18-year-old Anthony, my father's brother, had been lost at sea earlier that day.

In my father's treasured photograph of his younger brother, we see not one, but two smiling teenagers, Anthony and his nephew, Francis. Francis, the shy one, was regarded by the family more as younger brother than nephew. He had been raised for a time in the McCallig household after an earlier tragedy had widowed his mother.

By the time my father was thirty, the family had lost two brothers in two separate fishing accidents. It could have been worse. Father was supposed to go fishing on the earlier occasion, but he had a bad feeling. Perhaps he didn't like the look of the weather. In any case, he stayed ashore, and lived, but never spoke of that day again.

At one time, he and seven of his surviving brothers made their living from the sea. It might seem strange that they should continue to face that most capricious of elements. One evening, father came ashore from a three-day fishing trip to find a journalist waiting on the pier. *The Evening Press* wanted to profile the McCallig brothers from St John's Point. Weary as he was, father never declined an opportunity to express his affinity with the sea.

'Once you become a fisherman,' he told the reporter, 'the sea gets in your blood and you won't work at anything else.'

Francis Byrne, that shy boy in our precious family snap, that nephew who was like a brother, was to follow the family tradition.

He and his son, Jimmy, were aboard the *Skiford* in October 1982 when she foundered off the Donegal coast. They were among sixteen fishermen who lost their lives in that area, in one dreadful six-year period.

Soon after, my father sold his beloved *Angelique* and retired from fishing.

He stayed faithful to his habit of tuning-in to the shipping forecast. For me, it will always be associated with him. And the place names — Malin, Faroes, Fair Isle, Hebrides — are poetry to the ears of one old sea dog's daughter.

THE LIGHT SLEEPERS

Kevin Barry

On my frequent insomniac nights, when the bed is all rumpled like an angry sea, when my mind is zipping about like an unpleasantly lively little pup, when I flop from side to side like a dying trout on a river bank, it's on nights like these that I comfort myself with the thought that I am not alone in my torment.

There is a native gift here for insomnia. As a people, we don't quite trust the velvety embrace of sleep. If, as Shakespeare has it, sleep is the most blessed state, that which knits up the ravelled sleeve of time, then it's no wonder that we're the way we are … Going around the place gaunt and half mad-lookin' for the want of a kip, with the hair standing on end and the eyes outside our heads. There is a kind of honour to insomnia, though – show me the poet who's a sound sleeper.

It's a consolation, in the small hours, to picture one's fellow travellers through the wakeful night. And it's a comfort to imagine the life that continues throughout the night all over the island. I lie there, and I allow my mind to flit, and this is what I see:

I see a lone car on a mountain road under starlight – where's that fella headed for?

I see a worried mam sitting by the kitchen window, with the lights off, in a Midlands bungalow, and she peers out into the blue gloom – there's no sign of yer wan home yet from that party … Who was organisin' that party?

I imagine the minicabs trawling the quiet city streets, guided by the despatch voices, as they round up the last of the night's custom; the stragglers.

There is a man on flattened cardboard, in a doorway, with a bottle of own-brand supermarket vodka, and he's trying to remember the name of a Bay City Rollers hit from 1973. And then he tries to remember the name of a brother.

By water in the Claddagh there's a murmur of old voices. And I see the dead pubs in the night on Shop Street, with their shutters down, letting out a reek of stale beer and bleach.

And maybe there's a card game at a Chinese restaurant, after hours, somewhere in the medieval warren of the Waterford backstreets; bets being thrown down by a big chef from Szechuan in a sweet-and-sour-stained T-shirt.

And all the silent rants delivered to the bedroom ceilings … suddenly, you realise exactly what you should have said to that bitter auld aunt. (All that side of the family were bitter, of course.)

And there's a lonesome walker outside Poulgorm, and there's a weeper by the bus station in Cork, and there's a witch in a Salthill bedsit. A woman in Clonmel has a vision of Tonga. A window full of TVs in Drogheda shows a news channel's flickering: Taoist rebels are murderous in Nepal.

And all the 4 a.m. philosophers are in their murky lairs, and they lie there in staunch debate with the historical greats: Plato is put to rights in Dingle, Aristotle is shown the door in Portumna.

A bug-eyed kid works the joystick of an Xbox with dizzy quick fingers – there'll be no getting that yoke up for school.

There is moonfall on country ruins … see the moss-stained stones and the pagan carvings … a Sheela na Gig looking so rudely alive.

A stout old lad in Janesboro, in Limerick city, listens to show tunes from the 1950s on vinyl – 'Oh Cherry Pink and Apple Blossom White'. And he still has a full head of hair.

A lady under a sunbed has memories of Lanzarote. He told me he loved me, she thinks, and she torches another roll-up.

There's courting going on in the bushes of St Anne's Park in Raheny – the boat-club disco must have let out late. Then a powerful wingbeat overhead: a heron from the Bull Island mudflats, with an eel in its gob.

Lights from all the estates are put up against the sky, a dull sodium glow, the dream light of the suburbs. Beyond again, as the cities fade, the quiet of the fields and the hillsides. And relentlessly, always, somewhere in the distance, the lapping of the sea.

It's a joy to be awake for all this – these are the magic hours.

THE KISS

Grace Wells

'The kiss continued for miles beginning under city lights then further and further through suburbs then fields'

Shaindel Beers

Venus in the house of love, Saturn in rare alliance,
there were galaxies overhead and on them
destiny written in the fiery ink of shooting stars.
There was the sound of his voice and his life-story,
her answering echo of old hurts, waves falling
on the strand spiralling them deeper into courtship,
so at last his lips reached for hers – and get this nay-sayers –
his lips quivered, they actually shook
as there in that summer night the kiss began.
Swiftly the kiss became airborne, their lives
not yet conjoined, the kiss travelled back and forth,
on minute engines puttering endless Atlantic swell.
It might have tired, have ended there – only
that his mouth or hers flew forward to pull them on
over the last legendary miles. And yes, once or twice,
there were arguments, but the kiss healed them,
there was no room for bitterness in its harbour,
only tongues turning in the tight circle of its mouth.
The kiss had an appetite for travel. It loved Venice
and would have liked to visit Paris but there was never the time,
the kiss was too busy kissing in the centre of ordinariness.

It drove to the school bus. It waited at stations.
It survived supermarkets, delays at airports,
the frozen lock on a holiday cottage that would not open.
The kiss shuttled between dentists, lawyers, tax-accountants.
It bore up in the course of winter colds.
During migraines it tiptoed softly through darkened rooms.
In the safe garden of a shared life
the kiss did not diminish, always a chaste
mchw mchw mchw, dependable as a clock.
while sometimes the kiss rose in a crescendo of lips
so that doors had to close on the kiss,
trains dive into convenient tunnels,
for it was not the type to brag
that sometimes it was much more than just a kiss.
The kiss had to do with his neck's clean hair-line,
the smoothness of his jaw. Inherent also
was the softness of her lips.
Sometimes his eyes remained open
while hers did not, the kiss did not mind,
it was not a kiss to stand on ceremony,
you could take it anywhere. A kiss
that continued for miles, begun beneath shooting stars,
then further and further, through suburbs, through fields.

FOR WE RIDE DIFFERENT WAYS

Martina Devlin

We know him from Florence Wilson's ballad, 'The Man From God Knows Where'.

> Into our townlan' on a night of snow
> Rode a man from God knows where.

We know him from the words he spoke as he faced the hangman – confused, perhaps, after stepping from his prison cell into daylight.

'Is this the place?'

We know him from Mary Ann McCracken's somewhat breathless description: 'A model of manly beauty, he was one of those favoured individuals whom one cannot pass in the street without … staring in the face, and turning round to look at the receding figure.'

But there is more to Thomas Russell than a condemned man standing on a scaffold one October morning. Or a final resting place in Downpatrick, marked by a simple slab: 'The Grave of Russell', it reads. Or a patriot immortalised as a hard-riding stranger who chances upon a group of United Irishmen plotting in a County Down inn – neither side knowing they follow the same cause.

> But at screek o' day through the gable pane
> I watched him spur in the peltin' rain
> And I juked from his rovin' eye.

Thomas Russell was a revolutionary. But he was many other men besides.

He was a former officer in the British army. He was well travelled (India, Africa, Europe), his international perspective focusing his attention closer to home, on his own colonised people and their need for leadership.

He had religious conviction: Wolfe Tone nicknamed him PP, short for the parish priest. In the period preceding his execution, he read a Greek bible, and asked for a few days' grace to finish the Book of Revelations. The boon was withheld.

He was a librarian who promoted the collection of Irish-language songs. He was a bard, whose poem, 'The Fatal Battle of Aughrim', recounts the rout of the Gael in the Williamite wars – a defeat he hoped to overturn.

He was a contributor to Henry Joy McCracken's *Northern Star* newspaper. He was a pamphleteer: in his address, 'A Letter To The People Of Ireland On The Present Situation Of The Country', he insisted the earth's riches were given to benefit all men, not just a select few.

He was a restless spirit who spent years in captivity. He was a practical idealist. 'Poverty is a sort of crime,' he wrote.

He moved easily between north and south, between ascendancy and peasant, this son of an Anglican father and a Catholic mother, working for 'a communion of rights' between Irishmen of all creeds and classes.

All these facets, and others, contribute to the complicated man of straightforward principles who was Thomas Russell. Wolfe Tone admitted: 'I think the better of myself for being the object of the esteem of such a man as Russell.'

Towards the end of his short life, in 1803, he took on yet another role: as general and commander of the Northern forces in Robert Emmet's ill-fated revolt. That rebellion sent this roving man – celebrated in verse galloping through hail and rain to rouse the Ulster counties – on his final journey to the gallows.

'Governments proceed as if they were immortal,' he told the court that convicted him of high treason. Those words predicted a time when the regime would be toppled. Those words resonate today. More than two centuries later, governments continue to operate as if invested with immortality, and as if no one will ever scrutinise their record; even governments composed of our own people, as Russell would have wished.

Let us pause today to remember Thomas Russell: our man from God knows where, who drew breath first in Dromahane near Mallow in County Cork, in November 1767.

His last breath was exhaled at the age of thirty-five, in front of Downpatrick's granite jail, where he was hanged, then decapitated – a traitor's death for the friend of Tone, Emmet and McCracken.

Russell was among the last of the United Irishmen to die, captured in Dublin and transferred to the place where he had conspired, for trial and inevitable execution. It was intended as a warning to the population.

The rebuke underwent its own revolution, however, transformed into inspiration.

> He smiled in under his slouchy hat
> Says he: 'There's a bit of a joke in that,
> For we ride different ways.'

But the men in that ballad were all riding the same way, though they didn't yet realise it. As for us, in which direction do we go? And would Thomas Russell recognise the landmarks we steer by?

THE DARK VISITOR

Adrian Crowley

The rain pelted the frosted glass of the front door. The wind from the Atlantic droned and keened in ghastly polyphony down the stone chimney.

There in the hallway I stared as Mark pushed the door closed with his back, the wood shuddering to find its place in the frame.

He had something under his coat.

'I found it by the main road; I think its feathers lost their oils in the storm.'

I came closer and peered into the black recess of my brother's duffle coat.

'What is it?'

'A crow.'

I stared in silence, surveyed the bristling nape, the pulsing throat, the head lolling limply, the panting open beak like a burnished and split pumice stone.

We brought it to the store room at the back of the house and put it in a cardboard apple box. There were still a couple of Granny Smiths in there. Outside the window the stunted fir trees bucked and buffeted in the storm, and across the blackness of Galway Bay the distant lights of Kinvara, Doolin and the Aran Islands guttered like smugglers' lanterns.

The next morning we carried the box out to the back of the garden in a slow and silent procession of two. There was a scent of damp apple pie and wet bird.

We brought the box with its dull weight to a small grotto at the roots of a blackthorn and placed it on its side.

'Now that he's probably going to live, maybe you can think of a name?'

I knitted my brow in intense thought.

'I know, I'll call him "Crow".'

And there Crow lived for the coming weeks, miraculously.

I took on the role of provider and feeder, the gatherer of worms and saver of pork rinds. The semi-sharp bill scraping my palm became a familiar sensation. I tried all sorts of tasty treats: Marmite on toast, Curly Wurlys, mackerel guts, Batchelors baked beans, tapioca, macaroni cheese, *fettucine alfredo*, worms, moths …

Every day I'd deliver these bird meals making my way across the garden past the rotary washing line – crooked and askew from the prevailing Connemara wind, past the defunct Swingball pole, past the old Morris Minor – long since broken down with its windows all blackened out for its new role as mushroom factory – and through the privets and blackcurrant bushes to find the crow perched upright and waiting.

Crow slowly began showing vitality and the sheen gradually began to return to his feathers. I had learned the names of my mother's oil paints: crimson lake, Payne's grey, vermillion, alizarin, lampblack, Prussian blue and aquamarine. I could see them all in his feathers. His wings would stretch, his nape would bristle and the colours would shift again like petrol in a muddy pond.

The stench in that little cave hung like a limpid, dank, unmoving mist. It went from nasty to foul to morbidly oppressive. But not to me.

My two sisters couldn't stomach the smell though, and kept at bay. My little brother Q watched from our bedroom window.

The summer came and the storms subsided. The fields around the house were flush with burgeoning ferns – their viridian shoots curling up from the earth.

Then one Saturday morning I saw Crow making his attempts at flight. He heavily lunged and swerved and then he was above my head crossing the typically white sky of iridescent clouds. He shot through the archway in the privet and landed on the bonnet of the old Morris Minor. His squawk was tormented and excited as he lunged skyward again, his wingspan alarmingly wide, his talons hanging and limp. He shot up high over the lone fir tree that stood outside my mother's studio. The easels and stretched canvases leaned against dewy windows as I walked slowly across the damp grass, keeping my bird in sight. Then he came to rest on the boundary wall for a moment before taking off again towards the fern fields, sweeping lowly, and then he was gone. In the distance I saw the parliament of rooks and crows mingling on the telegraph wires and granite rocks that loomed out of the long grass and thorn bushes. An earthworm glistened and twirled in between my fingers and then as I turned away it dropped from my hand into the unkempt lawn.

It was late October the next time I saw Crow. I knew it was him but I didn't say a word when my little brother asked me what it was. Q and I had scaled the boundary wall and were walking along the top of it when he pointed to a cluster of bones and black feathers that lay among the rusty bracken.

THE RING OF THE BARM

Denise Blake

Barmbrack loaves, for me, were always about the ring. I was a teenager, so my food of choice contained chocolate-gateaux swiss rolls, Wagon Wheels or Curly Wurlys. Barmbracks were like the fruit-tea loaves that old people had on cold evenings beside the fire. But barmbracks held a ring. I ate whole packets just to be able to slice into the bread and accidentally discover the wee ring wrapped in white paper and find my future.

Since then I have always worn a ring, not for the ornamental bauble value but for something much deeper. At my barmbrack stage I wore a Claddagh with the heart facing outwards, searching. Eventually I was able to turn the ring around and wear it proudly with the taken heart placed towards me.

When I was young my mother told me that when she and Dad got engaged they knew a jeweller who let her take a few rings home to try them out. Mum wore the rings all that night and her hands felt awkward with the weight of most of them, except the one, with five diamonds in a row.

When I turned twenty-one, Dad gave me the present of Mum's ring that he had kept for me since her passing. It is my touchstone, a felt presence to turn on my finger like worry beads when I need her guidance.

And then came my engagement ring. The two of us going back to Letterkenny on the express bus after our day-trip to Dublin. I sat in at the window seat and stared at my ring with the ruby centre all the way home. My friends all tried it on and turned the stone towards them, towards their heart, three times as they made a wish.

After getting my engagement and my wedding rings I stopped buying barmbracks. I didn't want to eat fruit bread and neither did my husband or our young sons. But families need traditions and so we took on bobbing for apples instead. We had a plastic yellow baby bath full of tepid water placed on our kitchen floor. Green apples were floating about. It was the only time our sons had an interest in anything as healthy as fruit. Our eldest, Damien, would try his best to stay within the rules, down on his knees, hands behind his back, his mouth open, trying to catch any apple without getting soaked through. The other buck soaked himself, the floor, anyone near him and would have climbed into the bath just to get the only apple with a coin.

My boys didn't have any interest in token rings, just coins. I have two pictures from that time in our kitchen. A long chord is hanging from the door frame with an apple attached. In the first picture Damien is a blond curly headed 5-year-old in a blue tracksuit. He has his hands behind his back, mouth open, and he is trying to catch the apple in his teeth. In the next picture his brother is three, in a Man United football rig-out and blue wellies. He has given up trying to catch the apple by the rules of the game and he has only one hand behind his back. The other hand holds the chord firmly as he brings the apple towards him, mouth open, about to take a huge bite.

But all that is quite a while ago. On the day Damien got married I was aware that I was wearing my history on my hands; my rings; and the eternity ring from our twenty-fifty anniversary; Mum's ring and my Godmother's.

And when I look at our son I find it so strange to see his brand-new wedding ring. His ring says he has grown up, he is an adult; it says he loves his Mary, and it says his wife is now his nearest.

Damien's brothers aren't that far behind him. Maybe in a few years' time, when I feel like being mother of the groom again, I'll bring barmbracks back into our home, see which of them slices the bread and discovers the wee ring.

NOVEMBER

GHOSTS

Val Mulkerns

In the late 1950s my husband Maurice would be out Thursday nights presenting a programme called *Plays of The Week* from the old RTÉ studios in Henry Street. I would hear him letting himself in upstairs through the main hall, and walking across the as yet uncarpeted floor to the bathroom. This room, together with the kitchen beyond it, had been made from a tall-windowed back bedroom that used to be Mr Madden's room before he sold us his house. Little fragile plants were nurtured on the sunny granite window sills, and no doubt he had watched for signs of growth each morning before going out to work in the bank.

Horatio's footsteps used to disappear into that room. The fact that we had a ghost sharing this old house with us didn't particularly bother us because obviously he meant us no harm, but I can't pretend it wasn't spooky occasionally to look up from a book on hearing footsteps in the upper hall and go to the living room door to call hello to Maurice. No answering call from Maurice because it wasn't Maurice. Maurice would come in about fifteen minutes later after a drink, perhaps, with his producer in the Opal Bar, and he would run downstairs straight away to narrate the night's events.

There were no recorded radio programmes then; everything was live, and if some reviewer around the table had a cough you heard it all through the programme, partly muffled by a handkerchief.

If Horatio had already come in from a late mountain walk and gone straight into his own room, I would tell Maurice that, after he'd finished his story. A rationalist in every other way, he believed in ghosts. He had once seen a ghost at Moll Goggin's Corner near the lighthouse in

Youghal. He was a schoolboy then, down as usual with his grandparents on holiday, and with a few friends he had been on his way for a swim out near Clay Castle. A woman in a straggling long skirt had approached them at the corner, and, polite young fellow that he was, he stepped onto the roadway to let her pass.

'Why did you do that, Kennedy, with a car coming straight at you?' One of the friends asked.

'To let that old woman pass, of course,' said Maurice.

'What old woman?'

They all looked back. There was nobody there. Maurice crossed over the road to look back beyond the bend, but there was nobody. The friends were local fellows and quite blasé about the occurrence. 'It's only Moll Goggins, so,' said one of them. 'Some people see her and some don't. The da knows all about her. She used to wait for her man coming in on the boats just there below at the market dock. One wild night he didn't come in with the rest and she kept on waiting for his boat to appear around the headland ever after. Everyone knew about her when the old fella was at school, but I haven't heard tell of her in a long time.'

'She's no harm,' another voice said. 'She does no banshee wailing and she never says a word. She died astray in the head, they say.'

We never heard any hint of why our Horatio elected not to stay in the grave, and none of the children ever mentioned hearing anything. And so we absorbed Horatio in the same way we came to terms with the normal night-time sounds of an old house: the noisy lead pipes which dated form 1870; the creaking shutters which were always drawn on stormy nights; the three sighing steps in the middle of the stairs which led down to the lower hall; the actual settling of the old place into sleep, like the occupants. This is when you heard, also, the breathing of the beech tree like small breaking waves heard through open waves on summer nights.

There was this feeling which I remember well that we had, so to speak, bought them all with this house, that they absorbed us as benevolently as we did them. But once when we were all away on holiday there was a strange story waiting our return. Ronan Conroy was one of the school friends who loved cats, and he had kindly volunteered to come in everyday and feed ours. He had fallen asleep with the cat curled up beside him on a warm evening. He woke up later, feeling cold and scared and no cat beside him and footsteps coming across the hall, which was four steps above. He jumped up onto the landing which was colder still; no sign of the cat, no sign of any intruder. No sound now of any footsteps. Just this illogical cold as though he were inside a cloud on top of a mountain. He quickly checked the bathroom into which the footsteps had faded. Nobody. He checked the spare room. Nobody.

We didn't know what to make of this story, and at this stage I don't know whether or not Ronan knew of Horatio and embroidered this bad dream around him. I do know that the house was absolutely as we had left it when we came home.

We decided that Ronan's highly original and sceptical personality must have disturbed Horatio. He never bothered us anymore than he ever had, and eventually, he seemed to melt into eternity on one of his own mountain walks, or is it just that he didn't like a house with no children in it anymore?

THOMAS MOORE'S GENTEEL IRISH BLUES

P. J. Mathews

A few weeks ago, while clearing out a drawer stuffed with the random accumulations of many years, I came across a blank cassette tape, unused, and still pristine in its cellophane wrapper – a relic of the not-so-distant past. As I mused about whether to keep it or throw it away, I couldn't help thinking about my earliest memories of handling these wonderful pieces of audio storage equipment which have become obsolete in this digital era of CDs and MP3 players. Back in the early 1980s I could capture any sound within a range of ten feet by simply pressing, simultaneously, the 'Play' and 'Record' buttons on my silver and black Philips tape recorder. Very quickly I realised that this trusty device (my pride and joy at the time) could be deployed very usefully to record from the telly the latest hit music from *Top of the Pops*. Needless to say this became a weekly ritual of mine every Thursday evening.

I'm not sure if this practice could be conceived as 'illegal downloading – the early years' but one of the major challenges of the routine was to command total silence from other family members when recording was in progress. This proved particularly difficult because my grandfather (who lived with us at the time) was fond of passing comments at the crucial moment. For months I listened over and over again to my recording of that quintessential '80s song 'Pop Muzik' by M with my grandfather grumbling, 'Pity you wouldn't stay quiet when the news comes on' as the distinctive intro kicked in with all its pulsating, new-wave arrogance. Countless other hits were similarly marred by his standard quizzical reaction to the gender-bending fashions of the early 1980s, captured forever on tape: 'Bejasus, is that a man or a woman?'

Maurice Murphy loved Thomas Moore's *Irish Melodies* which, in the early 1980s, seemed dull and uninspiring to the ears of an 11-year-old boy discovering the delights of pop music for the first time. 'The Last Rose of Summer', 'The Meeting of the Waters' and 'The Minstrel Boy' were particular favourites of his. Knowing a bit more now, I realise that the lyrics that Moore wrote were not contrary to the spirit of pop music as I have known it – if anything they were early examples of the genre.

In many ways Moore was Ireland's first pop star. His 'albums' were the mass-produced booklets of sheet music that were reprinted many times throughout the nineteenth century, and were hugely popular in Ireland, Britain and the United States. Like many pop artists, Moore borrowed liberally from other sources without fully acknowledging them. He wasn't exactly a gangsta rapper, but he did associate with Robert Emmet who was considered to be a dangerous and seditious revolutionary. Songs like 'Oh! Breathe not his Name' played well with Irish nationalist audiences in the wake of Emmet's execution in the early 1800s, but Moore also cultivated the favour and patronage of wealthy members of the British establishment. Like many latter-day rock stars, he could trade on his anti-establishment credentials *and* cosy up to powerful figures of influence when it suited him. Many a homage has been paid to Moore in 'cover versions' by artists as diverse as John McCormack and Nina Simone – the latter recorded a memorable version of 'The Last Rose of Summer' in 1964.

Like an urbane Shane McGowan of the nineteenth century, Moore sang an entire nation's past into being, capturing something of the haunted mystique of old Ireland. His major innovation, for good or ill, was in bringing the plaintive concerns of the rebel balladeer into the bourgeois drawing room; in so doing he invented a genteel Irish blues tradition. Whether he emasculated or aggrandised the Irish nationalist cause in the process is a moot point. It takes quite a talent to square that circle, but like most enduring pop music Moore's appeal was founded on the carefully constructed ambiguity and open-endedness of his lyrics.

Tom Moore's melodies are still sung today, although not nearly as widely as they were a century ago. Nonetheless they endure as vestigial presences in contemporary culture, reasserting themselves with surprising regularity. 'Believe Me If All Those Endearing Young Charms' was immortalised in a Bugs Bunny cartoon in the 1950s, which is the equivalent of being name-checked in *The Simpsons* today. 'The Minstrel Boy', too, has featured on the soundtracks of many Hollywood movies with obvious Irish-American themes. In my own personal favourite example, Dexy's Midnight Runners used the opening bars of 'Endearing Young Charms' as a prelude to their biggest hit, 'Come on Eileen'. I recorded that song on my Philips tape recorder in the summer of 1982 when it reached No. 1 in the UK charts, but for some reason I didn't manage to catch the tribute to Moore at the start. I guess I was too busy shushing my grandfather.

BERLIN

Tim Carey

The reason for my first trip to Berlin was to see what remained of the Berlin Wall. But it was so long after the Wall had come down, in November 1989, that the person I was meeting was in the process of documenting and recording what remained of it in order to argue for its preservation, to retain proof for future generations that such a bizarre thing as the Wall had once existed in the heart of Europe.

My mental geography had put the iconic graffiti-covered façade as the front of the Wall. It was a view that agreed with the German Democratic Republic's spin that the Wall was an 'anti-fascist protection rampart'. But of course the Wall was to keep East Berliners in, not West Berliners out. And while there was precious little left of what was actually the back of the Wall, there were plenty of artefacts and sinister accoutrements of the front of the Wall.

The Wall came to dominate the image of the city, and in a sense it still does. But all the time we were on our tour of hinterland walls and roads, perimeter defences, marker posts, patrol tracks, foundations for various installations, lamps, electrical switch boxes and, probably the most defining part of the whole Wall complex, the void, the archaeological desert of the former death strip, I could not stop thinking of Berlin's past. Before the Wall. Before the war. Before the Nazis. To a time when Berlin was the centre of European culture, of European modernity which was a vision so at odds with what I was looking at.

As one of the city's chroniclers has written, 'There are times in history when a city transcends its earthly role and becomes the stuff of legend.' Berlin between 1919 and 1933, during the liberal and democratic era of the Weimar Republic, perfectly fits that description.

My first day in Berlin started on a bench in a train station looking across the tracks to the station's name in black tiles, set out in relief against white tiles: 'Alexanderplatz'. It was nearly impossible to read it without thinking of the title of the novel, by doctor, socialist and writer Alfred Döblin. *Berlin Alexanderplatz* was the first novel to be set in the city and it follows the attempt of released convict Franz Biberkopf to go on the straight and narrow in a seedy, poor, depraved Berlin. Another novel to come out of Berlin was Erich Maria Remarque's great anti-war novel *All Quiet on the Western Front*. In 1931 Nobel prize-winning writer Thomas Mann denounced the Nazis on the streets of the city. Anton Gill wrote in his book, *A Dance Between Flames: Berlin Between the Wars*, that there were over 800 writers living in Berlin. There were 149 newspapers.

Marlene Dietrich lived on Unter den Linden and starred in *The Blue Angel*. Film-maker Fritz Lang directed *Metropolis*, while his first talkie, *M*, launched the acting career of Peter Lorre. Meanwhile one Samuel Wilder began writing screenplays in the city. In later years and in another country he became Billy Wilder and directed films like *The Seven-Year Itch*, *The Apartment* and *Some Like it Hot*.

Painter Paul Klee's first major exhibition was in Berlin. Wassily Kandinsky lived there. Then there was the demonic, scathingly satirical cartoons of George Grosz, the bleak depictions of the darker side of Berlin life by Otto Dix and the politically charged photomontages of John Heartfield.

In theatre there was the great innovator Erwin Piscator and the collaboration between Kurt Weill and Bertolt Brecht that produced *The Threepenny Opera*. It premiered in Berlin in 1928 and the world heard 'The Ballad of Mac the Knife' for the first time.

Architect Mies van der Rohe, whose influence can be seen in every modernist building in the world, lived in Berlin during the entire Weimar period. Berlin-born architect Walter Gropius established the Bauhaus Art School whose influence on the world we live is everywhere: tubular steel chairs, flat roof architecture, almost every aspect of modern art, and also the design of a plethora of household items from the kettle we boil to the desk lamp that I write this piece by.

At the end of that first day in Berlin, which I can only describe as a confrontation with history, I took my seat in a booth in an art-deco theatre tent with mirror-lined walls near the Ku'damm, one of the main thoroughfares of Berlin.

I ordered a steak dinner and the first of a number of beers and watched the audience assemble. A pretty waitress effortlessly worked the tables, like that was what she was born to do.

I was soon joined in the booth by, on one side, two women in their late twenties with a woman I assumed to be their mother and, on the other side, a woman in her late thirties with a woman I assumed to be her mother. Neither group viewed my presence appreciably.

Dinner finished, another beer ordered, and the lights went down for the performance of *Das Kabaret*. Forget the sentimental Hollywood film version which is probably the best known cultural hand-me-down from Weimar Berlin. This was a far truer representation of the Berlin stories of Christopher Isherwood that were at its heart. It was a gritty, provocative, uncompromising performance and portrayal of the tensions that underlay Berlin life. At the end of it all, of course, the Nazis take power. And Weimar Berlin comes to an abrupt torch-lit end.

When the lights came up I didn't know what the Berliners in the audience were thinking as they put their coats on. Were they thinking of what had been lost? Or what was to come in their city? And I tried to comprehend what it must be like to live in a city with such a history as a city like Berlin.

ORANGE SEGMENTS

Peter Gillen

Heartbreak Hill is the fourth and final climb at twenty miles in to the Boston City marathon, so you can imagine how it got its name. Boston is the king of road marathons. A finisher's T-shirt is a treasure among marathon aficionados. I competed in the 108th Boston to raise money for Alzheimer's.

My father-in-law was my first introduction to Alzheimer's when he was diagnosed shortly after his retirement. Having a young family, visits for my wife meant a 150-mile round trip to the nursing home where he was placed when his wife could no longer cope. She would return exhausted with smudged mascara and tell-tale red eyes. Near the end I accompanied her with the children. Stunned by what I saw but attempting normality, I squeezed my 4-year-old son's hand and asked him to give Papa a kiss. Displaying a deeper understanding of the illness than mine he said simply, 'That's not the real Papa.'

Some years later we had a sense of déjà-vu. This time it was my own mother. Now my wife took over the primary carer role with a love and devotion no words of mine can describe. My mother became part of her daily routine. After dropping the kids off to school she would call and take her off by car to a variety of shops and restaurants where they were to become affectionately well known.

I had promised my mother I would never put her in a nursing home. The voices coming from the ceiling lights, the hidden chops in the wardrobe and the front door left open made me break that promise.

It poured rain the day I left her out to the nursing home. I managed to get her inside and, I thought, happily ensconced in her new room when she suddenly said, 'I have to go home now and make the dinner.' I don't recall which of the many excuses I was to use over the coming three years I gave to distract her while I exited. That first exit, though, was the hardest of all.

Sitting outside in my car it took me a few seconds to realise the wipers couldn't clear the water from in front of my eyes.

The 108th Boston marathon was a scorcher with temperatures in the mid-eighties. As I crested Heartbreak Hill I was brought to a standstill by agonising cramp. My hand clutched a knot of angry muscle where my hamstring used to be, and this time the tears in my eyes were for a very different reason.

Distraught and far from home I looked around for help. I saw an old lady sitting by the roadside holding a plastic bag in her lap. She opened it and offered me orange segments. There was something about her. The kindness, the assurances that I would be fine, but most of all the oranges. My mother adored oranges and cut and peeled them into identical segments all her life.

Duly fortified by oranges and some physiotherapy from a first-aid station, I hobbled the last six miles. In my confused and dehydrated state I convinced myself the old lady would be there at the finish line to congratulate me. I was mistaken.

I have long since mislaid the finisher's T-shirt from Boston, but the memory is still vivid.

That's the funny thing about Alzheimer's – it's your memory that goes first.

I know a lot about Alzheimer's now, but understand little. What I can't understand is how someone you love so much deserves to get it in the first place. Sometimes I like to imagine that you can cash in the 'lost' Alzheimer years on the other side. Maybe you can trade them in for a trip back to help someone you love make it to their finish line – whatever that might be in life. After all, who knows what an angel looks like?

Maybe all you need is a plastic bag and some orange segments.

TRAVEL BROADENS THE MIND

Kevin McAleer

Travel broadens the mind, or maybe it just makes your head bigger. Neil Armstrong went to the moon and back and ended up a farmer, so obviously it doesn't work for everybody. That was an awful waste of red diesel.

I left the North in 1974 – I'd had it with the violence, the beatings, the intimidation, and that was just the Christian Brothers. When I was living in London I'd come home for an odd flying visit, back to the small farm in Tyrone. Sometime in the early 1980s I got this weird idea of suggesting to my father that maybe he should come over and see me the next time. He never stepped on a plane in his life – he had the carbon footprint of a sheepdog. 'Ah,' he says, 'sure what would I see in London that I wouldn't see here.' I couldn't think of an answer to that.

Now I'm back in the home place myself, these last thirteen years, with my wife and kids, back where I started. I've travelled around a good few corners of the world and lived in a dozen cities, but I don't seem to be in any hurry to see any more. I'm turning into my father. Maybe I have enough strange and exotic pictures in my head to last me a lifetime. Besides, when you open your curtains in the morning, or in my case in the afternoon, the whole light of the universe is under your nose.

I'm not saying Northern Ireland is heaven on earth; anybody who thinks that needs to get out more. There's no place like home, but there's no place like India either. Anyway you don't travel the world looking for a replica of what you just left. You don't look at Sydney Harbour and think, 'Ah it's all right, but it's not Sixmilecross.' Or maybe you do.

My own kids are about to fly the nest, and I'd actively encourage them to travel far and wide – not that they need any encouraging; they've already conquered Europe and South-East Asia, and lost more passports, phones and money than I managed in fifty years.

I sometimes wonder though what I'd be like today if I hadn't travelled; would I have reached this advanced state of wisdom, serenity and hyper-awareness, not to mention an almost god-like humility, just by staying home and playing bingo? Who can tell.

I'll leave the last word to my father. It was 1987; I'd just come home from another of my epic 'gap years' (we knew how to do gap years – some of our gap years went on for decades, the young people nowadays don't know the half of it). I filled him in on how I'd flown to LA where people don't walk anywhere unless they're homeless, hitch-hiked to San Francisco, turned vegetarian, did some painting and decorating, bumped into Eugene McKenna in The Blarney Stone, drove 3,000 miles in ten days on Highway 80 in a bright yellow VW sports car, over George Washington Bridge in a thunderstorm, into Manhattan where you don't have to go to a show or a movie or a play because it couldn't possibly compare to what you'd see on the street for free, got a job in the kitchen of AT&T on someone else's green card, got fired on the first morning for getting my name wrong (it's hard to remember your name is Charlie at 6.30 a.m. when you've been too excited to sleep). Flew to Delhi, took a train to Varanasi, sat by the Ganges for a week drinking tea with cinnamon, cardamom, cloves, pepper and ginger in it – on my last morning the river had risen thirty feet during the night because the monsoon rains had arrived upstream and this brown flood with whole trees in it and a cow with a crow on its head drifting by in slow motion, the most moving thing I ever saw in my life. Then I flew to Amsterdam, peeled tulip bulbs, cleaned toilets in Amsterdam airport. One day the supervisor said 'the toilets are looking really good, Kevin'. I thought I have to get out of here, flew to Dublin, got the bus to Omagh, and here I am. My father says, 'Were there many on the bus?'

THE BACK WAY

Mary Morrissy

Instead of staying on the well-worn path, we often took a short cut as children on our way to the number 15 bus. We called it the back way; a narrow lane lined with garages and lock-ups, running behind a re-spectable red-brick avenue. The bollard at its entrance warned of its perils, a gatepost to a forbidden territory. We were warned never to take the back way. That was part of its attraction.

Once past the border, the high-walled laneway loudly announced its otherworldliness. In contrast to the neat, well-kept gardens out front, ragwort, dandelions and weeds sprouted between the cracks of the ridged and patched concrete. From the crevices of the walls, great spurts of evil-smelling valerian flourished, or rampant lilac in the summer. A couple of hundred yards along, there was a sharp right-angled turn and then, truly, you had passed into another country.

On one side were the garages, nearly always closed, though sometimes you would get a glimpse of the black holes of their interiors where do-mestic clutter reigned – rakes and yard brushes, tin baths or old bicycle frames hanging on hooks, tightly wound coils of hose, towers of orange boxes, a push mower. The odd one sported a car, or evidence of one in the oil-stained geography on the ground, but these were the exception. In between the garages there were single back doors, never opened, an-nouncing their redundancy by their peeling paint and rusting padlocks, adding to the shuttered air.

Here was the back stage of the known world. This part of the lane was dark with overhanging trees, the creeping menace of ivy. Jagged shards of glass glistened on the top of the walls, a deterrent to trespassers and a reminder to the suggestible child that from here there was no escape. The sight-lines were clear, despite the fact that the uneven walls, a mixture of cut stone and half-hearted pebbledash, sometimes bellied out unexpectedly, suggesting the unstable foundations of the world itself. You almost never met anyone taking this route, bar other children similarly testing the taboo.

But then the day came when your mother's words of warning – *don't go the back way, do you hear?* – became flesh. There he was. The man – it was always a man – coming towards you. You hold your breath, feel a sly prickling of sweat on your skin. What should you do? Quicken your step or slow down? Run back the way you came? Or stand still? You examine him as he approaches. He looks harmless enough. Not unlike your father. You breathe again. He wears an overcoat, a hat pulled down over his face so that you can't see his features. Impressions only – a graven chin, the suggestion of stubble, the mystery of a five o'clock shadow. His shoes, you notice, are mud-spattered, but there are creases in his pants and the glimpse of a white collar at his throat. You are reassured. He has a newspaper rolled like a baton under his arm. You stare ahead, determined that you will give him no excuse. But inside you are coiled. You wait for him to lunge at you, grab you by the throat and … well, it was never specified. Take you away, certainly. Never again, you promise yourself, never. You utter a prayer, well, more a bargain with God.

He draws level with you. You prepare to scream. But when you open your mouth, no sound emerges, only the silent howl of the dreamer. He passes by, wordless.

Relief has never been so sweet. You curb the temptation to run, in case now when the danger has almost passed you ignite his interest. You know enough not to look back. You have learned from the playground that feigned indifference is the way to stifle fear. Steadily you march on, trying to quieten your pounding heart. The far end of the laneway where it rejoins civilisation seems terribly far off. A mirage that seems to move as you do, like the destination in a nightmare. But finally you reach it. It is then and only then that you cast your eyes back. But the laneway is clear – the bogeyman has turned the corner and is out of sight. Or else you dreamed him up, a creature embodying all of your mother's warnings.

You never speak of these frights on the back way – well you can't, you weren't meant to be there in the first place. But several years later, you encounter a flasher on your way home from school one dark winter's evening on that respectable red-brick avenue where you *were* supposed to be. He is upon you before you realise, passing so close that the cuff of his coat brushes against your school gabardine. He strides by like a nineteenth-century *flâneur*, his coat-tails flying, a broad grin on his face, his flies agape and a great welcome for himself. You remember those dry runs on the back way – take no notice, keep walking, don't look back.

You say nothing when you get home. Why? Because you don't want to alarm your mother; your father, in the meantime, has died. That's another reason. But mostly it's because you realise the limited reach of your mother's protection and the fragility of her cautionary rules.

THE LAST OF THE LITERARY GIANTS

Anthony Glavin

I spent my first night ever in Ireland, some forty years ago, in Omagh, on the sofa of a kind couple who'd given me a lift from Cookstown. I even remember the date, 28 August 1967, if only because it happened to be my twenty-first birthday. I'd awakened earlier that morning from a dream in which rain was falling on my face, only to discover it actually was, a soft Scottish rain that'd already soaked through my sleeping bag in a field twenty miles north of Dumfries.

There was nothing for it but to arise and walk in the general direction of the Stranraer to Larne ferry, which I did, for ten miles or so, until a lorry finally acknowledged my outstretched thumb. And not just any lorry either, but one carrying a cargo of whiskey and cigarettes – just the kind of lorry you might expect to pull over and offer you a lift on the morning of your twenty-first.

That kind of surrealism, I realise now, wasn't unlike what you might find in the fiction of Benedict Kiely, only I didn't encounter Ben, neither his work nor himself, on that first fortnight's holiday in Ireland.

That happened later in 1974, when I returned to live for a time in County Donegal, and came upon in *The Irish Press* his marvellous short story, 'There Are Meadows in Lanark', a story set in Bundoran, and first published in *The New Yorker*. The idea of that honky-tonk Donegal seaside town, gaming machines and all, having featured in the august, not to mention glossy, pages of *The New Yorker*, entirely captivated me, and was the first thing I spoke of when I introduced myself to Ben after recognising him at a party in Monkstown, County Dublin, the following October. I recognised him instantly from the wee photo beside his wonderful, weekly travel column in *The Irish Times* that I'd been reading up in Donegal: the same leonine likeness, big head of hair, and distinctively hooded eyes. Yet mention Ben Kiely to friends, and chances are they'll comment on his remarkable aural gift, what Kiely himself described as 'my mournful Scots-Irish voice', that mellifluous Tyrone accent which I've seen, or rather heard, people try to take off from Ballyshannon to Boston.

In March 1979, I spotted Ben again on Stephen's Green where, in typically generous fashion, he promptly invited me into his company, remarking as we entered the Shelbourne Hotel, how 'this could be a good meeting for you' and 'I turn sixty this year!'. This last he offered with a slight air of astonishment, as if such numbers made no sense at all; a bewilderment I better understand myself now some thirty years on.

That afternoon proved not just 'a good meeting', but the start of a friendship I would treasure – for friendship was another of Kiely's great gifts, and his generosity to myself and many another younger writer was unbounded.

His erudite conversation had a kind of brilliant generosity too, and could effortlessly range from Charles Dickens to the American Civil War to his native Omagh as it did that day. 'It may be in contemplation of the things around that you begin to understand yourself,' Ben wrote about his beloved birthplace, but the search for self can also be abetted by having a place to go to – such as Dublin, where he lived for over sixty years.

And in his two memoirs about this double act, *Drink to the Bird* and *The Waves Behind Us*, Ben shows us how the way we see ourselves can include, nay embrace, all of who we are and might become – not just our accidental place of birth, our parentage, ethnicity, our religion or race, but also the entirety of all we experience and encounter as we grow up and out from these initial roots. And by refusing to see ourselves – and others – solely as members of one tribe or another, we give ourselves and others a greater space in which to grow, and hopefully prosper too. Something like that was seemingly possible in the Omagh Ben grew up in; where, speaking of political and sectarian grudges, he observed: 'In that town, we did, and do, go easy on the likes of that.'

One of Ireland's finest fabulists, he knew, better than most, how the longest way round is very much the shortest way home, and we are all of us the richer for that.

PORTADOWN 1641

Mary Russell

The sun gleams on the River Bann as it flows quietly through the town of Portadown. A few office workers sit on the bank eating their midday sandwiches. A dog paddles through the water chasing a red ball. A mother wheels her baby along in a stroller festooned with plastic shopping bags. A normal day, in a normal town, so why do I look intently at the bridge, gaze down from it at the waters below, trying to guess the drop? But then, way back in the winter of 1641, it was a different bridge, a timber one, so maybe the drop wasn't so far down. But to the frightened people standing on it that freezing November day, it was a place of terror, for one by one, men, women and children – 100 of them in all – were forced to jump into the icy waters. Those who hesitated were prodded with pikes and sticks until they too jumped to their death.

We talk a lot about climate change now, but Europe underwent a major shift in climate in the middle years of the seventeenth century with swings between drought and extreme cold resulting in failed harvests, famine and more poverty. So cold were some of the winters that the period was known as the Little Ice Age. In fact, in the mid-1640s, the harvests were the worst that had been recorded in the previous 600 years. So it was that these conditions were in force when the 1641 insurgency broke out in Ireland. Across the water, Charles I was on the throne, but his position as monarch was being challenged. The indigenous Irish-speaking poor were getting poorer; those Irish who still owned land feared for their precarious position between royalists and parliamentarians, not knowing which side might win the day in the upcoming English Civil War. So 1641, with all its uncertainty, seemed as a good a time as any to take advantage of a worsening situation. And so they struck, against the powerbases around the island and against the visible enemy – the settlers from Scotland who now lived in what had once been the insurgents' houses and farmed what had once been their lands. One of the leaders of the insurgency was Sir Phelim O'Neill and though his attempt to take over Dublin Castle failed for lack of support, Catholic insurgents in the northern counties carried through their plan of action which is how, on that fearful day in November, they rounded up a group of Protestant settlers in Portadown, stripped them of their clothes, locked them in a barn overnight, force marched them to the bridge over the Bann before pushing, shoving and throwing them into the waters below.

Incensed by this and other acts of rebellion all over Ireland, the English authorities set up a commission to which the settlers could come to give evidence. Five thousand people came to tell how land and cattle were taken, houses burned, family members attacked, abducted and killed. And because so many of those giving evidence were women, we now have a unique picture of domestic and social life at that time. Gathered together in thirty-one books, these documents are known as the *1641 Depositions* and are held in safe-keeping in Dublin's Trinity College.

Portadown, of course, has its own record of what happened. A plaque on the modern three-arched bridge tells us that the wooden bridge was destroyed by rebels in 1641, rebuilt in timber three times before being replaced by a sturdier stone bridge in 1763, though that too was damaged – by flooding.

Now you might think that these events create a sad impression of a town that has had its full share of disasters: the centre of Portadown has been rebuilt following the Troubles of the last century, the war memorial is surrounded with wreaths of red poppies in preparation for Remembrance Day, and among them lies a cushion of blue and white flowers – the St Andrew's Saltire – placed there by the Apprentice Boys of Derry. But beneath the bridge, the Bann flows quietly and peacefully, bordered by fuchsia-laden banks and green, grassy slopes – for though human beings may harbour memories, rivers flow onwards, carrying no trace of what has gone before.

A MAN IN THE FOREST

Michael Harding

He had lived with his wife for many years. Occasionally he went down to the village and smoked cigarettes and drank a few bottles of stout. Someone always gave him a lift home.

Now he lives alone in the forest. He still goes to the village, but less often. Someone still gives him a lift home at night, to the corner of the path where he turns off for the forest.

He lives in a prefab. It's an old box-shaped hut with a bed, a stove, and a small cooker. The council put it there years ago for an old woman who was blind in one eye, and had white hair, and a cow, which she walked with along the roads all day long, as it grazed on the ditches.

Then she died, and to everyone's surprise left him the hut. He was a teacher in those years, and married to a beautiful woman. And as the years went on he kept the little hut in the forest in good condition; fixing windows, painting it each summer, and lighting the stove each evening in the wintertime.

It gave him something to do, while his wife commanded the kitchen of their bungalow three miles away.

When their third beautiful daughter had reached the age of twelve, and the fragrance of four women in the house had grown so thick that they seemed to have a secret way of communicating, which he could not understand, he decided enough was enough.

The women always knew what the others were about to say. They always read each other's moods and emotions to perfection. And he walked like a bull in a china shop. So he decided one day that enough was enough. The hut in the forest beckoned.

It was difficult explaining to the neighbours and the villagers that there was nothing wrong with their marriage. It was just that he needed to be alone.

It was difficult explaining it to his daughters, who wanted him there all the time.

So he decided to give up teaching. He was old enough to take early retirement. And he was jaded from the job anyway. Twenty years is too long to spend in the same little classroom, looking at the endless flow of students, who are always the same age, as if the world were reborn every September.

But his real reason for quitting his job was that he thought it would give him an excuse to be alone in the forest. He put it about that his nerves were frayed. The gossips in the community filled out the details; he had suffered some kind of breakdown, they said; he wasn't able to teach anymore.

He looked out the window of his hut at the badgers and squirrels, under the shelter of leaves, and he smiled, knowing that there was nothing at all wrong with his mental health.

And after that it was plain sailing. The villagers left him alone.

But the truth was very different.

One night he saw his wife, by moonlight, in the forest outside his hut. At first he thought it was a deer, slipping through the trees. But then she stopped and their eyes met. And she smiled at him and he returned her smile, as if they were both wild animals, and were meeting there for the first time, and falling in love all over again.

IN THE PIG HOUSE

John Breen

My wife decided we should get pigs. We would feed them up in the spring and summer and then have lovely organic home-grown, fully traceable pork and bacon for the winter. Gloucester Old Spots. A fine breed. I volunteered to build the housing, called a pig ark, and a fenced-in enclosure. It would be a little summer project. What could possibly go wrong?

Hardware shops have a soporific effect on me. I wander the aisles dreamily, picking up and shaking objects that real men know how to use. I remember there was an ad on telly in the 1980s for a DIY magazine. The pitch was that if you buy this magazine you will know how to shop in a hardware store. They had the before and after shot of a hapless customer trying to describe a widget to a shop assistant. I really only remember the after shot. The customer says, 'I would like a robo-plegic rong guck with pallbeg shallots, please.' The assistant then looks at him with respect. He is a member of the freemasonry of the hardware store, and is not to be trifled with.

One of my neighbours is such a man. Fintan is building and renovating a Georgian manor and outbuildings practically single-handed. At the beginning of the summer he was working on an old coach-house and some stables. A Renaissance man. He repairs tractors, makes wine, keeps sheep and goats and paints delicate pictures of wild flowers which he sells in his gallery in Westport.

My pig project started to resemble a MasterCard commercial. The two by fours were very difficult to cut with a handsaw. Jigsaw, €54. I bought chicken wire, €36, felt nails and felt, €65. The pig ark was to resemble an isosceles triangle. I needed to calculate the angle at which to cut the ends of the two by fours so that they would fit snugly together at the top. No room for error, each length of two by four cost €12. I learn by doing and by the time I had finished cutting and screwing the rafters together I had gotten the hang of it. I simply stuck wedges in the tops of the rafters where my calculations had failed me. My wife bemoaned the fact that it didn't look very well. The pigs won't care, I said. It was to become my new mantra.

Then the fence. Shirt off, sea breeze blowing on my skin, the pleasing thud as the head of the sledge made contact. My kids came to watch and I put on a show. Grunting like Kournikova with each swing. Drinking deep from a bottle of water, then pouring some over my head. I was Charles Ingalls. A simple man bent to a humble task. I was so pleased with myself that I went out and bought thirty electric fence posts and some tape for when the pigs got too big for the chicken wire (€65).

Fintan called over while I was out and said that the posts were too long and weren't in deep enough. I bemoaned my fate to Derek, a fellow-Limerick man in exile in Mayo. 'This is what happens when you don't go to the pub,' he said. 'This is what we talk about.' His neighbours once had pigs. They used to break out and they would be up at all hours in their pyjamas hunting for the pigs in the dunes. 'Fencing is the most important part of the whole thing,' he said. 'You have to get a professional in for the fencing.'

We never got the pigs.

Fintan invited us over for lunch and gave us a tour of the refurbished property. He had used methods and materials from the period. He rebuilt old walls and chimneys using lime as cement. He reclaimed a seventeenth-century bread-oven and cooked pizza for us that evening which we had with his own elderflower champagne. We came home and gazed down the garden at my pig house. The wind had knocked it over and stripped some of the felt away, leaving it flapping in the summer breeze. It lay on its side. No longer was it an isosceles ark, now it looked more like … a wedge.

DEATH OF A COUNTRYWOMAN

Brian Leyden

While she was being treated for cancer, my mother stayed in our house by the sea in north Sligo. Earlier she'd wondered about the wisdom of our move from what she called the 'good Protestant' village of Droma-hair to such an exposed area without trees. To her way of thinking the absence of trees meant poverty. So, for instance, an Active-Age outing to the Aran Islands that we loved didn't appeal to her at all; but she'd take off gladly for Glenveagh National Park, where she'd never rob a cutting but 'liberate it', she said, to flourish in her own garden.

Life for her in Sligo meant months of treatment that she weathered resolutely; though the first time the nurse leading her to day oncology on the fifth floor of the hospital asked, 'Are you ready?' she said: 'I'd sooner be facing a bungee jump out that window.'

A lifetime of hill-farming and of walking to the shop for her weekly groceries – and more lately of walking to the post office for her pension – kept her so nimble she hopped into bed for the consultant's examina-tion like a child anticipating a fairy tale. Later, she told him that after the chemo there was enough fur on her tongue to make a hat.

'She's a concert,' said Bernie – the porter, and a part-time farmer – who was soon telling her about the neighbour who refused to part with a few bales of hay in the snowy weather because he'd 'sooner be looking at them than looking for them'.

All her life she'd been a devoted farmer: a hardy woman with a head-scarf tied under her chin out running marginal land by her own resources. Nobody knew cattle better, or had that grasp of animal ways and moods that only generations of livestock farming can teach. She had too what would locally be called the *conceit* of the McDermott's, her father's people: a proud nature that took pleasure in the condition of her livestock, and that the milk she and her husband Matt in his day sent in stainless-steel cans to the creamery passed the hygiene and quality tests for the bonus added to that all-important creamery cheque.

And when during her treatment she took an unquenchable craving for cold milk, she told the hospital staff she'd 'need a cow tied at the door'.

For a while the chemotherapy scalded her body into mending its ways. But the second time round her body wasn't having it. Against the grain of her worsening condition, however, she undertook a final journey back to her home on the mountain.

In a wheelchair she toured her garden to examine the health of her camellia, her hellebores and the snowdrops under the trees: their spring renewal contrasting with her decline. Then she sat at the coal-burning black Stanley Range that she'd always pampered like it was part of the family.

Her niece, Maureen, had arrived from America, and though Maureen maintained she was in Ireland to visit relations in the North, she had of course packed a black dress. Happy to be back amongst the familiar fixtures of her life, my mother reminded Maureen of her late father's favourite yarn about the boxer who made the sign of the cross, blessing himself before the big fight; and when the boy with the water bucket and sponge asked, 'Will that help?', the trainer said, 'not if he can't box.'

The deadlines we'd set were ignored for as long as the stories and her determination held up, and the pain held off. But then we really had to go.

Leaving the house, Maureen said to me, 'The hill will be empty without her.'

By the end of the following day her bed rest had deepened into a coma from which she could not wake. For two more days we were attentive but helpless, every few hours turning her body, now pliant as a rag-doll. The moment neared. And with her family present in our downstairs bedroom, the windows were showered with hailstones. A big gust of wind off the sea shook the house, as if taking her soul with it, and as she left us the heavens opened.

MONTE CASSINO IN KERRY

James Harpur

One year after the end of World War II, my parents honeymooned in Kerry. My father was showing off his homeland to his enchanted wife, a tide of homely Irishness softening his nerves still tuned to minefields, shells and split seconds.

My mother's letters say that the sky was a Mediterranean blue, with the Atlantic full of blue towards the Skelligs and beyond. The two of them were standing before a future neither could possibly imagine, a future that would end in divorce; but then, just then, the moment was exhilarating in that cliff-top field, with their easels, brushes, palettes, oils.

My mother paints a ruined cottage. My father paints from memory, preferring the paradise around his eyes, the Hades of war that his brain had shot in colour, but which it now recalls in black and white, grey and brown, and which it can't metabolise. It is a cut still fresh, jagged across his jangling soul. It is so deep and raw that no healing memory of childhood, the fields of Laois, and the country lanes of Timahoe and Stradbally, or newly married love could ever hope to cauterise it.

I can see his painting now. The framed mud and broken trees, and stumps, a glum defoliated Italian hill, with St Benedict's monastery, Monte Cassino, a burnt-out rump, harbouring the enemy. Its broken bits of walls, sculpted by bombs and shells, are so many tombstones for human lives, for life itself.

The painting came to live with us, above the fireplace in the dining room, a relic from a world closed off from questions. The war itself was a question mark, a mystery hinted at and leaking out: my mother waking up to hear my father shouting in his sleep, his voice another man's, a soldier crying 'Where am I? Where am I?'. My mother throwing out the door the junk-shop German helmet as if it were possessed of demons; my father in the cinema shaking and sweating at explosions on screen.

This was the war that dared not speak its name for fear of the unravelling, just like the spider's script I wished I'd never chanced upon scrawled across his diary page: 'No more bloody war'. It was a madman's jitters, a child's scratchings, and dated April 1944.

The painting followed him to London and the little flat he bought after the divorce. It resumed its role as a secret life, a skeleton on the wall, an alien to his second wife. It was his landscape of mortality that plugged the breach of memory: the bullet-whistling air; the heat of his Vickers machine-gun; smoke rising from the rubble; the smell of protein everywhere.

When my father died, the painting stayed in his flat, until his second wife died; the flat was cleared by unknown step-relations, the painting taken to a shop for bric-a-brac and junk.

And so the broken monastery of Monte Cassino may again be brought to life – by strangers' eyes on some new wall, in some new room. A curio of history appreciated only for the brush-strokes or composition.

Maybe its time had come. Its memory was no longer needed by its begetter, now removed from this earth, and it has turned from war's witness to simply a picture.

And perhaps the memory of evil the painting contained is now reduced to nothing but a fiction, a make-believe for children in an unknown house; a backdrop for a fairy story – the castle of the wicked witch. And maybe that is what the afterlife is like – we find past horrors were just scenery, a set for some absurdist play we happened to be cast in. And now, in some eternal place or state, we see paintings of the scenes we wanted when alive, the days we wished would never end; or the scenes we wished that we could change at the time: a picture, for example, of an intact monastery in spring, when pilgrims smell the season, the groves alive with olive light and Benedictine chanting.

Or a painting of a honeymoon on a summer's day near Waterville, in which my mother and father are absorbed in art, each moment present in their strokes and in their concentrating eyes and the flitting thoughts of happiness that only love can bring; and they not heeding past lives, and unaware the future will take them from the path they share, the one that started that summer – this is my picture, the one I paint right now.

A PLACE CALLED HOME

Vona Groarke

What does it mean to love a place? A place thinks nothing of you, is the same whether you're there or not, won't miss you when you're away, won't welcome your return. It is too busy being just the place it is, occupying its assemblage of buildings and history, arranging its sunlight and sounds. Every single place is full of itself, and couldn't care two hoots, in fact, for your presence or absence.

For all your screensavers and postcards, your photographs and words; for the flowers you transplant from its very soil; for the berries you picked there and froze, miles away; for the wall you painted a particular blue; for the driftwood you have on your bedroom bookshelf; for the fuchsia you pressed in your writing book; for all the rhymes you've made of its name; for all the times you set yourself down on a certain rock or a certain street to listen through the half-door of elsewhere for its goings-on and such, it isn't bothering with you, you know. It goes on without you.

The bread van delivers, the pub tap drips, the shutters are raised and are lowered again; a man in waders ticks off Lotto boxes, a child is handed a statuesque 99, a wrist flicks a fishing line, a sand-bucket is turned out, perfectly; the cappuccino machine up in the café spits and thrums; a woman slips into a call box; a bus brakes on the bridge; someone calls a name up a side-street, a radio bleats low prices from a car; mackerel glints in a pail; the river falls over itself; waves gossip with rocks; the last of the sunlight flits over the bay.

For all you imagine yourself part of it, it doesn't require you. You set down your other life like a sheet of tracing paper through which you find the significant lines of the place you want to be. You hear, in the noise of jets overhead, something of the deep sea's offshore boom. And sometimes a Sunday-evening sky looks for all the world like the cerulean bay, when it takes its ease.

A place is always occupied by the memories you've banked there. It's not just the sweet smell of fern and turf when you open the car-door, it's the fact that it's the same smell as hit you the last time, and the time before that, and twenty years ago. And the same view is laid out for you, give or take, as when you were a small girl, safe and sound in the world, your present self unimaginable, your future akin to a gold-wrapped parcel set under the Christmas tree. You love a place because you inhabit it in your imagination and your memory. You know things about it. You remember when the shrub was planted, the photo taken, the table set for different people with the same knives and forks. Maybe all attachments are sentimental, but all the same, that doesn't qualify or mediate their hold on you.

For all you know that your life will leave scarcely a trace behind when you have to go, you never quite believe it. That blue ring you were given for your twenty-first is still lost in the scrub. It's bound to show up eventually, and someone is bound to wonder whose it was and how it came to be here. Perhaps we enter the narrative of a place in only the smallest ways: a lost ring, a planted shrub, a bathroom extension, a new fridge. Perhaps it is all archaeology and the mark we make on the place we love is always in hindsight. Maybe it's only ever the past that we truly occupy.

But some places *are* more beautiful, more resonant, and more crucial than others. Some places simply matter more, however peripheral the reason: they define your everywhere else. I think you love a place, not just because of what it is, but because of what you were there: happy or young, in love or loved, up for the world, keen or more alive. And maybe, regardless of biographical fact, that place is what you call 'home'.

BORROWED PLUMAGE

Martina Devlin

My father never went to college, but his best hat did.

It's currently at Cambridge on his grandson's head – attending lectures and debates, maybe writing the odd essay (touch wood).

Not bad, for a hat belonging to a man who left school at thirteen.

Every day, his grandson wears his borrowed plumage: one of those narrow-brimmed felt trilbies with a feather in the band, whose natural habitat is an Irish market town. I nearly called it an aul' fellow's hat, except a 19-year-old student in England considers it the height of sophistication.

They wear it differently, mind you. My father plonked it on squarely – no cocking it over one eye, or any of that posturing. You'd never mistake him for Humphrey Bogart. The other day, I looked at a photograph of Patrick Kavanagh, and noticed he had a hat just like it. It sat on his head in the same, no-nonsense way.

Some hats wear the man and some men wear the hat.

My nephew, on the other hand, takes a rakish approach, tilting the trilby so far back it's a wonder gravity doesn't intervene.

His grandfather bought it in Todd's of Limerick, where he picked out all his hats. Usually he didn't care for department stores – they never gave him back the lucky penny he felt was his due after any business transaction – but he loved Todd's up there on O'Connell Street. It had row upon row of virtually identical trilbies.

I laugh out loud, to think what that hat must make of a student's life.

I daresay it's going to pubs with its new owner, though my father was a pioneer. I expect it's being taken to rock concerts, though my father believed a *céilí* was meat and drink enough for any music-lover.

The hat used to get brushed down with a toothbrush every morning, before being walked to 10 o'clock mass in the Sacred Heart Church. Many's the funeral it went to. It accompanied my father to GAA matches and to Lifford greyhound stadium; I wouldn't be surprised if it paid a visit to every dog track in Ireland.

Now, it saunters past Doric columns, to take its seat in a library built of honey-coloured stone, where its wearer is working his way through Shakespeare's sonnets. My father's taste ran to Zane Grey's cowboy books.

That hat must be looking on as its owner texts and tweets, surfs the net and updates his Facebook page. The man who bought it thought technology reached its pinnacle with the wireless.

He grew up in a cottage with an outside lavatory, and here's the new incumbent making himself at home amid quadrangles bordered by neo-classical buildings, whose old boys – except they call them *alumni* – include John Cleese and Michael Winner. That trilby has made the transition with ease.

Maybe it's being used to catch the eye of a girl. If not several girls. In the bird kingdom, peacocks spread their wings and strut during the mating ritual. In the student world, your grandfather's best hat might be just as dazzling an asset.

Seventy years separate its two wearers. Who could have guessed they'd end up sharing a hat?

Some grandchildren succeed to a lump sum, or a painting, or perhaps a watch. My nephew is heir to his granddad's favourite possession, shaped by his skull and smoothed by his fingers.

Now that's an inheritance.

After he died, I took his hat as a memento of my father. Until one day my nephew said he needed a cap to play an old codger in a school production. Could he have the loan of his granddad's?

I never got it back. He'd found his fit, you see. Once that hat went on his head, he knew it belonged there.

It seems a love of hats can be passed from one generation to the next. Indeed, the passion can lie dormant and skip an age bracket. My father would no more have stepped outside the door in his pyjamas than he'd be seen on the street with his head uncovered. His grandson applies the same standard.

When I look at my nephew, I don't see a boy in a man's hat. I see the spirit of my father, with a new lease of life.

I don't know if his best hat is picking up an education. But you don't have to be a Cambridge don to realise it's definitely getting one almighty eye-opener.

DECEMBER

LUXEMBOURG GARDENS

Gerard Smyth

Here in the Luxembourg Gardens
there are leaves to be gathered
and petals from the flowers of France.

There's a new transparency
that the time of blossoming lacked.
And perpetual motion: Sunday joggers

shuffling the gravel, running in circles
for the sake of their hearts.
Those at ease cast pallid shadows:

the blind man with cane and Labrador,
the book lover on the last chapter of Balzac.
Avenue and arbour, haunt of the *flâneur*

who walks in idle bliss on the way
to the Palace of Justice, the emperor's tomb,
a rendezvous at the other end of the metro tunnels.

Here in the Luxembourg Gardens
the early dusk is like a slow dance
when day and night are in each other's arms.

BRITISH QUEENS AND EPICURES

Niall Weldon

The year was 1933 and I was eleven years old. The way was now clear to undertake my first great odyssey. The trip was from Rush village, in North County Dublin where I lived, to Dublin city – a distance of eighteen miles.

My journey was to accompany my father on his horse and cart laden with vegetables to the Dublin Fruit and Vegetable Market. He and his trusty and faithful horse, named Raleigh, had been together on those roads for years and they knew every twist and turn along the way.

Rush was well known up and down the country for producing early-season vegetables and in particular for early and middle-crop potatoes: Epicures and British Queens.

Our adventure started at midnight. I was all a dither with excitement when having been woken by my mother I saw my father had already yoked Raleigh into the cart, which was heavily laden with scallions, cauliflowers, bundles of beetroots, carrots, radishes, parsley and thyme. He had made space for me in the middle of the load where I was sandwiched between kegs of potatoes. Before departing he attached a candle-lit lamp to one of the cart shafts and tied a nosebag filled with oats as well as a bag of hay to the protruding end.

As I settled into my make-shift bed, my mother sprinkled holy water all over me, my father and Raleigh. 'Make sure you don't lose him,' she said, and then added paradoxically, as was her wont, words to the effect that even if he did it wouldn't be the worst thing in the world! Then with a hup hup and a jerk of the reins, Raleigh moved forwards. I was in seventh heaven.

The village of Lusk and its renowned round tower were hardly notice-
able as we passed through with neither a soul nor a sinner in sight anywhere. I was still awake when we reached Swords, while my father had
dozed off for short periods. Raleigh truly amazed me with his uncanny
road sense and horse power. It seemed he didn't need a driver and, when
I later mentioned this to my father, I was told that he often made the trip
without the use of the reins.

Soon we were passing through Santry village, where I thought the
Swiss-like row of little houses looked trim and tidy in the early morning
mist. Here we were joined by other carts and carloads of neatly packed
cabbages from surrounding areas.

When Whitehall came into view my heart took an extra beat as I knew
we were on the outskirts of the city. Men on bicycles began to overtake
us, while others walked the road with us. We were now on the crest of a
hill with a long stretch of road leading down into Drumcondra. Straight
ahead there was a stunning panoramic view of the city, the Dublin
Mountains, and the Wicklow hills beyond. It was all serenely picturesque
in the coming early morning light. Ribbons of smoke eddied skywards
from factory chimney stacks and seemingly endless rows of houses.

Within an hour we arrived at our destination off Mary Street. Together with scores of other horses and carts, we lined up in a long queue
outside the market gate to await opening time at six in the morning.

Raleigh was watered and fed oats and hay which he devoured. Most of
the men, including my father, retired to a nearby pub which had a special
licence to serve drinks from an early hour. I was left minding Raleigh after
first being treated to a bottle of ciderette and a packet of plain biscuits.

In time, a bell clanged, signalling opening time, and a mad rush began
towards the prime locations on the various banks of the market, specific
open spaces leased by Dublin Corporation to the fruit and vegetable auctioneers, amongst them Lightfoots, Beggs and Fitzsimons. The bank my
father used was operated by Harry Lawlor and Son. Business was conducted at a frantic pace and the horse traffic was chaotic. Once my
father's vegetables were sold he went to Lawlor's office to collect his
'note' and cash. It was around midday when I was taken to an eating
house nearby and treated to a tasty meal of bacon and cabbage. Raleigh
was again watered and fed by one of the horse minders in an open field

called the Old Hole. It was aptly named, and a virtual health hazard for man and beast. The stench was indescribable.

Before heading for home I was taken on a short visit to the nearby Fish and Daisy Markets. The variety and size of some of the fish enthralled me. Everything from a needle to an anchor was for sale there, and trade in second-hand clothes stalls looked brisk. I recall pressing my father to buy me a little pellet gun, but he wasn't having any of it and smartly rushed me out of the place.

Raleigh's cart was then loaded with manure by the horse minder and, feeling the worse for wear, I was put sitting on top of a pile of sacks which would be my resting place for the six-hour journey home.

After my wonderful adventure into Dublin city by horse and cart with my father, the return trip was horrifying in the extreme. I fell into a deep sleep a short distance from the market and a nightmare took hold of me. I found myself pitched into hell where I witnessed an unforgettable scene of woe, misery and tribulation which I remember to this very day. Much of it is best described in John Milton's epic poem *Paradise Lost* which I read many years later:

> See'st thou you dreary plain, forlorn and wild,
> The seat of desolation, void of light,
> Save what the glimmering of these lurid flames
> Casts pale and dreadful.
> In that terror-stricken dungeon I saw angels fall from heaven:
> Thick as autumnal leaves
> That strew the brooks in Valambrosa.

It is unlikely I will ever forget those immortal lines. I woke up in a lather of cold sweat and my father, noticing my plight, was urging Raleigh on at a quickening pace. Immediately after reaching home my mother took over and rushed me to bed saying that I looked like death and would get pneumonia. She would not have been aware, of course, that I had already been to hell and back in my stupor.

It is well over seventy years since this episode took place. The old adage of 'never venture never win' was never far from my mind in those far-off days and I think I tested its veracity to the limit with varying results. However, I cannot be sure if my horse and cart trip merits a win.

Fortunately I didn't get pneumonia, but paid the price in other ways. I made a quick recovery and it was one occasion when running away from home was not an option. Perhaps it was just one trip too many in my calendar of rapscallion ventures.

WHEN EILEEN MET MAGS

Eileen Casey

English poet Francis Scarfe, in his poem 'Cats' had the right idea when
he wrote:

> Those who love cats which do not even purr,
> Or which are thin and tired and very old,
> Bend down to them in the street and stroke their fur
> And rub their ears and smooth their breast, and hold
> Their paws, and gaze into their eyes of gold.

I too have always adored cats. I love the ground they deign to pad across,
the relaxing preen of their t'ai chi movements. How their lithe backs arch
like quizzical eyebrows when stretching into yet another hour's blissful
slumber.

I love those deep, dark mysteries glazed in lazy amber slits, those tiny
lightning flashes of pink tongue onto fur. Washing away even the merest
hint of human disturbance. Surely the symmetry alone of their whiskers
is an engineering marvel? And what joy it is to watch that sleek sashay
across space and time. Even the most elegant women on the planet cannot emulate such lyrical motion. I'm in good company. Mark Twain,
Hemmingway, Doris Lessing, our own Hugh Leonard, together with legions of others, we have all succumbed to this charming icon of the animal world.

I recently heard there's a biopic film in the making. Concerning Philip
Treacy's link to Style Empress Isabella Blow, it promises to be a feast for
the senses. This welcome news soon had me searching for an old photograph album. The photographs are of my darling cat Mags, who even

at the ripe old age of nineteen was an acknowledged glamour puss in the family. And totally lionised from the very first moment she moved in with us. I invented stories about her when my children were younger. These harmless domestic narratives soon grew into adventures that placed her in deadly peril among lush, though treacherous, jungles in deepest Borneo or Madagascar.

Mags was oft the recipient of an Eastern prince's kiss which would transform her into – what else? – the beautiful princess we knew she already was beneath her layers of fur. But I and my beloved cat had our own private world too. A world when there was no one but ourselves in a six-in-the-morning house and nothing to hear but the contented purring from a cat who was happy in my company as I went about the morning tasks, stopping every so often to stroke her soft black and white body. Or to gently tweak the velvet fabric of her ears.

In November 2005, Philip Treacy's exquisite exhibition 'When Philip met Isabella' showed at the National Museum of Ireland. My young daughters and I went to the exhibition and were enthralled by Treacy's stunning works. One of the hats in particular, a replica of an eighteenth-century sailing ship with full rigging, caught my fancy. But all of the hats were millinery masterpieces, totally absorbing to look at and a great tonic for the imagination. It's rumoured that the milliner par excellence wants Brad Pitt to play him in the movie, and why not? I've certainly no quarrel with that!

Of course, when we arrived home from this stunning exhibition we set about including Mags in this fashion extravaganza.

As it was near Christmas, we took out our box of decorations and soon had our feline fashionista in hat heaven, every bit as statement-making and eccentric as the fashion writer herself. I think Treacy, whose devotion to his Jack Russell Mr Pig is legendary, would have appreciated the ensuing result. Some of the creations were assembled from ornamental peacocks with long pink feathers and shiny tinsel. One of the more spectacular pieces consisted of a miniature chandelier and a unicorn. We called this particular concoction 'Ballroom Blitz', deciding it revealed a more striking and contemporary version of the Cinderella story.

Another such masterpiece was constructed from an old piece of netting. Entitled 'Ms Havisham's Revenge', it could only have been worn by an ageing cat, with a full stomach and cushioned beside a warm fire. It's quite amazing the indignities a cat will suffer when creature comforts are completely satiated.

Soon, having run out of ideas on the decorations front, I raided the dolls' wardrobes and before long had an array of pillbox, cloches and chapeaux. We photographed the finished results, receiving a bored yawn for our troubles from our 'catwalk' Queen. Isabella Blow passed away in 2007, two years before our beloved Mags. Isabella Blow left an enduring legacy, not only in her own right but in the way she took the fledgling milliner under her wing and helped him develop as an artist. Lady Gaga is now one of Philip Treacy's best customers. Our own darling Mags, though no longer with us, lives on in fantasia images inspired by perhaps the greatest milliner of our time and also, more importantly, in the legacy she left us, of much fun and laughter.

THE GOODLY BARROW

Kerry Hardie

The deep cold has come early this winter. Early and hard. We wake to a world leached grey by the frosts that thicken the birch twigs and burden each grass blade. Ice glazes the water in bucket and butt and etches dead leaves with white rime. On the hill a dog barks, sheep cough in the field, the cattle move to the empty feeders and stand. The world has grown ancient and still. The valley fills with a whiteness that laps at our hillside like milk.

'I'm surprised that most people don't hear it,' This is the Czech novelist, Ivan Klima, writing of the voice of identity and place that he hears like a bell in his head.

Mountains – a river – birds – darkness – the cold season.

For Klima these bonds of place were stronger than those of race, faith, or ideas – so strong that he left the security and comfort he had found in America and returned to Czechoslovakia to live an impoverished and uncertain life.

For nearly twenty-five years now I've lived my life in the shadow of the Blackstairs Mountains, a mile from the River Barrow. I've woken each day to the same sounds and sights, the same light and dark, the same rain or sun as my neighbours. Yet as a teenager when we'd drive south from Belfast Lough for sea-side holidays or visits to relatives, I thought I would die if I had to live in rural Ireland.

Literally.

I would stare at lush fields and blue hills, at tangled hedges, untidy farms, unsigned crossroads set deep in the heart of nowhere. All that endless green, those endless small roads going back on themselves, those chains of low mountains stretching off in the endless distance. Even getting out of the car felt dangerously like drowning.

Winter is not the same as summer, what happens to a landscape in winter is more than loss of the sun on pasture, the leaves from the trees, the tangle of wild flowers and grasses in the ditches. The land withdraws into itself, its inhabitants tighten into a community, the bones of a more ancient way of life work their way closer to the surface.

I am writing now of the scattered dwellings and fields that lie between Graiguenemanagh in County Kilkenny and Borris in County Carlow – townlands that have kept a hold on their own way of being through these years of rapid, hectic change.

Here short roads wind back on themselves, family names repeat and repeat; there are faces in the present that have walked out of the past. The mountains that stand on our common horizon are the smoke-blue mounds of the Blackstairs; the valley now filling with frozen mist has been etched by the River Barrow. Winter is ancient and total. Horses move like wraiths behind ditches, cattle stumble the muddy hill-sides, magpies rattle across the land. Crows pick at the entrails of fox, newly dead on the frozen roads, then gather at dusk in their thousands, wheeling and cawing, before the whole sky seems to turn and flow home to the naked woods by a river grown pewter and swollen. Day creeps from the darkness, then turns and slinks like a renegade dog back into the night.

Mountains – a river – birds – darkness – the cold season.

I think I have long since died to that urban teenager who thought unsigned roads were something that people endured until they could leave them to go and live somewhere with cars and lights and a street name stuck on a plate on the wall. Or perhaps I slid into the waters of the River Barrow and drifted downriver past trailing meadow-sweet and nettles and agrimony; perhaps I simply forgot the 'real' world of where I had intended to live out my life.

As I grow older there is less and less I can be sure of; only the certainties which can't be proven stand like dolmens in my inner landscape. This is not the place I was reared, nor is it where I belong in the sense of faith or kin, but perhaps I have a belonging with the people who belong here, perhaps Ivan Klima is right and the sharing of a place is, above all, what matters.

When I am away from here I am away from home.

TRAVELLING A LINE

Jason Oakley

The seaboard edge of the Dún Laoghaire Rathdown local authority administrative area is where I live – in Sandycove. But do I really 'know' this place? I would say 'DLR' and me (to use the abbreviated parlance of the county council's email address) are just on nodding terms, like I am with most of my fellow Dart commuters.

On the platform, in the mornings – I don't know you, you don't know me. We are familiar strangers. Each of us a member of one another's cast of life's extras and bit-part players. If one of us fails to show – or if we find an unfamiliar crowd around us on the platform – we know something is up, or that indeed we are in the wrong place altogether.

This brings to mind an improbable occurrence and dilemma I experienced this April. I had flown to Berlin very early in the morning on a business trip – so it was around nine o'clock or so that I was on the train from Spandau Station to Alexanderplatz. Sitting only a few seats away was a woman I knew from the Dart platform – for the sake of argument, from the 8.45 a.m. crowd.

Our eyes met. There was an instantaneous exchange of understanding. We would not speak, and back home we would continue to dutifully ignore each other on the platform. It was as if the Dart platforms near Masonic conventions and rules – which indicate for us who are the initiates and the novice or outsiders – had been lassoed out across the Irish Sea to middle Europe.

The Dart line is clearly a major arterial connection in my personal geography. But maybe 'geography' is actually too grand a term as it suggests a richly complex and extensive topology. I find it more apt to talk in terms of snail trails – regular grooves and ruts; incised habitual routes. And routes don't get any more fixed than those along steel rails.

I work, socialise, consume and spectate mostly in Dublin city centre. Although for some reason I always call it 'town' when I am buying my Dart ticket. Dublin is hardly a mega-opolis by global standards, but its art galleries, cinemas, record shops, gentlemen's outfitters and drinking and eating places nonetheless exert a strong gravitational pull on me.

If I am honest, for me this Dart-link is an almost umbilical connection. I do hope that doesn't summon too many unpleasantly visceral images in your minds' eyes. OK then, I'm intravenously suckled by Dublin. I absorb her cultural nutrients, and I sup gratefully and lovingly on this pre-digested goo…

Or sometimes I think I am a 40-year-old adolescent – as the idea of cities hold for me the same abstract class of allure as that which motivates a typical 'youf' to be magnetically drawn to malinger in shopping malls, or sullenly cluster with their peers in oddly windswept public spaces.

You might understand better if I tell you that one time during a weekend spent on a small craggy island off the coast of Mayo a friend of mine attempted to nickname me 'City-Brit', after I inquired as to the availability of ATM machines. Isn't that such a neat, compound phrase? It should be the brand name of some kind of budget commuter rail or short-hop airline.

Thankfully 'City-Brit' didn't stick, but I do often snicker to myself at its aptness. I am indeed of the English persuasion, and I was reared in the bosom of the UK's fine infrastructural supports – such as postcodes; the naming of even small country roads; village hypermarkets and a plenitude of ATM machines in even the remotest of rambling spots.

But all this funny bluster aside, ironically enough I am, actually, originally from the countryside: a village in East Anglia between Norwich and Great Yarmouth. The landscape is fantastically linear and flat around this part of the world. We've no mountains, but by way of recompense we've the big skies, windmills and reed beds of the broad lands. And there is an especially amazing coastline, with wide-open beaches offering uninterrupted vistas of sea and landscape horizons.

So let me admit it, of course I love living by the sea here in Dún Laoghaire. I actually thanked Sandycove in my wedding speech. As if I knew the place – like a relative.

But we can't ever fully know places, can we? We can only know what we encounter, as we wander the lines and paths dictated by our own very peculiar pre-conceptions and habits.

THE HOLLY GATHERERS

Caroline Carey Finn

This year marks our eighteenth Christmas tree together. In December a fir tree is manhandled into the house to its pride of place, some adjustments having been made with an axe to its trunk in order that it fit in the iron stand that we inherited when my mother fell foul of a real tree and opted for the tidier, less vacuuming option of an artificial model some ten years earlier.

Inhaling up close and deeply, I try to rekindle memories of Christmases past from its pine-resin perfume. Looking a little worse for wear, beginning to show their age, toilet-roll holders covered in red crêpe paper and bearded with cotton wool, the Santas are hung from branches.

Among our baubles are the satin bows which had adorned the flower bouquets awarded on the birth of each of my babies. These are arranged among the bottom branches every year. One or two delicate ornaments are given places of prominence, having been bought the first Christmas we were married, when our decoration trousseau was initiated.

As our children grew up, requests from Santa became more materialistic with the inventions of PS1, 2 and 3 and Xbox 360.

I have managed to keep one memorable tradition going. It began thus: while tucking my young sons in at night, Steve, the eldest at six, asked, as he often did, 'Mum, what will we do tomorrow?'

Without fail, the reply would begin, 'Ge' up in the morning, pu' on the gear and head …'

This evening the reply was, 'Head down the fields to collect holly for Christmas.' That meant it was the first Sunday in December: we called it 'Holly Sunday'.

After their breakfast the boys and their mother pulled on old coats, boots, hats and gloves. Joe, aged four, was entrusted with plastic bags to carry the holly home. Baby Sam's little legs hadn't learnt to walk yet, so he was zipped into a cosy padded suit, strapped into the backpack and hoisted up on his mother's shoulders where he could bob along and see all around him. She'd wield one of their father's blackthorn sticks, steadying her balance across the rough ground.

Steve and Joe skipped ahead through familiar fields, the 'craft', the 'far field' and the one known as the 'twelve acres', where the best holly bush grew. During the year many leisurely diversions were taken from herding or fencing to see the holly bush. Opinions were expressed on the colour of the berries in October. Debates over what the profusion of berries indicated. If sparse, had birds already eaten them, signalling a mild winter? Or if in abundance, was a long hard winter forecast perhaps?

It was visible from a distance by its pronounced pointed shape unconnected to the hawthorn bushes growing either side. It grew on the far bank of a watery ditch.

Parking the backpack so Sam could see what was going on, wearing her green gardening gloves to protect her hands, Mother took rose clippers from her pocket. She snipped the shiny holly leaves, picking as many with berries as she could reach, and throwing them towards the bank where Steve gathered up the branches. His yellow football gloves, with their white rubber palm grips, protected him against the prickly leaves. Steve held his hand for his mother to grip as she clambered up out of the icy cold water on to the bank. She called him her 'banks man'!

After dinner on Holly Sunday, some of the holly was poked behind pictures along with ivy and draped over photographs in the house. Branches abundant with berries were put aside for Granny in Dublin, who relished her bit of country holly to go with her plastic tree. A round wreath was constructed; small silk flowers edged in golden glitter were secured to it. Joe helped by spraying some of the holly and ivy in gold paint, making it extra Christmassy. He held the wreath up while his mother tied it to the front door knocker with a large red ribbon. Standing back approvingly, they were satisfied with their work.

Now the house looked like Christmas.

CHRISTMAS TURKEY

Rita Ann Higgins

This was 1970s Ireland and the jobs were there for the taking. Everyone was singing the praises of the generous multinationals. New words, easy-to-say words, slide-off-the-tongue words, big-turkey words. Christmas was coming and the multinationals would look after you. They would big turkey you. And if you and your wife worked in the same factory, they big turkeyed you twice. You were fowled rightly; plucked, stuffed and roasted. You brought your own gravy.

Wonder was the only fruit in town. These were the exciting days when the only priority was washing the hair every day and slapping on the layers of make-up. Sexy was the word made fresh that dwelt amongst us, it was in the ether and on the factory floor. Energy was the second prayer of the day; have it, keep it, use it, waste it at your peril.

This was factory time. The industrial estate had its mechanical claws out for me and I embraced them with vigour and devil-may-care. Try our factory first girl and see what we have to offer, and if you don't like our factory go next door. We want you, we love you, slip inside and get addicted. The multinational needs you. Get Ireland off its knees with your young blood, was the vibe, and sexual awakening was the beat, and in the shirt factory we had the jive. In the buckle factory all the buckles were called after German rivers. On the outside we knew we could slip 'the Oder or the Danube or the Rhine' into conversation and it gave us a sense of importance. Then it was on to the nut and washer factory: a nut here, a washer there. A nut in this barrel, a washer in that barrel, never a nut with a washer be.

So I graduated up to the *crème de la crème* of factories and I arrived at Digital. More country girls and country lads, some townies. It was a community within a community. The factory floor was like a stadium. This was bigger than any other factory I had worked in: this was Multi Multi. The conditions were great; everyone talked about the conditions. They had their own nurse, for God's sake.

The canteen was like a posh restaurant: it had juices and fresh fruit on display. I thought fresh fruit was only for patients in hospitals. No more squashed sandwiches at the bottom of your bag. At Christmas time the multinationals were *flaithiúlach* – they gave us all big fat multinational turkeys.

Our turkey was so big it would not fit in the oven and we had to take a hatchet to it on Christmas Day. Key words were emerging: great company, big turkey, hatchet job. There was a 'no-union' echo sometimes floating around the multinational roadshow. Why would you need a union when you had big turkeys? As we later learned, the big turkeys were the red herrings in the end.

Some short years after that I started to hear 'pulling-out' stories. The multinationals were going to other countries where they didn't eat turkey. The multinationals made buckets full of money in Ireland because of a special love-in big-turkey relationship deal they had with the Irish government. As soon as the special incentives clock stopped ticking, the multinationals ran and took the turkey with them. They went to Morocco and Southeast Asia and other exotic sounding places and they never looked back.

Meanwhile a lot of the jiving girls married the country lads and they got big mortgages and had big babies after all the goodies the multinationals were throwing at them for years. Now they were left with nothing but the jive and the magical lingo that first brought them together. At least when they rolled over to meet each other in the king-size bed they bought on the never-never when the goose was not yet cooked, they still had each other and a lot of happy memories. But as one of the girls from the shirt factory said to me one day in town, 'Where can I cash that?'

THE *MORSEBY* TRAGEDY

Vivien Igoe

As the three-masted schooner, the *Moresby,* left Cardiff at 5 p.m. on 21 December 1895, the weather was moderate and fine with a fresh breeze from the east. She was bound for Pisagua, a port on the Chilean coast in South America, with a cargo of coal.

On board were 31-year-old Captain Coomber, his 29-year-old wife Isabella and their 2½-year-old daughter Ivy. Ivy was well used to ships and the sea as she was born on board the *Lady Lawrence*, off the River Plate, in South America. Like the skipper in Longfellow's poem 'The Wreck of Hesperus', Captain Coomber 'had taken his little daughter to bear him company'. The story of the *Moresby* is every bit as tragic as that of the schooner *Hesperus* that sailed the wintry sea.

Amongst the crew of twenty-two on board the *Moresby* was a first and second mate, a carpenter, a steward, a cook, a sail-maker and nine able-bodied seamen. Some of the crew members were as young as fourteen; three of them had never been to sea before, and four had made only one previous sea voyage.

The following day the wind increased, resulting in a heavy squall, which caused serious damage to the sails of the schooner. On 23 December, as the *Moresby* was approaching the south-east coast of Ireland, there was a very strong gale blowing and Captain Coomber decided to seek shelter. He followed a smaller two-masted schooner, the *Mary Sinclair*, which was also in distress, into Dungarvan Bay in County Waterford. Due to the poor visibility, Coomber was under the impression that he was entering Cork Harbour.

In the early afternoon, he dropped anchor near the Black Rock at the entrance to the harbour, three quarters of a mile from the lighthouse. At this stage, the three lower sails of the schooner were split. An hour and a half later, the Ballinacourty lifeboat arrived at the *Moresby,* and asked if the crew wished to leave and go ashore. But the captain did not want to abandon ship and he, his family and all his crew remained on board. The lifeboat with its brave crew returned to the shore.

During the stormy night, Allen Barker, the second mate, got his plum pudding, which had been sent to him from home. He divided it up between his fellow seamen and prophetically remarked, 'Here, boys, this is the last plum pudding you will ever eat.'

They all ate their share in solemn silence; their thoughts were far away with the families they had left behind a few days before. It was indeed a mournful feast. The wind howled and the gale increased in force and by half eleven that evening the tossing sea in the whole bay was eerily lit up with distress flares and burning blue lights sent up from the *Moresby.*

The gale continued on the following day, which was Christmas Eve. At around half past four in the afternoon, as the Christmas candles were beginning to flicker in the windows of the dwellings dotted on the dark hinterland, giving a welcoming glow, the anchor chains of the *Moresby* suddenly snapped – and with the continual bashing of the sea, she struck the Whitehouse sandbank, and keeled over on her side. The waves submerged her decks with water. Despite the distress flares, there was still no sign of a lifeboat from Ballinacourty.

The news of the *Moresby's* dilemma had now reached Dungarvan, where a volunteer crew comprising of twelve men was mustered. They hurried to Ballinacourty, where two members of the original crew joined them. The fourteen-man crew quickly donned their cork jackets, took over the lifeboat, and put to sea immediately with Captain John Veale from Dungarvan as coxswain.

In the meantime Captain Coomber had issued the order to abandon ship. His first mate Martin Losé, a powerful swimmer, jumped off with Isabella, his sister, attached to him with a rope, in a brave bid to swim the 400 yards to the shore. The Captain, who waited until almost last, wrapped his little daughter Ivy in a soft white blanket, which he tied securely to his back. He leapt overboard into the darkness and into a cruel sea with an ebbing tide, which only swept them further away from the shore.

By the time Captain Veale and his men reached the *Moresby,* the crew had already jumped off the riggings into the icy cold water in a last desperate attempt to reach safety. Seven men were rescued out of the twenty-five people who had originally been on board. Two of them died shortly after they reached land.

Captain Coomber's body was later washed ashore and found with an empty white blanket tied on his back; Isabella's was found at Rinn Ó gCuanach, and Ivy was found not far from her mother. Her little bonnet and one of her tiny shoes were later washed up on the strand. Martin Losé, with the sodden tangled rope still tied around his lifeless body, was found at Ardmore.

Captain Coomber, Isabella and little Ivy, along with most of the crew members, were buried in St Mary's Church of Ireland cemetery in Dungarvan.

Special honour was given to the volunteer crew of courageous men. Captain Veale, when later called to give evidence, said: 'I had only one life to lose … and I was prepared to sacrifice that to save the crew.'

These heroic men, who risked their lives in atrocious conditions, one hundred and fourteen years ago, are commemorated with a modest plaque on the wall at Dungarvan Harbour. It reads:

'To commemorate the bravery of the men who volunteered to man the lifeboat and rescue seven of the crew of the *Moresby*, wrecked in Dungarvan Harbour on Christmas Eve, 1895.'

MANDY

Gina Moxley

It's Christmas Eve during the glory days of drinking and driving. My parents are working flat out behind the bar of our country pub. It's jammed. Us kids were passed around between customers, their faces red as fires. They're laughing and crying, stinking of drink and fags; we're given money and sweets, kissed and squeezed. It's like being inside a burp. 'I saw Momma kissing Santa Claus' … I hope not, Daddy'd have a stroke. Outside, a man in a van is putting something into our coal-house like a thief in reverse. 'Rudolph the red nosed…' The turkey arrives, it's not plucked. My mother persuades the bread man to do it. 'You better watch out …' What's the good man going to bring you? Did you write to Santy? You did, you did. I certainly did.

We'd had a run-in with Santy a few years before when he gave us a mutant rocking horse. It didn't so much rock as buckle. My brother and I were distraught, but steeled ourselves to love it. When my father got up he noticed Santy had put the back legs on the wrong way round. Santy! This year we'd give Santy a smaller drink.

And I'd had a bad-present experience the previous August. My sixth birthday. I was on holiday with my grandmother when a man in a hat arrived to the hotel with this huge box addressed to me. It was my first experience of post. Very carefully I opened the package. Inside was a doll called Mandy. She was half the height of me. Hard plastic, cherubic lips, blue blinking eyes and curly hair. Half baby, half woman, her arms and legs slightly bent, as if crying out to be hugged. I hated her. Such was my disappointment it never crossed my mind to wonder who sent her. Or how. I glared at the man in the hat. The man who knew nothing about me. Mandy spent the rest of the holiday flung in the wardrobe, while I carried the box she came in everywhere, telling anybody who'd listen, 'Imagine, this box knew where I was.'

So yes, I had sent my letter to Santy. I don't want anything to do with dolls, I told him. I want something with wheels. A red scooter if you have one. Please.

In the darkness the spread of presents was huge. Somebody lifted somebody to turn on the light. My brother got Meccano, guns, a set of carpenters' tools. A trike for my sister, streamers from the handlebars. She smiled wanly and rubbed it. She had glandular fever.

And there was Mandy. Bold as you like. In a wedding dress. The baby bride. A veil covering where I'd hacked at her hair. The biro wounds to her neck were disguised with pearls. Her singed eyelashes just made her look more delighted with herself. She even wore make-up. There was a going-away outfit. An evening gown. A twin set. An Aran jumper. A kilt. Hat. Boots. Dressing-gown. Nightie. Slippers. A raincoat. Enough clothes for a lifetime of play.

Publicans have two days off a year. Since Good Friday was devoted to painting the toilets, Christmas Day was a big deal. A family day. By lunchtime it was mayhem; my brother had nailed the hot-press closed, my sister went back to bed, too sick to cycle, we continuously rang the bell of her bike to annoy her. People kept calling to the door gasping, begging for drink. When my mother realised I had swapped Mandy and her entire wardrobe for a game of Ludo, she lost it and marched me to the neighbours to swap it right back. Think how much work Mrs Claus put into making those clothes, she said; she's at it since August, every stitch by hand. Yes, but, I protested, it's not what I asked for. Can't she read? Did Mary and Joseph swap the gold, frankincense and myrrh for a board game or a night in a hotel? They did not. Their presents are still in a museum in Bethlehem. You ungrateful brat.

The next year I asked for a pogo stick. Nothing else. And that's what I got. Not even falling head first through our neighbours' front door on that pogo stick on Christmas morning dampened my delight.

THE HAPPIEST PLACE ON EARTH

Thomas McCarthy

Such intense happiness cannot be known anywhere on this earth. At this moment, 7 a.m. in Xuing Park, Shanghai. Music everywhere, smiling faces, elderly couples dancing slow foxtrots as the music falls gently, waves of sound falling from trees like so many autumn leaves. Nobody wants for a partner. At seventy years of age, in Shanghai, you'll never dance alone.

Less than fifty metres away, beside the pools of the now-faded lotus flowers and beneath the tall weeping willows and gnarled ginkgo trees, I pass by at least 300 serious but friendly, well-dressed middle-aged parents. They are the early morning match-makers. This is the Saturday marriage market. At this time of year – early autumn when the young return to their universities and the slightly older begin their first jobs – this marriage market is busier than ever.

A youngish mother holds up a notice, neatly written on quarto-sized typing paper, a public proclamation on behalf of her son in his late twenties. 'Born 1983. Tall. A graduate of Western university. Now working as an engineer with a monthly salary of ten thousand renminbi. Wishes to meet a tall woman, a woman who is gentle, one who dislikes loud music.'

And beside the oldest ginkgo tree, very close to a huge contemporary art installation of bamboos, there's a tall and very elegant man smoking a very long cigarette. He holds aloft, cheerfully and proudly, a placard declaring his daughter's eligibility and willingness to marry. She was born in 1988. She wishes for a tall husband, preferably a university graduate. She is working as a junior executive with an international bank in Shanghai. She holds a Shanghai resident's permit. This latter detail is a powerful asset, as powerful as the most expensive French perfume. A woman with such a permit qualifies for healthcare as well as guaranteed education for her unborn children, right up to university level. I look at her photograph, held aloft by her chic, chain-smoking father. It is an old-fashioned photograph, like a studio portrait of a bourgeois of Shanghai circa 1910. But these photos, I soon learn, are posed and printed to appeal, not to any would-be lover, but to the mothers of lovers.

Later in the morning, as I walk back that way again, I see these two marriage brokers deep in conversation. The first stage of the process is an exchange of photographs, the sharing of a larger portfolio of images so that the parent can choose the one most likely to appeal to a son or daughter. The whole event will turn upon a daughter's first reaction to that photograph: will she like the look of a boy or not? An entire lifetime, the begetting of children, the future of China itself, will turn upon the trained instincts of that Shanghai daughter: is there something in the look of him that unnerves her, or draws her in?

Beyond the ginkgo trees and the faded lotus flowers, around the pond of giant lilies, are dozens of caged birds singing wildly and sweetly. Their cages are hanging from trees and specially constructed poles. And around them, beneath them, are all the old men who can't dance, men who watch their own caged birds while smoking and gossiping in the morning sunshine. Every morning elderly men bring their caged birds to the park to hang beside other caged birds. In such company the birds of Shanghai sing, wildly and sweetly as I've said, the whole sound joined together in a great wave of energy. Any moment, I think, Respighi and his orchestra may burst through the bushes. But these birds sing on, hopping from blue and white porcelain water jars to blue and white porcelain grain jars.

These caged birds singing, seemingly perfectly contented and excited by the company of others, create a single great metaphor for China and its success: a success based on continuity, a mutually beneficial contract between the people and their own administrations. The administration, you must understand, is always a local one, a neighbourhood committee, a tenement work group. Then, still inside the first ring road, there's the district commune with its own mayor, and beyond that the city council, and, beyond the fourth ring road, the historic entities, the great lands of Fujian, Fukien, Guangdong, Hainan, Harbin Henan, Wuhan, Hunan,

Shenyang, Chinghai, Shandong, Jinan, Sichuan, Yunnan. Birds singing all the way to the Central Committee, to the Premier, to the President.

The young never left alone in their search for a life partner; the old never left alone in their need to dance. How can we ever understand what's going on? One thousand, three hundred million people. Growth, development, a sense of purpose and an atmosphere of confidence everywhere. This is merely one park in Shanghai. This is China on a sunny morning, between the ginkgo trees and the faded lotus flowers, in the year 2010.

STORIES LIKE THE LIGHT OF STARS

Éilis Ní Dhuibhne

January 1978. Bloody Foreland, Donegal. I am the only lodger in a Bed and Breakfast under *Cnoc na Naomh*. I booked in for a week because I have a seminar paper to write. For some weird reason I think it will be easier to write this paper in a B&B in Donegal than in a library in Dublin, even though in these days the internet doesn't exist and all research has to be done in libraries or archives. There are no PCs even – I carry a typewriter with me, on the bus. At least there is a bus.

But on my second day I abandon my seminar paper. After my tea of chips and pork chops and peas, eaten alone in the big dining room, I set off down the road and across the bog, a cassette recorder purchased that morning in Falcarragh under my arm. The *bean a tí* has told me that a storyteller, Joe, lives down the road, and he won't mind a stranger dropping in.

There is snow on the mountain, the sky is bright with stars and the air fragrant with peat smoke – that intoxicating smell of the Gaeltacht. Dogs bark furiously at every house I pass, but they don't bother to chase me, it being so cold.

After a while I reach a grey prefab, the kind you see on building sites or in school yards, nestling in the shadow of a derelict cottage. An old man with a long turfcutter's face and eyes like stars opens the door. His mouth twists for a second, uncertainly, but then he says, 'Come in, *a thaiscí.*' The kitchen is as cosy as a teapot. He introduces me to his aunt, who is about ninety, and is tucked up in a bed at the back of the kitchen, where she spends her days saying the rosary and smoking woodbine cigarettes.

I ask Joe, the old man, if he knows the story of the devil and the bailiff, which Chaucer heard in London in the fourteenth century and used as the basis for one of *The Canterbury Tales*. It's still known in Ireland, but no, Joe doesn't have it. But he cocks his head on one side and asks me, 'Have you heard of *Maighdean an tSolais*?'

This story lasts for about an hour. It is – I find out later – a version of *The Girl as Helper in the Hero's Flight*, one of the great wonder tales of Ireland and of the world. It includes episodes like the 'Impossible Tasks', which were known to Homer several centuries before Christ. At least 700 versions of it have been collected in Ireland – we always have more versions, hundreds more, of any tale than any country in the world. These can be read in the archive of the National Folklore Commission collection. Joe's version is there too.

That night, walking back across the bog, I felt I knew how all the collectors must have felt, down through the years – Séamus Ó Duilearga going to Seán Ó Conaill in Cill Rialaig, Robin Flower going to Peig Sayers on the Great Blasket and John Millington Synge going to Pat Derrane on Inis Meaín. I thought it must have been like this for the Brothers Grimm, making their way through the snow – it must have been snowing – to cottages in the countryside around Münster, to collect what became *Kinder und Hausmärchen*, the first collection of folk tales to take the world by storm in 1812.

Few experiences in life are as exhilarating as collecting. This is a thing not many people know! Hearing an ancient story told by a good narrator, in a cabin in Donegal, as it might be, or in Iceland, or Nigeria or Nebraska, is like being handed a precious, beautiful object that has been passed on from storyteller to storyteller across the centuries and around the globe, because folk tales know no national boundaries.

An oral story, a folk tale, is more fragile than most objects, however. It is a complex work of art that is carried in the human memory, transmitted by the human voice, received by human ears. Recreated each time it is told and dependent on interested listeners. What is the right metaphor for the migratory stories? Not butterflies or birds or wild salmon, although they are a bit like all those things. I think they are most like lights; like the flickering will-o'-the-wisp or the souls of dead children who, in legends, flutter around the bogs and mountains after dark in search of their mothers.

Joyce used the word 'epiphany' about his short stories. They illuminate life like the star of knowledge that guided the Magi to the great illumination in the stable of Bethlehem. That is a good metaphor. But it suits all good stories, not just modern novella. All good stories are flashes of light, stars of knowledge. They are the light in the eyes of a storyteller and of those who love stories, the creative spirit that does not go out as long as people want to be entertained and know how to entertain themselves by weaving words and memories and ideas into interesting patterns.

Of course, what the Irish Folklore Commission did and what the National Folklore Collection continues to do, was to preserve them on cylinder and tape, in manuscripts and books. Pin them down, like butterflies under glass. But again the analogy is not quite correct. Out of the covers of books and manuscripts, the stories emerge again to inspire writers and artists, and composers, and students and scholars, and new kinds of storyteller; the luminous messages from the imagination of the past go on flying from mind to mind, from mouth to mouth, from mouth to pen to page to screen. The stories are not swallows or salmon, but immortal, like the light of stars. They cannot be snuffed out so easily.

AN TEACH TUÍ

Vona Groarke

Thistledown, fuchsia, flagstone floor:
this noun house

has the wherewithal
to sit out centuries,

squat between bog-water darkness
and rooms turned inside out into summer,

straw-coloured months of childhood
answering each other

like opposite windows in thickset walls
that sunlight will cajole.

Tea roses bluster the half-door.
rain from eaves footfalls the gravel.

A robin, cocksure of himself,
frittered away all morning in the shrub.

If I knew how to fix in even one language
the noise of his wing in flight

I wouldn't need another word.

CONTRIBUTOR BIOGRAPHIES

SILE AGNEW: Originally from Dublin, lives in Kildare with her family. Writes with Sapphire Writing Group in the Irish Writers' Centre. Currently working on her first novel, she enjoys painting and cooking. An avid reader with Marietta Book Club, she wrote a prize-winning piece last year for the Ennis Book Club Festival's competition to find the Book Club of the Year (p. 187).

LIAM AUNGIER: Has been published in *The Irish Times* and in *THE SHOp*. His first book, *Apples in Winter*, was published by Doghouse in 2005 (p. 1).

JOHN BANVILLE: A novelist, reviewer and screenwriter. His latest novel is *The Infinities*. His crime novels, written under the pen-name Benjamin Black, include *Christine Falls* and *Elegy for April* (p. 192).

KEVIN BARRY: Born in Limerick and currently living in Sligo. *There are Little Kingdoms*, his first short story collection, won The Rooney Prize for Literature. His stories have been published in *The New Yorker*. His first novel is published in 2011 (p. 330).

DENISE BLAKE: Born in Ohio, USA in 1958. Moved back to Ireland in 1968 and grew up in Letterkenny, County Donegal. Her poetry collections include *Take a Deep Breath* and *How to Spin without Getting Dizzy*, published by Summer Palace Press (p. 340).

JOHN BOLAND: A literary and television critic for the *Irish Independent* and an arts broadcaster. His collection of poetry, *Brow Head*, was published in 1999 (p. 43).

PAT BORAN: Born in 1963 in Portlaoise. Lives in Dublin where he is the publisher of the Dedalus Press. He has written numerous books of poetry, fiction and memoir, and most recently *The Invisible Prison: Scenes from an Irish Childhood* (p. 115).

JOHN BREEN: A playwright and theatre director best known for his hit comedy *Alone it Stands*. He is currently Artistic Director of TEAM Educational Theatre Company in Dublin (p. 367).

CATHLEEN BRINDLEY: Born in India and educated in Ireland, where she received a degree in Modern Languages. Enjoys travel and has written extensively on the subject (p. 85).

MARY ROSE CALLAGHAN: Has written nine novels, including *Billy, Come Home* (2007) and *A Bit of a Scandal* (2009). She is also a short story writer, playwright and biographer (p. 27).

CAROLINE CAREY FINN: Attended Coláiste Bríde in Clondalkin. Lives in County Meath with husband and four children. A member of the Boyne Writers Group, she has had several pieces published in their *Boyne Berries* magazines (p. 394).

TIM CAREY: American-born author and historian, whose books include *Mountjoy: The Story of a Prison* and *Croke Park: A History*. He is currently Heritage Officer with Dún Laoghaire–Rathdown County Council (p. 351).

EILEEN CASEY: Currently a post-graduate student in Trinity College. Her debut poetry collection *Drinking the Colour Blue* was published by New Island. *From Bone to Blossom*, a collaborative work with visual artist Emma Barone, is the recipient of the 2010 Bursary for Artists Scheme awarded by Offaly County Council and is published by Altents, South Dublin (p. 386).

KEVIN CASEY: Kevin's most recent novel, *A State of Mind*, was published in 2009 (p. 64).

MAURICE CASHELL: Maurice has lived in Switzerland, France and Belgium as well as in Ireland. His publications include short stories and travel features and also studies on labour law and industrial relations (p. 182).

ANNE CHAMBERS: Author of several biographies, a novel, short story collection, stage drama and screenplays, her books have been translated and published abroad and have been the subject of international television and radio documentaries (p. 149).

Michael Coady: Lives in Carrick-on-Suir and is a member of Aosdána. His most recent book is *Going by Water*, a collection of poems, prose and photographs published by Gallery Press (p. 239).

Mary Coll: From Limerick, a former Director of the Belltable Arts Centre and has worked as an arts consultant, theatre and visual arts critic and radio contributor. *All Things Considered*, her poetry collection, was published by Salmon in 2002. Her first play, *Excess Baggage*, short-listed for the Stewart Parker Award, was produced in Limerick in 2009, followed in 2010 by *Anything But Love* (p. 79).

Evelyn Conlon: Set her last novel among the lowest of the dead on Death Row, but the next one will have birds, boats and a lot of sky in it. She lives in Rathmines (p. 102).

Pádraic Conway: Director of the UCD International Centre for Newman Studies and a Vice-President of University College Dublin (p. 267).

Amanda Coogan: A performance artist living in Dublin. Her practice is represented in the Irish Museum of Modern Art's collection, by the Kevin Kavanagh Gallery in Dublin and Galleria Safia in Barcelona (p. 81).

Claire Coughlan: A graduate of UCD's MA in Creative Writing. In 2009 she was awarded an Arts Bursary in Literature from Dublin City Council. She is originally from County Kildare (p. 135).

Adrian Crowley: Born in Malta and grew up in County Galway. A professional musician and songwriter and has released five albums to date. He lives in Dublin with his wife and two children and is currently working on his first collection of prose (p. 337).

Brian Crowley: The Curator of the Pearse Museum, Rathfarnham, County Dublin. His article, 'I am the son of a good father: James and Patrick Pearse' appeared in *The Life and After-Life of P. H. Pearse* in 2009 (p. 143).

Catherine Ann Cullen: Has written two books for children, *The Magical Mystical Marvelous Coat* and *Thirsty Baby*, both published by Little, Brown in the US. Her first collection of poetry, *A Bone in My Throat*, was published by Doghouse in 2007 (pp. 104, 141).

LEO CULLEN: Author of *Clocking 90 on the Road to Cloughjordan* and *Let's Twist Again* (Blackstaff Press). A frequent broadcaster on RTÉ Radio and BBC. He hails from County Tipperary and lives in Monkstown, County Dublin (p. 276).

GERALD DAWE: Born in Belfast, a lecturer in Trinity College Dublin, where he is a director of the Oscar Wilde Centre for Irish Writing and co-director of the graduate Creative Writing Programme. He has published numerous books of essays and poetry. He is a member of Aosdána and lives in Dún Laoghaire (pp. 77, 235).

JOHN F. DEANE: Born in Achill Island, founder of Poetry Ireland, poet and fiction writer; *Where No Storms Come*, a novel, Blackstaff Press 2010; *Eye of the Hare*, poems, Carcanet, June 2011 (pp. 36, 127).

MARTINA DEVLIN: Born in Omagh, a novelist, non-fiction writer and columnist. Her latest book is the historical novel *Ships of Dreams* (pp. 334, 375).

JOHN S. DOYLE: Journalist, born in Dublin. He was one of the founders of *In Dublin* magazine and presents *It Says in the Papers* on RTÉ Radio 1 (p. 46).

NOEL DUFFY: Born in Dublin. His debut poetry collection, *Passage,* was published by Ward Wood in June 2011 (p. 84).

CHRISTINE DWYER HICKEY: An award-winning short story writer and novelist. Her sixth novel, *Cold Eye of Heaven*, will be published in autumn 2011 by Atlantic Books. (p. 319)

NOEL ELLIS: A primary school teacher in Lucan, County Dublin. He originally hails from Carlow town, but he is now residing in Beaumont, Dublin with his wife and three children (p. 270).

BERNARD FARRELL: A playwright whose twenty-one plays have been mainly premiered at the Abbey and Gate theatres. *I Do Not Like Thee Doctor Fell* (1979) was his first play, and *Bookworms*, his latest, both at the Abbey (pp. 53, 130).

MICHAEL FEWER: Born in County Waterford, he is the author of numerous books relating to nature, landscape and the environment, most recently *The Wicklow Military Road* and *Rambling Down the Suir: The Past and Present of a Great Irish River* (p. 251).

CIARÁN FOLAN: Born in Newtowncashel, County Longford. Author of the short story collection *Freak Nights*. Has won the RTÉ Francis MacManus short story competition twice, most recently in 2009. He has published fiction in *New Irish Writing* and in *The Dublin Review*, and non-fiction in Irish in *The Irish Times* (p. 133).

CATHERINE FOLEY: A full-time writer and broadcaster, and a former staff journalist with *The Irish Times*. She has presented and co-produced documentaries for TG4. She is a regular presenter on TG4's arts programme, *Imeall*. Her third Irish-language novella, *Samhradh an Chéasta*, was published recently. Her two earlier ones are *An Cailín Rua* and *Sorcha sa Ghailearaí* (p. 56).

HEDY GIBBONS LYNOTT: Writer and broadcaster, lives in Clarinbridge, County Galway, and finds inspiration for her essays and poetry in the people and places she loves (p. 156).

PETER GILLEN: Born in Drogheda, he is a medical surgeon in Our Lady of Lourdes Hospital in Drogheda, County Louth (p. 354).

ANTHONY GLAVIN: Author of two short story collections, *One for Sorrow* and *The Draughtsman & The Unicorn*, and a novel, *Nighthawk Alley* (p. 361).

BRENDAN GRAHAM: His songs 'Rock 'n' Roll Kids', 'The Voice', 'Isle of Hope', 'Isle of Tears', 'Winter, Fire & Snow' (with Macdara Woods) and 'Crucán na bPáiste' will be known to many. His 'You Raise Me Up' (music by Rolf Lovland) has become one of the most successful songs in the history of popular music. He has also written a trilogy of historical novels for Harper Collins, the first of which – *The Whitest Flower* – was a No. 2 bestseller in Ireland (p. 230).

VONA GROARKE: Born in Edgeworthstown, County Longford, she is an award-winning poet and a member of Aosdána. Her most recent collection is *Spindrift*, published by the Gallery Press. She teaches at the Centre of Creative Writing at the University of Manchester (pp. 216, 373, 409).

MARIE HANNIGAN: Born in London and grew up in Killybegs, County Donegal. Her first stories were published in *New Irish Writing* and she was twice winner of Listowel Writers' Week short story award. She has written drama for radio, television and the Balor Theatre Community Arts programme (p. 327).

KERRY HARDIE: The author of two novels, *Hannie Bennet's Winter Marriage* and *The Bird Woman* (Harper Collins). She has published five books of poetry with the Gallery Press. A *Selected Edition* of her poetry will be published in February by the Gallery Press and Bloodaxe Books (p. 389).

MICHAEL HARDING: Has written a couple of books of fiction, numerous plays for The Abbey Theatre and other theatre companies. He is a regular contributor to *The Irish Times* (p. 365).

JAMES HARPUR: A poet with four collections of poetry published by Anvil Press. He has won a number of awards, including the 2009 Michael Hartnett Award and the British National Poetry Competition (p. 371).

DONAL HAYES: Restaurateur, husband, dad, brother, writer, contrary, unkempt, ex-banker, cheesemonger, bad driver, big, optimistic, sailor, libertarian, chef, corny and sanguine (p. 296).

MARGARET HAWKINS: A Wicklow-born journalist and health writer with the *Irish Farmers Journal.* Her first book, *Restless Spirit: The Story of Rose Quinn,* was published in 2006. She is currently completing her rural-based novel, *Kingdom of Abe* (pp. 70, 248).

NUALA HAYES: Actor, storyteller and independent radio producer. She is currently touring Ireland with *Dear Frankie* by Niamh Gleeson, a play based on the life of Frankie Byrne, radio's first and much-loved agony aunt (p. 299).

MONICA HENCHY: A retired assistant librarian in Trinity College Dublin, she was president of the Dublin Spanish Society for several years. Her special interests are writing, and lecturing about the Irish colleges of Spain (p. 73).

RITA ANN HIGGINS: Rita Ann Higgins is from Galway. Her first collection, *Goddess on the Mervue Bus* made an indelible mark on Irish poetry. Since then she has published numerous other collections as well as the recently published collection of essays, *Hurting God*, in 2010. She is a member of Aosdána (p. 396).

JOSEPH HORGAN: Born in Birmingham, England, of Irish parents. Has lived in Ireland since 1999, is the author of two books, a poet, writer and journalist, and a past winner of the Patrick Kavanagh Award (p. 200).

DECLAN HUGHES: A playwright, a novelist and the co-founder of Rough Magic Theatre Company. His work includes the plays *Digging for Fire, Twenty Grand* and *Shiver*, and the novels *The Wrong Kind of Blood, All The Dead Voices* and *City of Lost Girls* (p. 322).

VIVIEN IGOE: A Dubliner, a graduate of University College Dublin. Author of four books, and working on her fifth, she first contributed to *Sunday Miscellany* in 1991. (p. 398).

MARK JOYCE: Born in Dublin in 1966, he studied painting at the Royal College of Art, London, and has had solo shows in Ireland, UK and the USA. His work is in the collections of the Irish Museum of Modern Art and Arts Council. The works explore optical and perceptual aspects of colour, and the physical nature of light (p. 22).

COLBERT KEARNEY: A Dubliner who recently retired as Professor of English at UCC to have more time for writing (pp. 3, 67).

JOE KEARNEY: Born in Kilkenny, he is a full-time writer and has made numerous award-winning documentaries for RTÉ Radio 1. He teaches creative writing and is currently completing a Ph.D in Creative Writing in UCD. His latest collection, *The Bend of The Road*, will be published shortly (pp. 16, 50).

CYRIL KELLY: Born in Listowel, taught in Dublin. Now retired and serving time as a scribbling apprentice (p. 119, 194).

MARY KENNY: A veteran journalist working in Dublin and London. In recent years, she has developed her interest in history and has written a biography of 'Lord _Haw-Haw', *Germany Calling*, a history of Irish values, *Goodbye to Catholic Ireland*, a play about Winston Churchill and Michael Collins in 1921–22, *Allegiance*, and *Crown and Shamrock: Love and Hate between Ireland and the British Monarchy*. See www.mary-kenny.com.(p. 164).

CLAIRE KILROY: One of Ireland's finest young writers, she is the author of three acclaimed novels, most recently *All Names Have Been Changed* (p. 189).

CHUCK KRUGER: Has six books to his name – poetry, short story, thriller, island history – all set on Cape Clear. For details, unexpurgated reviews, radio pieces, and fun photos, feel free to browse his website at www.chuckkruger.net (p. 170).

ANNE LE MARQUAND HARTIGAN: Born in England and living in Ireland for many years, she is a poet, playwright and painter. *To Keep the Light Burning*, her sixth collection of poetry, was published in 2009. She has a family of six children (p. 243).

MAE LEONARD: Originally from Limerick, she now lives in Kildare. A broadcaster, award-winning writer and poet, her publications include *My Home is There*, *This is Tarzan Clancy* and *Six of Gold*. Amongst the many honours received for her writing are the Scottish International, Francis McManus, Belmont and Cecil Day Lewis Awards (p. 92).

BRIAN LEYDEN: Lives in Sligo. He is the author of *Departures*, *Death & Plenty* and *The Home Place*. See http://brianleyden.blogspot.com (p. 369).

NICOLA LINDSAY: Published works includes a children's book and a collection of poetry. She is the author of five novels. Her work has been broadcast and anthologised in Ireland and Britain (p. 172).

TRISH LONG: Grew up in St Mary's Park, Limerick, lives in Dublin and Wicklow and is married to Paddy Woodworth. She is the general manager and vice president of Walt Disney Studios, Ireland (p. 197).

LOUISE LYONS: Her interests are hill-walking, cycling and growing organic vegetables. A long-time member of Toastmasters. Though widely travelled, her favourite places in the world are West Cork, Kerry and Connemara (p. 202).

MARGUERITE MACCURTIN: From County Galway, Marguerite is a broadcaster, writer and passionate traveller (p. 117).

DOLORES MACKENNA: A writer and critic. She has written a number of educational books and is the author of *William Trevor: The Writer and his Work*, published by New Island (p. 324).

JOHN MACKENNA: A novelist, short-story writer and playwright. His work has won the *Irish Times* Fiction Award; Jacobs Radio Award; Hennessy Award and Cecil Day Lewis Award. He lives in Kildare (p. 227).

SHEILA MAHER: Sheila Maher lives in Dublin, where she teaches in Dún Laoghaire

VEC. A regular contributor to *Sunday Miscellany*, she has recently completed a memoir of growing up in 1970s Dublin (pp. 94, 184).

P. J. MATHEWS: Lectures in Anglo-Irish Literature and Drama at University College Dublin. He is the editor of *The Cambridge Companion to J. M. Synge* (p. 348).

KEVIN MCALEER: A writer and comedian from Omagh, County Tyrone. One of the founding fathers of modern Irish stand-up, he is still going strong with his writing and live performances (p. 356).

JOSEPHINE MCARDLE: A teacher, born and living in Athlone. Married, mother of three daughters, a Jesse James fan, enjoys writing short stories and is gearing up for the novel commitment! (p. 272).

THOMAS MCCARTHY: Born in Cappoquin, County Waterford, he is a poet, novelist and critic. He has written numerous collections of poetry, plays and novels. His most recent poetry collection is *The Last Geraldine Officer* published by Anvil. He lives in Cork city where he works in the City Libraries (p. 403).

LARRY MCCLUSKEY: Was a keen sportsman in youth; has had a lifelong involvement in amateur theatre, with Drumlin Players. His career in education spanned forty-five years in Ireland and Ghana. Now retired, he still supports Cavan. An optimist! (p. 279).

IGGY MCGOVERN: Associate Professor of Physics at Trinity College. He has authored two poetry collections, *The King of Suburbia* and *Safe House*, both published by Dedalus Press (p. 25).

MARK MCGOWAN: Specialist in the religious, social, migration, and educational history of Canada. Co-editor of the award-winning books *Catholics at the Gathering Place: Historical Essays on the Archdiocese of Toronto* and *The Waning of the Green: Catholics, the Irish and Identity in Toronto, 1887–1922* (McGill-Queen's); *Michael Power: The Struggle to Build the Catholic Church on the Canadian Frontier* (McGill-Queen's). He has recently completed a revisionist work on the Irish Famine migration to Canada and a short book for the Ireland Park Foundation: *'A Calamity to the Province': The Irish Famine Migration of 1847 and Toronto*. He is currently principal of St Michael's College, Toronto (p. 167).

PÁDRAIG MCGINN: A retired school principal, living in Carrick-on-Shannon, County Leitrim. His stories have been published in *The Leitrim Guardian* and *First Cut*. He has been short-listed in a number of writing competitions, including The Bard of Armagh and the Strokestown Poetry Award (p. 6).

ANDREW MCKIMM: A Dublin-based maths teacher and writer. Apart from his family, his main interests are music, travel and *Star Wars* (p. 262).

ALEX MILLER: Born in 1936 in London of Irish parentage, he emigrated to Australia when he was sixteeen. A graduate of The University of Melbourne, he is an award-winning writer of numerous novels, including *Lovesong*, published in 2010. He participated in the *Sunday Miscellany* live event at the Mountains to Sea Writers Festival 2010 (p. 286).

SEAN MOFFATT: A full-time script writer who worked for many years on RTÉ's *Fair City* as well as dramas for stage and radio (p. 245).

MARY MORRISSY: A journalist and author of the novels *Mother of Pearl*, *The Pretender* and of the short story collection *A Lazy Eye*. She works as a journalist and teaches creative writing (p. 358).

GINA MOXLEY: An actor and playwright. Her most recent play, *The Crumb Trail*, was produced by Pan Pan Theatre. Her theatre piece, *Map of M*, revised, was performed in Rome in 2011 (p. 401).

GERRY MORAN: From Kilkenny, he is a former primary-school principal and the author of *Kilkenny City & County*. His work has appeared in a variety of publications (p. 260).

VAL MULKERNS: Born in Dublin in 1925, she moved to London after working in the civil service. She returned to Ireland in 1952 as the associate editor of *The Bell*. A novelist and short story writer, she jointly won the AIB Prize for Literature, and her writing is included in the recently published *The Granta Book of the Irish Short Story* edited by Anne Enright. She is a member of Aosdána (p. 345).

COLIN MURPHY: A journalist in Dublin. He contributes regularly to *The Dublin Review*. His radio series, *From Stage to Street*, was recently broadcast on RTÉ Radio 1. See www.colinmurphy.ie (p. 30).

PETER MURPHY: Writer, musician and journalist from Enniscorthy, County Wexford. His first novel, *John the Revelator*, was published in the UK and Ireland by Faber & Faber and in the US by Houghton Mifflin Harcourt, and has been nominated for the 2011 IMPAC Literary Award and shortlisted for the 2009 Costa Book Awards. One of Ireland's most respected arts writers, his journalism has been published in *Rolling Stone*, *Music Week* and *The Irish Times*, and he currently serves as contributing editor with Dublin's *Hot Press* magazine. He is also a regular guest on RTÉ's arts review show, *The View*, and has contributed liner notes to the forthcoming remastered *Anthology of American Folk Music* (p. 174).

DYMPNA MURRAY FENNELL: From County Westmeath, she now lives in Lucan. She is a retired teacher, having taught in many parts of Ireland and in Africa (pp. 8, 122).

NUALA NÍ CHONCHÚIR: Her debut novel *You* (New Island, 2010) was called 'a heart-warmer' by *The Irish Times* and 'a gem' by *The Irish Examiner*. Her third poetry collection, *The Juno Charm*, appears from Salmon Poetry in 2011 (p. 288).

MÁIRÉAD NÍ CHONEANAINN: Born in east Galway and a civil servant for years. Married an Islander and lived on Inis Mór. Has been a regular actor in An Taibhdhearc and has a long interest in literature (p. 90).

ÉILIS NÍ DHUIBHNE: Born in 1954, she is the author of numerous award-winning novels, short stories, literature for children and plays for stage and radio. Her work is translated into numerous languages. For many years she worked as a librarian in The National Library of Ireland. She is now Writer Fellow in University College Dublin where she teaches on the MA in Creative Writing. She is a member of Aosdána (p. 406).

SUE NORTON: Having grown up in America, she now lectures in the Dublin Institute of Technology (p. 19).

JACKIE NUGENT: Has finally realised that a lifetime's attraction to bold boys has got her nowhere and is now seeking the help that she so obviously needed from a very young age. Jackie lives in Dublin and now loves Tim, a West Highland Terrier. Tim is a very good boy (p. 59).

JASON OAKLEY: Art writer, editor and critic, Jason Oakley, born in East Anglia, UK, 1968, is publications manager with Visual Artists Ireland. Teaches on the Visual Art Practices BA at IADT and is a member of the curatorial panel of Temple Bar Gallery and Studios (p. 391).

MEGAN O'BEIRNE: A writer and visual artist, her work is represented in national and county collections. A regular contributor to The Tree Council of Ireland's publication *CRANN*, she is currently preparing an illustrated book on Irish heritage (p. 210).

CONOR O'CALLAGHAN: His most recent collection of poems is *Fiction* (Gallery Press, 2005). His comic memoir about Ireland's 2002 World Cup campaign, *Red Mist* (Bloomsbury 2004), was adapted into a documentary for Setanta TV in 2007. He lives in Manchester (p. 153).

JOSEPH O'CONNOR: His novel *Ghost Light* has been chosen as Dublin's One City One Book novel for 2011. He broadcasts a weekly radio column on RTÉ Radio 1's *Drivetime* with Mary Wilson and appears with the musician Philip King in the acclaimed stage show *Whole World Round* (p. 290).

JOHN O'DONNELL: His work has been published and broadcast widely and his awards include the Irish National Poetry Prize, the Ireland Fund Prize and the Hennessy/*Sunday Tribune* Poetry Award. A barrister, he lives in Dublin (p. 312).

CLODAGH O'DONOGHUE: Studied law at Trinity College Dublin and has worked as an actor with the Abbey, Project, Fishamble, Second Age, Pan Pan, Bewley's Cafe Theatre, RTÉ and BBC. She has written short stories for children for RTÉ and co-edited *Contemporary Irish Monologues* for New Island Books (p. 11).

BAIRBRE O'HOGAN: Born in Dublin. She has worked in education and in tourism and is now a State-accredited translator to/from Irish. Her main writing focus is on memoir, hoping that the material will give her sons access to their family stories (p. 282).

ÉAMONN Ó HUALLACHÁIN: Lives on the border between Louth and Armagh. Has long had enthusiastic love of the culture, language and history of his place. Often takes groups around this scenic and historically interesting place (p. 207).

EMER O'KELLY: A critic and commentator, mainly for the *Sunday Independent*, where she specialises in drama and public affairs. She was a member of the Arts Council of Ireland 1998–2003, and 2003–2005, and is currently serving a second term as board member of the Irish Museum of Modern Art (p. 224).

COLETTE OLNEY: From Cork, teaches writing. She has won major poetry prizes and has had work published in *Poetry Ireland Review*, *Cyphers*, *The Irish Times* and *Best Irish Poetry 2010* (pp. 109, 179).

MARY O'MALLEY: Born and reared in Connemara, she now lives in the Moycullen Gaeltacht. She broadcasts, travels and lectures widely and is a member of Aosdána. She has written six collections of poetry and teaches on the MA in Writing and in Arts Administration in NUI Galway (pp. 158, 219).

JOE Ó MUIRCHEARTAIGH: Born in Dublin, a writer/journalist based in Ennis and is Deputy Editor/Sports Editor of *The Clare People* (pp. 254, 315).

KARL O'NEILL: Born in Armagh, is an actor, and author of a children's book *The Most Beautiful Letter In The World*. Among other writings, he has contributed translations to *The Irish Catullus* (p. 87).

JOSEPH O'NEILL: The author of four books, most recently the novel *Netherland* (winner of the 2008 Kerry Fiction Prize) and the non-fictional *Blood-Dark Track: A Family History* (p. 176).

JULIE PARSONS: The author of six novels, including *Mary, Mary*, *Eager to Please* and, most recently, *I Saw You*. A former radio and television producer with RTÉ, she has also written two plays for radio. She was born in New Zealand but has lived in Ireland for most of her adult life (p. 237).

CATHY POWER: Lives in Kilkenny with her family. Has worked as a journalist, and as a radio producer (pp. 124, 293).

FIONA PRICE: From Terenure in Dublin, emigrated shortly after she graduated from UCD during the last recession, returning home at the height of the Celtic Tiger. Fiona is a prize-winning short story writer and is a founder member of Eblana Writers, www.eblana-writers.com (p. 39).

MARK ROPER: Has published five collections of poetry. *The River Book: A Celebration of the Suir*, a collaboration with the photographer Paddy Dwan, appeared in October 2010 (p. 241).

MARY RUSSELL: A journalist and writer with a particular interest in travel. Born in Dublin, her books include *The Blessings of a Good Thick Shirt*, *Please Don't Call it Soviet Georgia* and *Journeys of a Lifetime*. She lives in Oxford and Dublin (p. 363).

DENIS SAMPSON: A long-time resident of Montreal, he now spends a major part of the year in County Kilkenny. He is the author of books on John McGahern and Brian Moore as well as many personal essays. A new book, *Young John McGahern: Becoming a Novelist*, will be published in 2011 (p. 305).

BARBARA SCULLY: A writer, Reiki therapist and full-time mother to three daughters who range in age from twenty-three to ten years. She is also slave to four cats and master of one not very bright dog (p. 14).

ORLA SHANAGHY: Lives in Waterford. Her work has featured in various shows on RTÉ radio, *The Stinging Fly* literary magazine and several local anthologies. She blogs at curmumgeon.wordpress.com and orlashanaghy.wordpress.com (p. 284).

ANNE SHARPE: A psychologist who lives in County Wicklow (p. 48).

TED SHEEHY: A freelance journalist, critic, script writer and editor born in Limerick and living in County Roscommon. He has contributed to *Sunday Miscellany* since the early 1990s (pp. 61, 112).

PETER SIRR: Lives in Dublin where he works as a freelance writer and translator. His most recent collection of poems, *The Thing Is*, was published by Gallery Press in 2009 (pp. 96, 161).

ELAINE SISSON: Grew up in Rathfarnham and now lives in Kilmainham, Dublin, both places associated with the Pearse Brothers. She is a writer on early twentieth-century Irish cultural history (p. 146).

GERARD SMYTH: His poetry has appeared widely in publications in Ireland, Britain and America, as well as in translation. *The Fullness of Time: New and Selected Poems*

(Dedalus Press, 2010) is the most recent of his seven collections. He is a member of Áosdana (p. 381).

SUSAN STAIRS: Lives in Dublin and has written various publications on Irish art. She has an MA in Creative Writing from University College Dublin. Her short story 'The Rescue' was one of six shortlisted for The Davy Byrnes Irish Writing Award in 2009. Her work has been featured on *Sunday Miscellany* since 2008. She is currently working on a novel (p. 99).

BILL TINLEY: Received the Patrick Kavanagh Poetry Award in 1996 and published *Grace* in 2001. He is working on a collection of short stories (p. 308).

GEMMA TIPTON: Independent writer on art and architecture, writing regularly for *The Irish Times* and other Irish and international publications. Works as a curator, and is Guest Artistic Director for Kinsale Arts Week for 2011 (p. 213).

NIALL WELDON: Born in Rush, County Dublin, he worked in Aer Lingus for over forty years. He is the author of *Lengthening Shadows*, published by the Linden Press, and *Poineers in Flight*, published by Liffey Press (p. 382).

GRACE WELLS: Born in London in 1968, she is an award-winning writer of literature for children. Her first collection of poetry, *When God Has Been Called Away to Greater Things*, was published by Dedalus Press in 2010 (pp. 257, 332).

MARIAD WHISKER: Although better known for awards in fashion design, since earning her MA in Creative Writing at University College Dublin, Mairead has been short-listed for Fish Flash Fiction and long-listed for The Seán Ó Faoláin Prize (p. 221).

BERT WRIGHT: Has worked in the books industry for twenty-five years. He is currently administrator of the Irish Book Awards and events curator for Mountains to Sea dlr Book Festival in Dún Laoghaire. He is married with two children and lives in Dalkey, County Dublin (p. 33).